SELECTED
PLAYS
AND PROSE
OF
AMIRI BARAKA/
LEROI JONES

SELECTED
PLAYS
AND PROSE
OF
AMIRI BARAKA/
LEROI JONES

WILLIAM MORROW AND COMPANY, INC.

NEW YORK   *1979*

Copyright © 1979 by Amiri Baraka

Grateful acknowledgment is made for permission to use material as specified below:

From *Tales,* Copyright © 1963, 1964, 1965, 1967 by LeRoi Jones, Grove Press, Inc., New York, N.Y.

From *Raise, Race, Rays, Raze,* by Imamu Amiri Baraka (LeRoi Jones). Copyright © 1969, 1970, 1971, by LeRoi Jones. Reprinted by permission of Random House, Inc.

Library of Congress Cataloging in Publication Data

Baraka, Imamu Amiri, 1934-
 Selected plays and prose of Amiri Baraka.

 Includes bibliographical references.
 I. Title.
PS3552.A583A6   1979   818'.5'409   79–18309
ISBN 0-688-03495-0
ISBN 0-688-08495-8 pbk.

Book Design by Michael Mauceri

Printed in the United States of America.

First Edition
1 2 3 4 5 6 7 8 9 10

Self-Determination
  for the Afro-American Nation
    in the Black Belt South!

Equal Rights for the Black Oppressed Nationality
  Wherever They May Be!

& for Kellie, Lisa & Dominique,
  Three 20th-Century Foxes!

CONTENTS

SELECTED PLAYS AND PROSE OF AMIRI BARAKA/ LEROI JONES

CUBA LIBRE
from *Home, Social Essays*

Preface

If we live all our lives under lies, it becomes difficult to see *anything* if it does not have anything to do with these lies. If it is, for example, true or, say, honest. The idea that things of this nature continue to exist is not ever brought forward in our minds. If they do, they seem, at their most sympathetic excursion, monstrous untruths. Bigger lies than our own. I am sorry. There are things, elements in the world, that continue to exist, for whatever time, completely liberated from our delusion. They press us also, and we, of course, if we are to preserve the sullen but comfortable vacuum we inhabit, must deny that anyone else could possibly tolerate what we all agree is a hellish world. And for me to point out, assuming I am intrepid enough, or, all right, naïve enough to do so, *i.e.,* that perhaps it is just this miserable subjection to the fantastic (in whatever fashion, sphere, or presence it persists) that makes your/our worlds so hellish, is, I admit, presumption bordering on insanity. But it is certainly true . . . whether I persist or no . . . or whether you believe (at least the words) or continue to stare off into space. It's a bad scene either way.

* * * *

(What I Brought to the Revolution)

A man called me on a Saturday afternoon some months ago and asked if I wanted to go to Cuba with other some other Negroes, some of whom were also writers. I had a house full of people that afternoon and since we had all been drinking, it seemed pretty silly for me to suddenly drop the receiver and say, "I'm going to Cuba," so I hesitated for a minute, asking the man just why would we (what seemed to me to be just "a bunch of Negroes") be going. For what purpose? He said, "Oh, I thought that since you were a poet you might like to know what's *really* going on down there." I had never really thought of anything in that particular light. Being an American poet, I suppose, I thought my function was simply to talk about everything as if I knew . . . it had never entered my mind that I might really like to find out for once what was actually happening someplace else in the world.

*   *   *   *

There were twelve of us scheduled to go to Habana, July 20. Twelve did go, but most were last-minute replacements for those originally named. James Baldwin, John Killens, Alice Childress, Langston Hughes, were four who were replaced. The only other "professional" writer on this trip was Julian Mayfield, the novelist, who went down before the main body with his wife.

At Idlewild airport, the 20th, we straggled in from our various lives, assembling at last at 3 P.M. We met each other, and, I suppose, took stock of each other. I know I took stock of them, and was disappointed. First, because there were no other, what I considered, "important" Negro writers. The other reasons were accreted as the trip went on. But what I could get at that initial meeting was: One embarrassingly dull (white) communist, his professional Negro (*i.e.,* unstraightened hair, 1930's bohemian peasant blouses, etc., militant integrationist, etc.) wife who wrote embarrassingly inept social comment-type poems, usually about one or sometimes a group of Negroes being mistreated or suffering in general (usually in Alabama, etc.). Two middle-class young Negro ladies from Philadephia who wrote poems, the nature of which I left largely undetermined. One 1920's "New Negro" type African scholar (one of those terrible examples of what the "Harlem Renaissance" was at its worst). One 1930's type Negro "essayist" who turned out to be marvelously un-lied to. One strange tall man in a straw hat and feathery beard (whom I later got to know as Robert Williams and who later figured very largely in the trip, certainly in my impressions of it). The first Negro to work for the *Philadelphia Inquirer*—I think probably this job has deranged him permanently, because it has made him begin to believe that this (the job) means that white America (*i.e.,* at large) loves him ... and it is only those "other" kinds of Negroes that they despise and sometimes even lynch. Two (white) secretaries for an organization called the Fair Play for Cuba Committee, who I suppose are as dedicated (to whatever it is they are dedicated to) as they are unattractive. One tall skinny black charming fashion model, who wore some kind of Dior slacks up into the Sierra Maestra mountains (she so reminded me of my sister, with her various younger-generation liberated-type Negro comments, that it made any kind of adulterous behavior on my part impossible). One young Negro abstract expressionist painter, Edward Clarke, whom I had known vaguely before, and grew to know and like very much during this, as he called it, "wild scene." Also at the terminal, but not traveling with us, a tall light-skinned young, as white liberals like to say, "Negro intellectual." It was he, Richard Gibson, who had called me initially and who had pretty much arranged the whole trip. (I understand now that he has just recently been fired from his job at CBS because of his "Cuban activities.")

* * * *

We didn't get to leave the 20th. Something very strange happened. First, the airline people at the desk (Cubana Airlines) said they had no knowledge of any group excursion of the kind Gibson thought he had arranged. Of course, it was found out that he, Gibson, had letters from various officials, not only verifying the trip, but assuring him that passage, etc., had been arranged and that we only need appear, at 3 P.M., the 20th, and board the plane. After this problem was more or less resolved, these same airline people (ticket sellers, etc.) said that none of our tickets had been paid for, or at least, that the man who must sign for the free tickets had not done so. This man who was supposed to sign the free passes to make them valid was the manager of Cubana Airlines, New York, who, it turned out, was nowhere to be found. Gibson raged and fumed, but nothing happened.

Then, a Señor Molario, the head of the July 26th movement in New York City appeared (he was supposed to accompany us to Habana), and the problem took on new dimensions. "Of course," Señor Molario said, "there are tickets. I have a letter here signed by the Minister of Tourism himself authorizing this trip. The passes need only be signed by the manager of the New York office of Cubana."

Gibson and the airline people told Molario about the manager's inconvenient disappearance. Molario fumed. Gibson and Molario telephoned frantically, but the manager did not appear. (His secretary said she had "no idea" where he was.) Finally, when it was ascertained that the manager had no intention of showing up by plane time, Señor Molario offered to pay for all our tickets out of his own pocket. Then the other dimension appeared. The two men behind the desk talked to each other and then they said, "I'm very sorry, but the plane is all filled up." Molario and Gibson were struck dumb. The rest of us milled around uncertainly. At 4:30 P.M., the plane took off without us. Five hours later, I suppose, it landed in Habana. We found out soon after it took off that there were thirteen empty seats.

The communist and his wife were convinced that the incident represented an attempt by the U.S. government to discourage us from going to Cuba at all. It seemed a rational enough idea to me.

* * * *

There was no trouble at all with our tickets, etc., the next day. We took off, as scheduled, at 4:30 P.M. and landed at José Martí airport five hours later

(8:30 P.M. because of the one-hour time difference). At the airport we were met in the terminal by a costumed Calypso band and a smiling bartender who began to pass out daiquiris behind a quickly set up "Bacardi bar" at an alarming rate. There were also crowds of people standing outside the customs office, regular citizens they looked to be, waving and calling to us through the glass. Between daiquiris, we managed to meet our official interpreter, a small pretty Cuban girl named Olga Finlay. She spoke, of course, better English than most of my companions. (I found out later that she had lived in New York about ten years and that she was the niece of some high official in the revolutionary government.) We also met some people from Casa de las Americas, the sponsoring organization, as well as its sub-director, a young architect named Alberto Robaina. I met two young Cuban poets, Pablo Armando Fernandez, who had translated one of my poems for *Lunes de Revolución,* the literary supplement of the official newspaper of the revolution, and Guillermo Cabrera Infante, the editor of the supplement.

From the very outset of the trip I was determined not to be "taken." I had cautioned myself against any undue romantic persuasion and had vowed to set myself up as a completely "objective" observer. I wanted nothing to do with the official type tours, etc., I knew would be waiting for us and I had even figured out several ways to get around the country by myself in the event that the official tours got to be too much. Casa de las Americas, the government, was paying all our bills and I was certain that they would want to make very sure that we saw everything they wanted us to see. I wanted no part of it. I speak Spanish fairly well, can't be mistaken for a "gringo yanqui" under any circumstances, and with the beard and without the seersucker suit I was wearing, I was pretty sure I'd be relatively free to tramp around where I wanted to. So of course with these cloak-and-dagger ideas and amidst all the backslapping, happy crowds (crowds in the U.S. are never "happy" . . . hysterical, murderous, duped, etc., viz. Nathanael West, yes, but under no circumstances "happy." A happy crowd *is* suspect), government-supplied daiquiris, Calypsos, and so forth, I got extremely paranoid. I felt immediately sure that the make was on. (See preface.)

*   *   *   *

In New York we were told that we would probably be staying at the Hotel Riviera, one of the largest luxury hotels in Habana. However, the cars took us to another hotel, the Hotel Presidente. The Presidente is hardly what could be called a luxury hotel, although I'm sure it was one of the great *turista* places during the 1930's. Now, in contrast to the thirty-story Hilton and the other newer "jeweled pads" of Habana, the Presidente looked much like the 23rd Street YMCA. It had become, after the advent of the skyscraper hotels, more or less a family residence with about thirty-five permanent guests.

When we got out of the cars and realized that by no stretch of the imagination could we be said to be in a luxury hotel, there was an almost audible souring throughout the little band. The place was fronted, and surrounded, by a wide, raised awning-covered tile terrace. There were rattan chairs and tables scattered all over it. At the top of the stairs, as we entered, a small glass-enclosed sign with movie schedules, menus for the dining room, and pictures of the entertainers who worked (only weekends now) in the hotel bar. There was one working elevator run by a smiling, one-armed, American slang-speaking operator. The sign-in desk was exactly the way they are in movies and I was startled for a moment by the desk clerk, who in his slightly green-tinted glasses and thin eyes looked exactly like pictures of Fulgencio Batista.

*   *   *   *

To further sour our little group, the men were billeted two in a room. Clarke and I managed to get into a room with a connecting door to another room. As soon as we got into our room, the other door opened and the model came through smiling and mildly complaining. She definitely missed the Riviera. However, the three of us established an immediate rapport and I called room service and ordered two bottles before we even took off our jackets.

The liquor was brought upstairs and when I opened the door to let the bellhop in, the essayist and the tall bearded man were standing outside the door also. We invited them in and everyone reintroduced himself. As the evening moved on, and more liquor was consumed, we talked more and more about ourselves. I was most interested in the tall man. His name, Robert Williams, was vaguely familiar. I remembered just where it was, and in what context, I had seen Williams' name. He was the president of the Monroe, North Carolina, branch of the NAACP. He was also the man who had stated publicly that he didn't hold too much with "passive resistance," especially as championed by Rev. Martin Luther King, and he had advocated that the Southern Negro meet violence with violence. He had been immediately suspended by the home office, but the people in his branch had told the New York wheels that if Williams was out so were they. He had been reinstated, but very, very reluctantly. Williams had gone on, as he told us in some detail later, to establish a kind of pocket militia among the Negroes of Monroe, and had managed to so terrorize the white population of the town that he could with some finality *ban* any further meetings of the local Ku Klux Klan. The consensus among the white population was that "Williams was trying to provoke them and they weren't going to be provoked."

Somehow, people in Cuba heard about Williams' one-man war in Monroe and invited him to see for himself what was happening in Cuba. Apparently, when the people who were in charge of trying to attract U.S. Negro tourists to Cuba found out that they drew blanks in their dealings with NAACP people and other "official" Negroes, viz. the tragedy of Joe Louis, they thought Williams would be a good risk. He was. He came down to Habana with Richard Gibson and toured the entire country at government expense, meeting Fidel Castro as well as most of the other important men in the revolutionary government. There were many pictures of Williams in most Cuban newspapers, many interviews given to newspapers and over the various television networks. In most of the interviews Williams put down the present administration of the U.S. very violently for its aberrant foreign policy and its hypocritical attitude on what is called "The Negro Question." He impressed almost all of Cuba with the force of his own personality and the patent hopelessness of official Uncle Sham.

On his return to the States, Williams, of course, was castigated by whatever portion of the American press that would even bother to report that there had been an American Negro "leader" who had actually gone down to Cuba and had, moreover, heartily approved of what he had seen. The NAACP people in New York called Williams in and said he was wasting his talent down in that small town and offered him a good job at the home office in New York. When he was offered a return trip to Cuba, Williams jumped at the chance.

*   *   *   *

Later in the evening, the two middle-class ladies from Philadelphia turned up, drawn I suppose by all the noise that must have been coming out of our room. The one pretty middle-class lady talked for a while about not being at the Riviera, and what people in Philadelphia had said when she told them she was going to Cuba. I was pretty surprised, in one sense, at her relation of those comments, because the comments themselves, which I suppose must have come from people pretty much like herself, *i.e.*, middle-class, middlebrow young Negroes living in Philadelphia, were almost exactly the same as the comments that had been tossed my way from the various beats, bohemians and intellectuals in Greenwich Village, New York City (of course, given that proper knowing cynicism that is fashionable among my contemporaries). It made me shudder. I mean to find how homogenous most thinking in the U.S. has become, even among the real and/or *soi-disant* intellectual. A New York taxicab driver taking me out to Idlewild says, "Those rotten commies. You'd better watch yourself, mister, that you don't get shot or something. Those guys are mean." And from a close friend of mine, a young New York poet, "I don't trust guys in uniforms." The latter, of course, being more reprehensible because he is supposed to come up with thought that is alien to the cliché, completely foreign to the well-digested particle of moral engagement. But this is probably the biggest symptom of our moral disintegration (call it, as everyone else is wont, complacency), this so-called rebellion against what is most crass and ugly in our society, but without the slightest thought of, say, any kind of direction or purpose. Certainly, without any knowledge of what could be put up as alternatives. To fight against one kind of dullness with an even more subtle dullness is, I suppose, the highwater mark of social degeneracy. Worse than mere lying.

* * * *

In 1955, on leave from an airbase in Puerto Rico, I came into Habana for three days. I suppose, then, probably next to Tangiers, Habana was the vice capital of the world. I remember coming out of my hotel and being propositioned by three different people on my way to a busstop. The first guy, a boy around fifteen, wanted to sell me his sister. The second guy, also around fifteen, had a lot of women he wanted to sell. Probably not all of them were his sisters. The third guy had those wild comic books and promises of blue movies. The town was quieter in the daytime; then it was only an occasional offer to buy narcotics. No one even came out on the streets except billions of beggars and, of course, the Americans, until the sun went down ... then it was business as usual. The best liberty town in the world. I remember also blowing one hundred bucks in the casino and having some beautiful redhaired woman give it back to me to play again. She was the wife of a bigtime British film maker who said she was in love with Africans. She was extremely dragged when she found out I was just an American G.I. without even money enough to buy a box of prophylactics.

* * * *

(What I Brought Back Here)

The next morning I was awakened by the phone on the night table next to my head. It was the historian, who had assumed the role of official spokesman, etc., and, I suppose, co-ordinator of the group. He said that the group was waiting for Clarke and me to come down, hadn't we been advised as to what time to meet in the lobby, etc.

Our official guides and interpreters were waiting, Olga Finlay and the architect, Robaina. Robaina, about twenty-eight years old and blond, wore a fairly expensive Italian suit and was driving a white Jaguar. He spoke almost no English, though he understood it perfectly, but had to go along with us because he was sub-director of the sponsoring organization.

That was our first stop, Casa de las Americas. It was housed in a large white building about three blocks from the Presidente. The organization itself is responsible for disseminating and promoting Cuban culture throughout the Americas. It is also responsible for such things as intercultural exchanges between Cuba and other countries: traveling art shows, arranging visits to Cuba by American (North and South) persons from all the arts, setting up writers' conferences (such as the one that included Simone de Beauvoir and Jean Paul Sartre), running an adult education center, discussion groups, lecture series, and hundreds of other things. They've had a few North Americans down to lecture and perform: William Warfield gave several concerts all over the country, Waldo Frank lectured, and Maya Deren, the experimental film maker, was down in May, showing her films and lecturing. Many more North American artists, etc., have been invited to come down just to see what's going on in the country, but most have refused or been very busy.

The adult school, which is run very much like the New School for Social Research, specializes in what's known as "Cultura Para el Pueblo" (Culture for the People). The courses of study are French, English, Portuguese, American History, Cuban History, Cuban Literature, Political Geography, Latin-American Literature, Music, North American Literature, and one in Film. The library, which specializes in "Asuntos Americanos," has about 25,000 volumes, including literary magazines from all over the Americas.

La Casa also maintains a record library of Latin-American music, classical as well as folk. They also serve as a publishing house for Latin-American authors, having just conducted this spring an intra-Latin-American competition for the best new books, poetry, drama, short stories, a novel, and a collection of essays. The prizes were $1000 and publication of the work. Two Argentines, a Cuban, a Guatemalan and an Ecuadorian won the first prizes.

The place is a jumble of activity. Even early in the morning when we got there, there were secretaries running through the various offices speaking Spanish, Portuguese, English and French. We were introduced to the director of La Casa, Señora Haydee Santamaria, a blonde buxom woman of about forty. The first thing she told us, through Olga, was that although special tours had been arranged for our party, we were free to go anywhere we could. This brought a low roar of approval from the group, although the communist and his wife said they hoped the official tour would include at least one peasant's home and a typical Cuban Negro family. Señora Santamaria said that if the tours did not already include these things, she would make sure they were added. She talked to us briefly about La Casa's functions and had small pamphlets passed around which went into these functions in detail. We were also given copies of the five prizewinning books I mentioned before, even though the only members of our party who could read or speak Spanish were the essayist and myself.

The small demitasse cups of Cuban coffee were served and we asked Señora Santamaria questions as well as the other employees of La Casa who were present for just that purpose. Robaina was standing next to me so I began to ask him about Cuban poets. Were there any literary magazines in Cuba? What were the young poets like? What was Cuban painting like? Would I get a chance to meet Nicolas Guillen (the best known Cuban poet—he and Neruda are considered the best living Latin-American poets). Robaina's English conversation was mostly Spanish, but we got on very well. He answered almost all of my questions energetically and even offered to take me around to see some of the young Cuban painters and poets.

We hung around La Casa another hour then went downstairs to the production offices of *Arma Nueva,* the organ of La Comisión Nacional de Alfabetización, the organization in charge of elementary adult education. This organization is attempting to educate the great masses of illiterate Cubans concentrated mostly in rural areas. They number more than two million throughout the country. *Arma Nueva* is "a review for rebel soldiers, workers, and farmers." Most of the articles in the magazine deal with popular heroes, current events and sports and are written the way a child's primer is. In the edition I received, there were articles on Great Cuban Women, Great Cuban Sports Figures, The Seas Around Cuba, What is a Biography?, The Life of Camilo Cienfuegos, The Agrarian Reform, A History of Cuba in 10 Paragraphs, The Battle of "El Uvero," What Is a Cooperative?, The Rebel Army, and many features like crossword puzzles, double crostics, etc. Each article, as well as giving basic information, attempts to point out the great changes in Cuba since the revolution. Each article is, of course, trying to do two things at once, educate as well as proselytize. For example, one of the word games went: "Who is the chief of the Cuban revolution?–FIDEL." "What is the principal product of Cuban economy?–SUGAR." "What is the hope of all the people?–LIBERTY."

These offices were small and in the basement of La Casa. There were about five young men busily stapling mimeographed announcements inside the current issue of *Arma Nueva.* They all got up to shake our hands and greet us when we came in. The only young woman in the office gave us a brief talk about the magazine and the adult education program in Cuba. Most of the people in the office seemed to recognize Robert Williams immediately, and after the young woman's talk, some of the young men left their stapling to ask Robert about the U.S. and why he thought U.S. newspapers told so many lies. One of them asked, "Are they paid to lie? Don't they ever tell the truth about what's happening down here? That man in the *Times* (Tad Szulc) is a filthy liar. He should be kicked out of the country and an honest man brought down." Robert thought this was funny and so did I, but I could see the possible headlines in the *New York Times* if said Szulc were to have overheard this exchange. CUBAN EXTREMISTS ADVOCATE EXPULSION OF U.S. NEWSMEN.

We drank some more Cuban coffee and hit the road again.

* * * *

At the Ministry of Education, a prewar, Spanish-style office building in old Habana, we met the assistant minister (or subsecretary) of education, Dr. José Aguilera. The minister, a short dark man in his forties, talked about an hour, with frequent interruptions, about the educational situation in Cuba. He compared the status of the Cuban educational system as of January 1, 1959, with the system as it stood now; outlining the many changes the revolutionary government has brought about. The statistics were staggering. In their excellent book *Cuba: Anatomy of a Revolution,* Leo Huberman and Paul M. Sweezy give exact facts and figures, comparisons outlining precisely how far, not just the educational system has come since the first days of the revolutionary government, but just how much extreme progress has been made in all areas of economic, social and cultural adjustment. It would seem to me that since the *New York Times* is usually so fond of facts and statistics, it would reprint a few of the innumerable graphs, charts and tables in this book instead of printing long, tiresomely untrue "reports" by middle-class Americans suffering from that uniquely American sickness called "identification." This is a disease wherein the victim somehow thinks that he receives monies or other fringe benefits from Standard Oil, Coca-Cola, Du Pont, U.S. Steel, etc., and feels genuinely hurt if some of "their properties" are expropriated. "They're taking *our* oil and *our* Coca-Cola."

Dr. Aguilera talked softly and convincingly, smoking constantly. The Cuban coffee came in, and he had some pamphlets passed around the table, as well as a few examples of new Cuban schoolbooks. (This had been a country of notoriously few schoolbooks.) He gave us copies of what had been the first first-aid book printed in Cuba for general use, then went on calmly and confidently citing statistics as only a government official can. "In the last seven-year period," he said, "a total of only 400 classrooms were created. The revolutionary government by September 1960 will have created almost 10,-000. As Fidel said, we're changing every former Batista military fortification into a school. School cities we call them. You'll probably get a chance to visit a few before you leave. [We did the next day.] To show you the amount of blatant corruption that infested this country before the revolution, the educational budget during the years 1907–08, the beginning of the republic, was $4,208,368. The index of illiterates then was 31.47 per cent. Fifty years later, in 1958–59, the budget was $88,389,450, twenty-two times larger, but the index of illiterates remained the same. Only about 8.9 per cent of people between the ages of twelve and nineteen (secondary school age) received any schooling at all. That meant only about 9 out of 100 young people were receiving any secondary schooling at all."

Most of the ladies in our group gasped politely, genuinely impressed. The minister went on: "Another very, very amusing fact about the Cuban education system is that in 1959, just before the revolutionary government took over, there were 24,011 teachers in Cuba, but 1,514 of them were school inspectors." The minister briefly turned the pages of one of the pamphlets he had given us and then with a broad smile resumed his statistics. "Yes, 1,514 inspectors in this little country. Do you know that in the countries of Belguim and France combined they have only 760 inspectors." Everybody in the office broke up. "Well, we've reduced the number of inspectors to around 400, which still means we've got about 80 more than France, a country whose population is eight times larger than ours."

Robert Williams poked me in the side. "Ol' Fulgencio must have had a bunch of relatives."

The group then began to ask questions of the minister. He answered most of them very thoroughly, sometimes asking the opinions of some of his aides who were in the room. More statistics were cited, photographs of old, now demolished school buildings were shown, photos of the new school city in Oriente, "Camilo Cienfuegos," other new school cities just being built. Then the communist's wife wanted to know if in the new schoolbooks that were being manufactured, little Negro children were portrayed as well as white. The minister did not understand at first, or rather, his interpreter did not. The wife said, "I mean, to show the little Negro children that they are not inferior, I think you should have little colored boys and girls in schoolbooks as well as little white boys and girls." I began to laugh very impolitely, and the woman silenced me with a cold look of dignity. When the interpreter got through explaining to the minister again, the puzzled look did not leave his face, but he picked up a few new geography books and thumbed quickly through them. When he reached the page he wanted, he pressed it down and handed it to the woman. She smiled ecstatically and showed the book to her husband. The minister handed her a newly printed notebook for elementary schools; on the cover were five children at a blackboard, two of them black. The woman almost swooned. The minister laughed and shook his head.

*　*　*　*

We scrambled into waiting cabs and Olga told us our next stop was the National Agrarian Reform Institute (INRA). The Agrarian Reform Law is the basic law passed by the revolutionary government. And it is the application of this law, and its subsequent repercussions that have been largely responsible for the shaping of public opinion (*i.e.,* opinions of specific governments and their subsequent popularization throughout the populations controlled by these governments) about the new Cuban government, whether pro or con. The Agrarian Reform Law *is* radical social legislation. As Fidel Castro himself admitted. "I *am* a radical," he said, "a very radical young man. But I am right."

The INRA is responsible for seeing that the statutes of the Agrarian Reform Law are carried out. The head of the institute, Dr. Antonio Nuñez Jiménez, is responsible only to Fidel Castro. Once one is in Cuba it becomes more than vaguely apparent that the Agrarian Reform and its continued fulfillment by the new government is the key to their success, and that as long as this law is upheld, the majority of the Cuban people will love Fidel Castro even if it were proven that he was Lucifer himself.

We left old Habana and passed the huge white monument to José Martí, the father of the Cuban republic. The institute is a massive white building still in the last stages of completion. It was begun by Batista for some now obscure purpose, but after the revolution the INRA offices were moved in immediately.

The entire front walk of the glass and stone building was covered with milling crowds. Mostly the crowd was made up of rebel soldiers and *campesinos* (peasant farmers). The *campesinos* had probably come from one of the many rural areas of the country to settle some business affair at the institute. They wear the traditional big straw hats with the front brim turned up and all carry the also traditional machete. As we got out of the cabs, a small unit of *miliciana* marched by. The *miliciana* are the female contingent of the home guard that has been formed all over the island. The various units are usually made up of particular age groups. Some, like the one that was passing us, were made up of teen-age girls, others include older women, some even younger girls. This unit wore dark skirts, maroon shirts, and dark berets. They moved by in perfect step; a pretty young red-haired girl stepping beside the main body called out cadence loud and clear.

There were two soldiers sitting just inside the glass doors. They smiled at us as we went by, one pointing over his shoulder toward an information desk. Another soldier sat behind the information desk reading a newspaper, beside him one of the young girl *miliciana*. Olga spoke to the soldier briefly and he waved us on. The elevators were so crowded we had to go up in smaller groups. Everywhere in the building there were young soldiers, many of them bearded, all of them carrying some sort of firearm. There were also hundreds of farmers walking around, some even with their wives, children, and huge lunch pails. The noise in the lobbies was unbelievable.

We went into a quiet air-conditioned office with great windows looking out at the sea. A speaker on one of the walls kept up a steady hum of music as well as news broadcasts and announcements. A very dark Negro welcomed us in Cuban English as did a tall blond man who sounded like an Irishman. We were given chairs, and the Irishman, after talking to Olga, dragged out a huge wooden map of Cuba. Another man came out of an inner office, very tall and thin with a neat Latin mustache. He greeted everyone in the office very warmly. He was about thirty, and wore a loose-fitting Brooks Bros. type suit, with an open-collared button-down shirt. He was one of the directors of one agency of the institute. He spoke very bookish English, but seemed to become embarrassed when he couldn't find proper adjectives so he asked Olga to interpret.

Using the huge map, which showed how the country was divided into provinces, he began to outline INRA's responsibilities and the different problems that confronted it. He too began citing reams of statistics, and the Irish-sounding man joined in. Soon, we were having a joint lecture, neither of the men seeming to get in the other's way. "The reason Cuban economy and thereby most of the people were in such bad shape," said the Irishman, "is that before the revolution we were a monoculture, most of the cultivated land being given over to the growing of sugar cane. Do you know we even imported rice from the United States. Somebody was paying off. Most of the land was owned by large corporations that employed the Cuban labor force for only three months a year, leaving them to starve in the off season. And most of the people did starve. The average per capita income in 1950–54 was about $312 per year. Small farms under twenty-five acres made up only about 3.3 percent of total land holdings. They were almost nonexistent. The majority of farms in the country were being planted and worked by people who did not own the land: sharecroppers. We were a nation of sharecroppers and squatters. Most of the workable land was in the hands of absentee landlords, in some cases foreign corporations."

The tall man butted in "That's why the Agrarian Reform Law was so important. That's also why it was so controversial." He went to a desk and picked up copies of a mimeographed booklet, and beckoned for one of the uniformed young men to pass them around to us. "The first article of the law is the basis for our revolution. It is the only thing that makes us a sovereign country." He read it to us. "Article one. Latifundium (uneconomic and extensive production of large land holdings) is hereby proscribed. The maximum area of land that may be possessed by a natural or juridical person shall be thirty *cabellerias* (about 1,000 acres). The lands belonging to a natural or juridical person that exceed that limit will be expropriated for distribution among the peasants and agricultural workers who have no land."

This meant of course that United Fruit, American Sugar, etc., got burnt immediately. The tall man went on, "And of course, the direct complement to this basic tenet of the reform law is Article Sixteen. It says that an area of two *cabellerias* (about 66 acres) of fertile land, without irrigation and distant from urban centers, is established as the "vital minimum" for a peasant family of five persons engaged in crops of medium economic yield."

"That *is* communism," one of the ladies next to me said half jokingly.

"Is it wrong?" the tall man wanted to know. The woman agreed that it was not.

After more questions, a soldier came into the office and said a few words to Olga. She stood up and our interview with these young men was over. "We're in luck," she said. "We're going to be able to get in to see Antonio Nuñez Jiménez, the executive director of INRA, for about ten minutes." We all got up, finished our coffee, and began shaking hands with everyone in the office. Nuñez Jiménez' office was directly across the hall from the office we were leaving. In the outer office, a large, smoothfaced Negro soldier sat at a desk typing. He had a huge pearl-handled .45 strapped to his hip and faultlessly polished boots. When we came in, he spun around in his secretary's chair and let us have all thirty-two teeth. He recognized Robert Williams immediately and shook his hand vigorously. While we sat in the outer office waiting for our interview, Williams enthralled him, at his request, with unbelievable tales about separate toilets and chromatic buses. The soldier was obviously too intelligent to believe all of the stories. He kept saying, "Ah, mon, go on!"

Finally, another soldier, this one carrying what Williams described to me as "a new Belgian automatic rifle," came out of the inner offices and beckoned to Olga. There were two more offices inside the one we had waited in. They were filled with clerical workers and soldiers. The door to Nuñez Jiménez' office was standing open and we all crowded in. There were two other soldiers in the office besides the executive director, both with .45's. There were also two young Negroes in civilian clothes talking to each other very animatedly. When we came through the door, Dr. Jiménez wheeled away from his conversation and made a polite Latin bow with both hands extended in greeting. Everyone shook his hand. After the many handshakes he began talking pleasantly to our interpreter. She conveyed his greetings to the group and then began to laugh as she contined to translate the captain's words. "Dr. Nuñez says that he is glad there are still Americans who want to see Cuba even though the travel agencies no longer think of it as the paradise just five hours from Manhattan. From a paradise to a hell in little over a year . . . we're making progress no matter how you look at it."

While we laughed, one of the soldiers passed out cigars to the men from a box that was on Dr. Nuñez' desk. Some of the group began to ask questions. The captain did his best to answer all of them. While he was doing this, the model leaned over to me and whispered, "God, he's beautiful! Why're all these guys so good-looking?" And she was right, he was beautiful. A tall, scholarly-looking man with black hair and full black beard, he talked deliberately but brightly about everything, now and then emphasizing a point by bringing his hands together and wringing them in slow motion, something like college English professors. He wore the uniform of the rebel army with the black and red shoulder insignia of a captain. A black beret was tucked neatly in one of his epaulets. He also carried a big square-handled .45.

Finally one of the secretaries asked, "Dr. Jiménez, why is it everyone, even high-ranking officials like yourself, still carry weapons?" There were embarrassed titters from other people in the group, but I thought it the highwater mark of most of the questioning so far.

The captain smiled cheerfully and ran the fingers of one hand from his mustache to the tip of his beard with that gesture characteristic of most men with beards. "Well, señorita, we are still a revolutionary government and as such we are still liable to attack by our enemies. Actual physical attack, not just terrible speeches a thousand miles away. We have to be ready for such developments, and we have to let our enemies know that we're ready."

"But don't you think there's been enough killing?" the woman continued.

Nuñez Jiménez stopped smiling for a second and looked down at his shiny-handled weapon. "I've never killed anyone in my life. I was a professor at the University. But it is just because I feel that there's been enough killing that I and the other members of the revolutionary government carry these weapons. We have to carry them until we are strong enough to defend ourselves diplomatically. There are people all over the world who would like for us never to become that strong."

After he had stopped answering questions, the captain passed out copies of a book he had written that had just been published called *La Liberación de las Islas*. Most of the group had him autograph their copies; when I filed past I took the book, tucked it under my arm and shook the minister's hand. He said, "No autograph?" I answered in Spanish, telling him that I thought the speech and handshake were fine enough souvenirs. He asked was I an American? and I told him that I was an American poet, which meant that I wasn't a real American like Señor Nixon or Arthur Godfrey but that I had certainly been born in that country. He slapped his sides laughing and shouted my answer to his aides.

*   *   *   *

The last stop was the Ministry of Housing. We were talked to there by a young man of about twenty-seven in a tattersall vest and desert boots. He was one of the subdirectors of the ministry. He used charts, pamphlets, and scale models of new housing to illustrate his points. He talked earnestly and excitedly for an hour and then we left for the hotel. As we were leaving I didn't see Ed Clarke, so I thought he had gotten separated from the party. I went back upstairs with Robaina, the architect, to try and locate him. We met the subdirector in the elevator and after he had helped us look vainly around the now empty halls for Clarke (he had left earlier), we began to talk about the States where, it turned out, he had lived for about six or seven years. One thing he was extremely interested in was whether Miles Davis, the trumpet player, was playing again and healthy after the terrible beating a policeman had given him outside of a nightclub where Miles was working. I told him that Miles was fine and playing as well as ever. "Wow," the subdirector of housing said, "that place is turning into a real police state."

* * * *

After dinner, Clarke, the essayist and I went into Old Habana to look around. We walked down almost every narrow street and back alley in that section of the city, peering into cafés, ogling the women, talking to bus drivers, thinking we looked pretty Cuban. The essayist and I spoke Spanish, and Clarke is the kind of light-skinned, straight-haired Negro that looks very Latin. Finally we stopped in one particularly grubby bar in the real 42nd Street part of town.

We went in and I said to the bartender, "Tres cervezas, por favor."

The bartender asked, "Qué clase?"

I looked at Ed and said, "Hey, what kind of beer you want?" He told me and the bartender whipped around and got them.

We had barely begun to sip the beer when a large stocky man across the bar, who was drunker than he should have been, raised his head, probably for the first time in three hours, and stared across the bar at us. Then he growled very drunkenly, "Abajo imperialismo yanqui! Viva Cuba Libre!" Then his head slumped again unwillingly. The three of us on the other side of the bar looked at each other with whatever expression comes into people's faces in that kind of situation and tried to continue sipping calmly. The man raised his head again. "Abajo imperialismo Yanqui! Viva Fidel! Viva Cuba Libre!" His head slumped. Clarke nudged me. The essayist made a face. I looked at my food. "Cuba Sí, Yanqui No! Cuba Sí, Yanqui No! Venceremos!" (We will win.) The head was up again.

Other people in the bar began to look up at us and smile or happily nudge their friends. This time the essayist called across to the man in Spanish. "Look, friend," he said firmly, "if you're talking to us, there's no need to, we readily agree with you. Down with Yankee imperialism. Cuba Yes, Yankee No! It's true." I tried to find my cigarettes.

The man seemed to gather strength from my companion's intrusion and began to shout even louder, then he began to come around the bar toward us. The essayist repeated what the man had just said and Clarke put the newspaper he'd been carrying on the bar. I turned to face the man, hoping I was smiling. But the man sidestepped me and walked around to the essayist and began to talk very loudly, waving his newspaper, instructing my friend on the spot in the virtues of the Cuban revolution and the evils of American imperialism. The essayist agreed and agreed. Clarke and I were agreeing also, but the man never turned to face us. He went on and on. Finally, the bartender came over and told him to be quiet. He lowered his voice one half decibel and continued his seemingly endless tirade. I thought the only sensible thing was to get out of the place, so I dumped the rest of the beer down my throat, pointed at Clarke's and tried to step between the loud man and his prey. The prey resisted, shaking his finger in the man's face, stopping only long enough to tell me that he was trying to tell this fellow that not all Americans were

John Foster Dulles, and that there were still some intelligent people left in the country. That seemed like a pretty farfetched idea to try to convince a Cuban of, so I ordered another beer and tried to relax. The two men wailed on and on.

Presently a shabbily dressed Negro, who was obviously a drifter, came in the bar with a sketchbook under his arm. He came over to where the discussion was raging, stood for a second, then looked over at Clarke and me. Finally he said to me, "Hey man, you American?" I nodded resignedly. "Yeh, yeh, no kidding?"

"That's right," I mumbled, "but only if you don't want to argue."

"Argue?" He pulled up a stool and sat in front of us. "No, man, I don't argue. You my brother." He pointed at his dark arm and then my own. "I just want you to tell me about Harlem. Tell me about Harlem, man."

This was the wildest thing I'd heard all night. I almost fell off the stool laughing. "What's the matter, didn't you read Jimmy Baldwin's article in *Esquire*?"

"What?" He looked at me quizzically. "Qué dice?"

"Oh, forget it." I then proceeded to tell him about Harlem as best I could, not even leaving out Hulan Jack and Adam Clayton Powell. While I told him about Harlem, he drew an awful little sketch of me on the back of a matchbook cover which he titled "The Comic." I also bought him two beers and promised to show him around Harlem if he ever got to the States.

When we got to leave the bar around four in the morning, the essayist and his assailant were still agreeing violently. When we left the bar, the man followed us all the way to the bus stop, promising to show us Habana.

*   *   *   *

The next day toward afternoon, we drove out first to a beach club called El Obrero Círculo, one of the hundreds of formerly privately owned beach clubs that have since been expropriated and turned into public resorts. "La Playa es por El Pueblo," a big sign outside the beach house said. (The beach is for the people.) It was a marvelous white beach with unbelievably blue water and hundreds of beautiful women, but true to my American heritage, I sat in the bar and drank daiquiris till it was time to leave.

*   *   *   *

When we got back to the hotel bar, Ed Clarke between sips of beer asked me, "Hey, have you seen any old people? There's nothing but young people running this country. What is Fidel, thirty-three? Ché, Nuñez Jiménez, both in their early thirties. Raúl's not even that old. What'd they do to all those old people?"

I laughed. "They must all be in Miami." But it was true, the wild impression one gets from the country is that it is being run by a group of young radical intellectuals, and the young men of Latin America are *radical.* Whether Marxist or not, it is a social radicalism that they want. No one speaks of compromise. The idea has never occurred to them. The many so-called friends of Castro who have run out since the revolution were in most cases people who were prepared to compromise. People who knew that Fidel's radicalism would make him dangerous to the "free world." That free world of bankers, political pawns, grasping industrialists and liars. The free world that cited the inhumanity of the government of Fulgencio Batista an "internal problem," just as they now condone the hateful willfulness of Generalissimo Trujillo (whose picture, until a few months ago, was plastered up all over Cooper Square in New York City).

The weird stupidity of this situation is that in most cases the so-called American intellectual is not even aware of what is happening anyplace in the world. Not anyplace where it serves the interests of the various trusts and gangsters that situations be obfuscated. The intelligent American reads an "account" of what is happening someplace in the world, say in the *New York Times.* He is certainly aware to a certain extent that some of what is being "accounted" is slanted in the general direction of American "well-meaning-ness." The most severe condemnation of American leaders by the American intellectual is that they are "bumblers," unintelligent but well-meaning clowns. But we do not realize how much of the horrible residue of these paid liars is left in our heads. Who is it in the U.S. that is not afraid of China? Who is that does not believe that there is such a thing as "the free world"? That West Germany is "freer" than East Germany? That there *are* communist influences in the Cuban government? We reject the blatant, less dangerous lie in favor of the subtle subliminal lie, which is more dangerous because we feel we are taking an intelligent stance, not being had. What do we know about China? Who told you about the communist influences in the Cuban government? How do you know the Indian people love Nehru? We go to Mexico for a vacation. The place is a haven for bearded young men of my generation to go and make their "scene," but not one in a hundred will come back realizing that there are students there getting murdered and beaten because they are protesting against the fraudulent one-party regime that controls the country, which is backed to the hilt by our "well-meaning" government.

It is sad, and there is nothing I can even suggest as an alternative. We've gone too far. There is a certain hopelessness about our attitude that can even be condoned. The environment sickens. The young intellectual living in the United States inhabits an ugly void. He cannot use what is around him, neither can he revolt against it. Revolt against whom? Revolution in this country of "due processes of law" would be literally impossible. Whose side would you be on? The void of being killed by what is in this country and not knowing what is outside of it. Don't tell me about the dead minds of Europe. They stink worse than our own.

* * * *

It was late at night, and still Habana had not settled down to its usual quiet. Crowds of people were squatting around bus stops, walking down the streets in groups headed for bus stops. Truckloads of militia were headed out of the city. Young men and women with rucksacks and canteens were piling into buses, trucks, and private cars all over the city. There were huge signs all over Habana reading "a la Sierra con Fidel ... Julio 26." Thousands of people were leaving Habana for the July 26th celebration of Sierra Maestra all the way at the other end of the island in Oriente province. The celebration was in honor of Fidel Castro's first onslaught against Moncada barracks, July 26, 1953, which marked the beginning of his drive against the Batista government. Whole families were packing up, trying to get to Oriente the best way they could. It was still three days before the celebration and people clogged the roads from Habana all the way to the Eastern province.

The night of our departure for Oriente we arrived at the train station in Habana about 6 P.M. It was almost impossible to move around in the station. *Campesinos,* businessmen, soldiers, *milicianas,* tourists—all were thrashing around trying to make sure they had seats in the various trains. As we came into the station, most of the delegates of a Latin-American Youth Congress were coming in also. There were about nine hundred of them, representing students from almost every country in Latin America. Mexicans, Colombians, Argentines, Venezuelans, Puerto Ricans (with signs reading "For the Liberation of Puerto Rico"), all carrying flags, banners, and wearing the large, ragged straw hat of the *campesino.* We were to go in the same train as the delegates.

As we moved through the crowds toward our train, the students began chanting: "Cuba Sí, Yanqui No ... Cuba Sí, Yanqui No ... Cuba Sí, Yanqui No." The crowds in the terminal joined in, soon there was a deafening crazy scream that seemed to burst the roof off the terminal. Cuba Sí, Yanqui No! We raced for the trains.

Once inside the train, a long modern semi-air-conditioned "Silver Meteor," we quickly settled down and I began scribbling illegibly in my notebook. But the Latin Americans came scrambling into the train still chanting furiously and someone handed me a drink of rum. They were yelling "Venceremos, Venceremos, Venceremos, Venceremos." Crowds of soldiers and militia on the platform outside joined in. Everyone was screaming as the train began to pull away.

The young militia people soon came trotting through the coaches asking everyone to sit down for a few seconds so they could be counted. The delegates got to their seats and in my coach everyone began to sing a song like "Two, four, six, eight, who do we appreciate ... Fidel, Fidel, Fidel!!" Then they did Ché (Guevara), Raúl, President Dorticos, etc. It was about 1,000 kilometers to Oriente and we had just started.

Young soldiers passed out ham sandwiches and Maltina, a thick syrupy sweet beverage that only made me thirstier. Everyone in the train seemed to be talking excitedly and having a wild time. We were about an hour outside Habana and I was alternating between taking notes and reading about ancient Mexican religion when Olga Finlay came up to my seat accompanied by a young woman. "I told her you were an American poet," Olga said, "and she wanted to meet you." I rose quickly and extended my hand, for some reason embarrassed as hell. Olga said, "Señora Betancourt, Señor LeRoi Jones." She was very short, very blond and very pretty, and had a weird accent that never ceased to fascinate me. For about thirty minutes we stood in the middle aisle talking to each other. She was a Mexican delegate to the Youth Congress, a graduate student in economics at one of the universities, the wife of an economist, and a mother. Finally, I offered her the seat next to mine at the window. She sat, and we talked almost continuously throughout the fourteen-hour ride.

She questioned me endlessly about American life, American politics, American youth—although I was jokingly cautioned against using the word *American* to mean the U.S. or North America. "Everyone in this car is American," she said. "You from the North, we from the South." I explained as best I could about the Eisenhowers, the Nixons, the Du Ponts, but she made even my condemnations seem mild. "Everyone in the world," she said, with her finger, "has to be communist or anticommunist. And if they're anticommunist, no matter what kind of foul person they are, you people accept them as your allies. Do you really think that hopeless little island in the middle of the sea is China? That is irrational. You people are irrational!"

I tried to defend myself. "Look, why jump on me? I understand what you're saying. I'm in complete agreement with you. I'm a poet ... what can I do? I write, that's all, I'm not even interested in politics."

She jumped on me with both feet as did a group of Mexican poets later in Habana. She called me a "cowardly bourgeois individualist." The poets, or at least one young wild-eyed Mexican poet, Jaime Shelley, almost left me in tears, stomping his foot on the floor, screaming: "You want to cultivate your soul? In that ugliness you live in, you want to cultivate your soul? Well, we've got millions of starving people to feed, and that moves me enough to make poems out of."

*　　*　　*　　*

Around 10 P.M. the train pulled into the town of Matanzas. We had our blinds drawn, but the militia came running through the car telling us to raise them. When I raised the blind I was almost startled out of my wits. There were about 1,500 people in the train station and surrounding it, yelling their lungs out. We pulled up the windows. People were all over. They ran back and forth along the train screaming at us. The Mexicans in the train had a big sign painted on a bedspread that read "Mexico is with Fidel. Venceremos." When they raised it to the windows young men leaped in the air, and women blew kisses. There was a uniformed marching band trying to be heard above the crowd, but I could barely hear them. When I poked my head out of the window to wave at the crowds, two young Negro women giggled violently at first, then one of them ran over to the train and kissed me as hard as she could manage. The only thing to do I could think of was to say "Thank you." She danced up and down and clapped her hands and shouted to her friend, "Un americano, un americano." I bowed my head graciously.

What was it, a circus? That wild mad crowd. Social ideas? Could there be that much excitement generated through all the people? Damn, that people still *can* move. Not us, but people. It's gone out of us forever. "Cuba Sí, Yanqui No," I called at the girls as the train edged away.

*   *   *   *

We stopped later in the town of Colón. There again the same mobs of cheering people. Camaguey, Santa Clara. At each town, the chanting crowds. The unbelievable joy and excitement. The same idea, and people made beautiful because of it. People moving, being moved. I was ecstatic and frightened. Something I had never seen before, exploding all around me.

*   *   *   *

The train rocked wildly across and into the interior. The delegates were singing a "cha cha" with words changed to something like "Fidel, Fidel, cha cha cha, Ché Ché, cha cha cha, Abajo Imperialismo Yanqui, cha cha cha." Some American students whom I hadn't seen earlier ran back and forth in the coaches singing, "We cannot be moved." The young folk-song politicians in blue jeans and pigtails.

About two o'clock in the morning they shut the lights off in most of the coaches, and everybody went to sleep. I slept for only an hour or so and woke up just in time to see the red sun come up and the first early people come out of their small grass-roofed shacks beside the railroad tracks, and wave sleepily at the speeding train. I pressed my face against the window and waved back.

*   *   *   *

The folk singing and war cries had just begun again in earnest when we reached the town of Yara, a small town in Oriente province, the last stop on the line. At once we unloaded from the train, leaving most luggage and whatever was considered superfluous. The dirt streets of the town were jammed with people. Probably everyone in town had come to meet the train. The entire town was decorated with some kind of silver Christmas tree tinsel and streamers. Trees, bushes, houses, children, all draped in the same silver holiday tinsel. Tiny girls in brown uniforms and red berets greeted us with armfuls of flowers. Photographers were running amok through the crowd, including an American newsreel cameraman who kept following Robert Williams. I told Robert that he ought to put his big straw hat in front of his face American ganster style.

From the high hill of the train station it was possible to see a road running right through Yara. Every conceivable kind of bus, truck, car, and scooter was being pushed toward the Sierra, which was now plainly visible in the distance. Some of the *campesinos* were on horses, dodging in and out of the sluggish traffic, screaming at the top of their lungs.

The sun had already gotten straight up over our heads and was burning down viciously. The big straw *campesino* hats helped a little but I could tell that it was going to be an obscenely hot day. We stood around for a while until everyone had gotten off our train, and then some of the militia people waved at us to follow them. We walked completely out of the town of Yara in about two minutes. We walked until we came to more railroad tracks; a short spur leading off in the direction of Sierra Maestra. Sitting on the tracks were about ten empty open cattle cars. There were audible groans from the American contingent. The cars themselves looked like movable jails. Huge thick bars around the sides. We joked about the American cameraman taking a picture of them with us behind the bars and using it as a *Life* magazine cover. They would caption it "Americans in Cuba."

At a word from the militia we scrambled up through the bars, into the scalding cars. The metal parts of the car were burning hot, probably from sitting out in the sun all day. It was weird seeing hundreds of people up and down the tracks climbing up into the cattle cars by whatever method they could manage. We had been told in Habana that this was going to be a rough trip and that we ought to dress accordingly. Heavy shoes, old clothes, a minimum of equipment. The women were told specifically to wear slacks and flat shoes because it would be difficult to walk up a mountain in a sheath dress and heels. However, one of the American women, the pretty young middle-class lady from Philadelphia, showed up in a flare skirt and "Cuban" heels. Two of the Cubans had to pull and tug to get her into the car, which still definitely had the smell of cows. She slumped in a corner and began furiously mopping her brow.

I sat down on the floor and tried to scribble in my notebook, but it was difficult because everyone was jammed in very tight. Finally, the train jerked to a start, and everyone in all the cars let out a wild yell. The delegates began chanting again. Waving at all the people along the road, and all the dark barefoot families standing in front of their grass-topped huts calling to us. The road which ran along parallel to the train was packed full of traffic, barely moving. Men sat on the running boards of their cars when the traffic came to a complete halt, and drank water from their canteens. The train was going about five miles an hour and the *campesinos* raced by on their plow horses jeering, swinging their big hats. The sun and the hot metal car were almost unbearable. The delegates shouted at the trucks, "Cuba Sí, Yanqui No," and then began their "Viva" shouts. After one of the "Vivas," I yelled, "Viva Calle Cuarenta y dos" (42nd Street), "Viva Symphony Sid," "Viva Cinco Punto" (Five Spot), "Viva Turhan Bey." I guess it was the heat. It was a long slow ride in the boiling cars.

*   *   *   *

The cattle cars stopped after an hour or so at some kind of junction. All kinds of other coaches were pulled up and resting on various spurs. People milled about everywhere. But it was the end of any tracks going further toward Sierra. We stood around and drank warm water too fast.

Now we got into trucks. Some with nailed-in bus seats, some with straw roofs, others with just plain truck floors. It was a wild scramble for seats. The militia people and the soldiers did their best to indicate which trucks were for whom, but people staggered into the closest vehicle at hand. Ed Clarke and I ran and leaped up into a truck with leather bus seats in the back. The leather was too hot to sit on for a while so I put my handkerchief on the seat and sat forward. A woman was trying to get up into the truck, but not very successfully, so I leaned over the rail and pulled her up and in. The face was recognizable immediately, but I had to sit back on the hot seat before I remembered it was Françoise Sagan. I turned to say something to her, but some men were already helping her back down to the ground. She rode up front in the truck's cab with a young lady companion, and her manager on the running board, clinging to the door.

The trucks reared out onto the already heavily traveled road. It was an unbelievable scene. Not only all the weird trucks and buses but thousands of people walking along the road. Some had walked from places as far away as Matanzas. Whole detachments of militia were marching, rout step, but carrying rifles or .45's. Women carrying children on their shoulders. One group of militia with blue shirts, green pants, pistols and knives was carrying paper fans, which they ripped back and forth almost in unison with their step.

There were huge trucks full of oranges parked along the road with lines of people circling them. People were sitting along the edge of the road eating their lunches. Everyone going *à la* Sierra.

Our trucks sped along the outside of the main body of traffic, still having to stop occasionally when there was some hopeless roadblock. The sun, for all our hats, was baking our heads. Sweat poured in my dry mouth. None of us Americans had brought canteens and there was no water to be had while we were racing along the road. I tried several times to get some oranges, but never managed. The truck would always start up again when we came close to an orange vendor.

There was a sign on one of the wood shack "stores" we passed that read "Niños No Gustan Los Chicle Ni Los Cigarros Americanos Ni El Rocan Rool." It was signed "Fondin." The traffic bogged down right in front of the store so several French photographers leaped off the truck and raced for the orange stand. Only one fellow managed to make it back to our truck with a hat full of oranges. The others had to turn and run back emptyhanded as the truck pulled away. Sagan's manager, who had strapped himself on the running board with a leather belt, almost broke his head when the truck hit a bump and the belt snapped and sent him sprawling into the road. Another one of the correspondents suddenly became violently ill and tried to shove his head between the rough wooden slats at the side of the truck; he didn't quite make it, and everyone in the truck suffered.

After two hours we reached a wide, slow, muddy river. There was only one narrow cement bridge crossing it, so the trucks had to wait until they could ease back into the regular line of traffic. There were hundreds of people wading across the river. A woman splashed in with her child on her shoulders, hanging around her neck, her lunch pail in one hand, a pair of blue canvas sneakers in the other. One group of militia marched right into the brown water, holding their rifles above their heads. When our truck got on the bridge directly over the water, one of the Cuban newspapermen leaped out of the truck down ten feet into the water. People in the trucks would jump right over the side, sometimes pausing to take off their shoes. Most went in shoes and all.

Now we began to wind up the narrow mountain road for the first time. All our progress since Yara had been upgrade, but this was the first time it was clearly discernible that we were going up a mountain. It took another hour to reach the top. It was afternoon now and already long lines of people were headed back down the mountain. But it was a narrow line compared to the thousands of people who were scrambling up just behind us. From one point where we stopped just before reaching the top it was possible to look down the side of the long hill and see swarms of people all the way down past the river seeming now to inch along in effortless pantomime.

The trucks stopped among a jumble of rocks and sand not quite at the top of the last grade. (For the last twenty minutes of our climb we actually had to wind in and out among groups of people. The only people who seemed to race along without any thought of the traffic were the *campesinos* on their broken-down mounts.) Now everyone began jumping down off the trucks and trying to re-form into their respective groups. It seemed almost impossible. Detachments of *campesino* militia (work shirts, blue jeans, straw hats and machetes) marched up behind us. *Milicianas* of about twelve and thirteen separated our contingent, then herds of uniformed, trotting boys of about seven. "Hup, hup, hup, hup," one little boy was calling in vain as he ran behind the rest of his group. One of the girls called out "Hup, hup, hup, hup," keeping her group more orderly. Rebel soldiers wandered around everywhere, some with long, full beards, others with long, wavy black hair pulled under their blue berets or square-topped khaki caps, most of them young men in their twenties or teen-agers. An old man with a full gray beard covering most of his face, except his sparkling blue eyes and the heavy black cigar stuck out of the side of his mouth, directed the comings and goings up and down this side of the mountain. He wore a huge red-and-black-handled revolver and had a hunting knife sewn to his boot. Suddenly it seemed that I was lost in a sea of uniforms, and I couldn't see anyone I had come up the mountain with. I sat down on a rock until most of the uniforms passed. Then I could see Olga about fifty yards away waving her arms at her lost charges.

There was a public address system booming full blast from what seemed the top of the hill. The voice (Celia Sánchez, Fidel's secretary) was announcing various groups that were passing in review. When we got to the top of the rise, we could see a large, austere platform covered with all kinds of people, and at the front of the platform a raised section with a dais where the speakers were. Señora Sánchez was announcing one corps of militia and they marched out of the crowd and stopped before the platform. The crowd cheered and cheered. The militia was commended from the platform and then they marched off into the crowd at the other side. Other groups marched past. Young women, teen-age girls, elderly *campesinos,* each with their own militia detachment, each to be commended. This had been going on since morning. Hundreds of commendations, thousands of people to be commended. Also, since morning, the officials had been reading off lists of names of *campesinos* who were to receive land under the Agrarian Reform Law. When they read the name of some farmer close enough to the mountain to hear it, he would leap straight up in the air and, no matter how far away from the platform he was, would go barreling and leaping toward the speaker. The crowd delighted in this and would begin chanting "Viva Fidel, Viva Fidel, Viva Reforma Agraria." All this had been going on since morning and it was now late afternoon.

After we walked past the dais, introduced to the screaming crowd as "intellectual North American visitors," we doubled back and went up onto the platform itself. It was even hotter up there. By now all I could think about was the sun; it was burning straight down and had been since early morning. I tugged the straw hat down over my eyes and trudged up onto the platform. The platform itself in back of the dais was almost overflowing, mostly with rebel soldiers and young militia troops. But there were all kinds of visitors also, the Latin American delegates, newsmen, European writers, American intellectuals, as well as Cuban officials. When we got up on the platform, Olga led us immediately over to the speakers' dais and the little group of seats around it. We were going to be introduced to all the major speakers.

The first person to turn around and greet us was a tall, thin, bearded Negro in a rebel uniform bearing the shoulder markings of a *Comandante*. I recognized his face from the papers as that of Juan Almeida, chief of the rebel army, a man almost unknown in the United States. He grinned and shook our hands and talked in a swift combination of Spanish and English, joking constantly about conditions in the United States. In the middle of one of his jokes he leaned backward, leaning over one man to tap another, taller man on the shoulder. Fidel Castro leaned back in his seat, then got up smiling and came over to where we were standing. He began shaking hands with everybody in the group, as well as the many other visitors who moved in at the opportunity. There were so many people on the platform in what seemed like complete disorder that I wondered how wise it was as far as security was concerned. It seemed awfully dangerous for the Prime Minister to be walking around so casually, almost having to thread his way through the surging crowd. Almost immediately, I shoved my hand toward his face and then grasped his hand. He greeted me warmly, asking through the interpreter where I was from and what I did. When I told him I was a New York poet, he seemed extremely amused and asked me what the government thought about my trip. I shrugged my shoulders and asked him what did he intend to do with this revolution.

We both laughed at the question because it was almost like a reflex action on my part: something that came out so quick that I was almost unaware of it. He twisted the cigar in his mouth and grinned, smoothing the strangely grown beard on his cheeks. "That *is* a poet's question," he said, "and the only poet's answer I can give you is that I will do what I think is right, what I think the people want. That's the best I can hope for, don't you think?"

I nodded, already about to shoot out another question, I didn't know how long I'd have. Certainly this was the most animated I'd been during the entire trip. "Uh"— I tried to smile—"what do you think the United States will do about Cuba ultimately?" The question seemed weird and out of place because everyone else was just trying to shake his hand.

"Ha, well, that's extremely difficult to say, your government is getting famous for its improvisation in foreign affairs. I suppose it depends on who is running the government. If the Democrats win it may get better. More

Republicans . . . I suppose more trouble. I cannot say, except that I really do not care what they do as long as they do not try to interfere with the running of this country."

Suddenly the idea of a security lapse didn't seem so pressing. I had turned my head at a weird angle and looked up at the top of the platform. There was a soldier at each side of the back wall of the platform, about ten feet off the ground, each one with a machine gun on a tripod. I asked another question. "What about communism? How big a part does that play in the government?"

"I've said a hundred times that I'm not a communist. But I am certainly not an anticommunist. The United States likes anticommunists, especially so close to their mainland. I said also a hundred times that I consider myself a humanist. A radical humanist. The only way that anything can ever be accomplished in a country like Cuba is radically. The old has been here so long that the new must make radical changes in order to function at all."

So many people had crowded around us now that it became almost impossible to hear what Fidel was saying. I had shouted the last question. The young fashion model brushed by me and said how much she enjoyed her stay in Cuba. Fidel touched his hand to the wide *campesino* hat he was wearing, then pumped her hand up and down. One of the Latin-American girls leaned forward suddenly and kissed him on the cheek. Everyone milled around the tall young Cuban, asking questions, shaking his hand, taking pictures, getting autographs (an American girl with pigtails and blue jeans) and, I suppose, committing everything he said to memory. The crowd was getting too large. I touched his arm, waved, and walked toward the back of the platform.

I hadn't had any water since early morning, and the heat and the excitement made my mouth dry and hard. There were no water fountains in sight. Most of the masses of Cubans had canteens or vacuum bottles, but someone had forgotten to tell the Americans (North and South) that there'd be no water. Also, there was no shade at all on the platform. I walked around behind it and squatted in a small booth with a tiny tin roof. It had formerly been a soda stand, but because the soda was free, the supply had given out rapidly and the stand had closed. I sat in the few inches of shade with my head in my hands, trying to cool off. Some Venezuelans came by and asked to sit in the shade next to me. I said it was all right and they offered me the first cup of water I'd had in about five hours. They had a whole chicken also, but I didn't think I'd be able to stand the luxury.

There were more speakers, including a little boy from one of the youngest militia units, but I heard them all over the public address system. I was too beat and thirsty to move. Later Ed Clarke and I went around hunting for water and finally managed to find a small brown stream where the soldiers were filling up their canteens. I drank two Coca-Cola bottles full, and when I got back to Habana came down with a fearful case of dysentery.

Suddenly there was an insane, deafening roar from the crowd. I met the girl economist as I dragged out of the booth and she tried to get me to go back on the front platform. Fidel was about to speak. I left her and jumped off the platform and trotted up a small rise to the left. The roar lasted about ten minutes, and as I got settled on the side of the hill Fidel began to speak.

He is an amazing speaker, knowing probably instinctively all the laws of dynamics and elocution. The speech began slowly and haltingly, each syllable being pronounced with equal stress, as if he were reading a poem. He was standing with the *campesino* hat pushed back slightly off his forehead, both hands on the lectern. As he made his points, one of the hands would slide off the lectern and drop to his side, his voice becoming tighter and less warm. When the speech was really on its way, he dropped both hands from the lectern, putting one behind his back like a church usher, gesturing with the other. By now he would be rocking from side to side, pointing his finger at the crowd, at the sky, at his own chest. Sometimes he seemed to lean to the side and talk to his own ministers there on the platform with him and then wheel toward the crowd calling for them to support him. At one point in the speech the crowd interrupted for about twenty minutes, crying, "Venceremos, venceremos, venceremos, venceremos, venceremos, venceremos, venceremos, venceremos." The entire crowd, 60,000 or 70,000 people all chanting in unison. Fidel stepped away from the lectern grinning, talking to his aides. He quieted the crowd with a wave of his arms and began again. At first softly, with the syllables drawn out and precisely enunciated, then tightening his voice and going into an almost musical rearrangement of his speech. He condemned Eisenhower, Nixon, the South, the Monroe Doctrine, the Platt Amendment, and Fulgencio Batista in one long, unbelievable sentence. The crowd interrupted again, "Fidel, Fidel, Fidel, Fidel, Fidel, Fidel, Fidel, Fidel, Fidel, Fidel, Fidel, Fidel." He leaned away from the lectern, grinning at the chief of the army. The speech lasted almost two and a half hours, being interrupted time and again by the exultant crowd and once by five minutes of rain. When it began to rain, Almeida draped a rain jacket around Fidel's shoulders, and he relit his cigar. When the speech ended, the crowd went out of its head, roaring for almost forty-five minutes.

* * * *

When the speech was over, I made a fast move for the platform. Almost a thousand other people had the same idea. I managed to shout something to Castro as he was being whizzed to the back of the platform and into a car. I shouted, "A fine speech, a tremendous speech."

He shouted back, "I hope you take it home with you," and disappeared in a host of bearded uniforms.

* * * *

We were told at first that we would be able to leave the mountain in about three hours. But it had gotten dark already, and I didn't really fancy shooting down that mountain road with the same exuberance with which we came ... not in the dark. Clarke and I went out looking for more water and walked almost a mile before we came to a big pavilion where soft drinks and sandwiches were being served. The soft drinks were hot and the sandwiches took too long to get. We came back and lay down at the top of a hill in back of the speakers' platform. It drizzled a little bit and the ground was patently uncomfortable. I tried to go to sleep but was awakened in a few minutes by explosions. The whole sky was lit up. Green, red, bright orange: the soldiers were shooting off fireworks. The platform was bathed in the light from the explosions and, suddenly, floodlights from the rear. The public address system announced that we were going to have a show.

The show was a strange mixture of pop culture and mainstream highbrow *haute culture*. There was a choral group singing a mildly atonal tone poem, a Jerome Robbinsesque ballet about Hollywood, Calypso dancers, and Mexican singers and dancers. The last act was the best, a Mardi Gras scene involving about a hundred West Indian singers and dancers, complete with floats, huge papier-mâché figures, drummers, and masks. The West Indians walked through the audience shouting and dancing, their many torches shooting shadows against the mountains. When they danced off and out of the amphitheater area up toward a group of unfinished school buildings, except for the huge floodlights on stage, the whole area was dark.

* * * *

Now there was great confusion in the audience. Most Cubans were still going to try to get home that night, so they were getting themselves together, rounding up wives and children, trying to find some kind of transportation off the mountain. There were still whole units of militia piling into trucks or walking off down the hill in the dark. The delegates, our group and a couple more thousand people who didn't feel like charging off into the dark were left. Olga got all the Americans together and we lined up for what was really our first meal of the day: beans, rice, pork, and a small can of fruit juice. At that time, we still had some hopes of leaving that night, but soon word was passed around that we weren't leaving, and it was best that we slept where we were. "Sleep wherever you want," was what Olga said. That meant the ground, or maybe cement sidewalks around the unfinished school buildings and dormitories of the new "school city." Some of the Americans started grumbling, but there was nothing that could be done. Two of our number were missing because of the day's festivities: the young lady from Philadelphia had to be driven back to Habana in a station wagon because she had come down with diarrhea and a fever, and the model had walked around without her hat too often and had gotten a slight case of sunstroke. She was resting up in the medical shack now, and I began to envy her her small canvas cot.

It was a very strange scene, about three or four thousand people wandering around in semidarkness among a group of unfinished buildings, looking for places to sleep. The whole top of the mountain alive with flashlights, cigarette lighters, and small torches. Little groups of people huddled together against the sides of buildings or stretched out under new "street lamps" in temporary plazas. Some people managed to climb through the windows of the new buildings and sleep on dirt floors, some slept under long aluminum trucks used for hauling stage equipment and some, like myself and the young female economist, sat up all night under dim lights, finally talking ourselves excitedly to sleep in the cool gray of early morning. I lay straight back on the cement "sidewalk" and slept without moving, until the sun began to burn my face.

We had been told the night before to be ready by 6 A.M. to pull out, but when morning came we loitered around again till about eight o'clock, when we had to line up for a breakfast of hot milk and French bread. It was served by young militia women, one of whom wore a big sidearm in a shoulder holster. By now, the dysentery was beginning to play havoc with my stomach, and the only toilet was a heavy thicket out behind the amphitheater. I made it once, having to destroy a copy of a newspaper with my picture in it.

By nine no trucks had arrived, and with the sun now beginning to move heavily over us, the crowds shifted into the few shady areas remaining. It looked almost as if there were as many people still up on the mountain as there had been when we first arrived. Most of the Cubans, aside from the soldiers, stood in front of the pavilion and drank lukewarm Maltina or pineapple soda. The delegates and the other visitors squatted against buildings, talking and smoking. A French correspondent made a bad joke about Mussolini keeping the trains running on time, and a young Chinese student asked him why he wasn't in Algeria killing rebels.

The trucks did arrive, but there were only enough of them to take the women out. In a few minutes the sides of the trucks were almost bursting, so many females had stuffed inside. And they looked terribly uncomfortable, especially the ones stuck in the center who couldn't move an inch either way. An American newspaperman with our group who was just about to overstay his company-sanctioned leave began to panic, saying that the trucks wouldn't be back until the next day. But only a half-hour after the ladies pulled out, more trucks came and began taking the men out. Clarke, Williams, another member of our group, and I sat under the tin roof of an unfinished school building drinking warm soda, waiting until the last truck came, hoping it would be the least crowded. When we did climb up into one of the trucks it was jammed anyway, but we felt it was time to move.

This time we all had to stand up, except for a young *miliciano* who was squatting on a case of warm soda. I was in the center of the crowd and had nothing to hold on to but my companions. Every time the truck would stop short, which it did every few yards we traveled, everyone in the truck was slung against everyone else. When the truck did move, however, it literally zoomed down the side of the mountain. But then we would stop again, and all of us felt we would suffocate being mashed so tightly together, and from all the dust the trucks in front of us kicked up. The road now seemed like the Exodus. Exactly the same as the day before, only headed the opposite way. The trucks, the people on foot, the families, the militias, the *campesinos,* all headed down the mountain.

The truck sat one place twenty minutes without moving, and then when it did move it only edged up a few yards. Finally the driver pulled out of the main body of traffic and, honking his horn continuously, drove down the opposite side of the road. When the soldiers directing traffic managed to flag him down, he told them that we were important visitors who had to make a train in Yara. The truck zoomed off again, rocking back and forth and up and down, throwing its riders at times almost out the back gate.

After a couple of miles, about five Mexicans got off the truck and got into another truck headed for Santiago. This made the rest of the ride easier. The *miliciano* began opening the soda and passing it around. We were really living it up. The delegates' spirits came back and they started their chanting and waving. When we got to the train junction, the cattle cars were sitting, but completely filled with soldiers and farmers. We didn't even stop, the driver gunned the thing as fast as it would go and we sailed by the shouting soldiers. We had only a few more stops before we got to Yara, jumped down in the soft sand, and ran for the big silver train marked "CUBA" that had been waiting for us since we left. When we got inside the train we discovered that the women still hadn't gotten back, so we sat quietly in the luxurious leather seats slowly sipping rum. The women arrived an hour later.

*   *   *   *

While we were waiting in Yara, soldiers and units of militia began to arrive in the small town and squat all around the four or five sets of tracks waiting for their own trains. Most of them went back in boxcars, while we visitors had the luxury of the semi-air-conditioned coach.

The ride back was even longer than the fourteen hours it took us before. Once when we stopped for water, we sat about two hours. Later, we stopped to pick up lunches. The atmosphere in the train was much the same as before, especially the Mexican delegates who whooped it up constantly. They even made a conga line up and down the whole length of the train. The young

Mexican woman and I did a repeat performance also and talked most of the fifteen or sixteen hours it took us to get back to Habana. She was gentler with me this time, calling me "Yanqui imperialist" only a few times.

Everyone in the train was dirty, thirsty, and tired when it arrived in Habana. I had been wearing the same clothes for three days and hadn't even once taken off my shoes. The women were in misery. I hadn't seen a pocket mirror since the cattle cars.

The terminal looked like a rear outpost of some battlefield. So many people in filthy wrinkled clothes scrambling wearily out of trains. But even as tired as I was I felt excited at the prospect of being back in the big city for five more days. I was even more excited by the amount of thinking the trip to the Sierra was forcing me to. The "new" ideas that were being shoved at me, some of which I knew would be painful when I eventually got to New York.

The idea of "a revolution" had been foreign to me. It was one of those inconceivably "romantic" and/or hopeless ideas that we Norteamericanos have been taught since public school to hold up to the cold light of "reason." That reason being whatever repugnant lie our usurious "ruling class" had paid their journalists to disseminate. The reason that allows that voting, in a country where the parties are exactly the same, can be made to assume the gravity of actual moral engagement. The reason that permits a young intellectual to believe he has said something profound when he says, "I don't trust men in uniforms." The *residue* had settled on all our lives, and no one can function comfortably in this country without it. That thin crust of lie we cannot even detect in our own thinking. That rotting of the mind which had enabled us to think about Hiroshima as if someone else had done it, or to believe vaguely that the "counterrevolution" in Guatemala was an "internal" affair.

The rebels among us have become merely people like myself who grow beards and will not participate in politics. Drugs, juvenile deliquency, complete isolation from the vapid mores of the country, a few current ways out. But name an alternative here. Something not inextricably bound up in a lie. Something not part of liberal stupidity or the actual filth of vested interest. There is none. It's much too late. We are an *old* people already. Even the vitality of our art is like bright flowers growing up through a rotting carcass.

But the Cubans, and the other *new* peoples (in Asia, Africa, South America) don't need us, and we had better stay out of their way.

* * * *

I came out of the terminal into the street and stopped at a newsstand to buy a paper. The headlines of one Miami paper read, "CUBAN CELEBRATION RAINED OUT." I walked away from the stand as fast as I could.

The Heretics
from *The System of Dante's Hell*

"The whole of lower Hell is surrounded by a great wall, which is defended by rebel angels and immediately within which are punished the arch-heretics and their followers."
      And then, the city of Dis, "the stronghold of Satan, named after him, . . . the deeper Hell of willful sin."

Blonde summer in our south. Always it floats down & hooks in the broad leaves of those unnamed sinister southern trees. Blonde. Yellow, a narrow sluggish water full of lives. Desires. The crimson heavy blood of a race, concealed in those absolute black nights. As if, each tiny tragedy had its own universe / or God to strike it down.

*   *   *   *

Faceless slow movement. It was warm & this other guy had his sleeves rolled up. (You cd go to jail for that without any trouble. But we were loose, & maybe drunk. And I turned away & doubled up like rubber or black figure sliding at the bottom of any ocean. Thomas, Joyce, Eliot, Pound, all gone by & I thot agony at how beautiful I was. And sat sad many times in latrines fingering my joint.
      But it was dusty. And time sat where it could, covered me dead, like under a stone for years, and my life was already over. A dead man stretched & a rock rolled over . . . till a light struck me straight on & I entered some madness, some hideous elegance . . . "A Patrician I wrote to him. Am I a Patrician?"

*   *   *   *

We both wore wings. My hat dipped & shoes maybe shined. This other guy was what cd happen in this country. Black & his silver wings & tilted blue cap made up for his mother's hundred bogus kids. Lynchings. And he waved his own flag in this mosquito air, and walked straight & beauty was fine, and so easy.

/   33

He didn't know who I was, or even what. The light, then (what george spoke of in his letters ... "a soft intense light") was spread thin over the whole element of my world.

Two flyers, is what we thot people had to say. (I was a gunner, the other guy, some kind of airborne medic.) The bright wings & starched uniform. Plus, 24 dollars in my wallet.

That air rides you down, gets inside & leaves you weightless, sweating & longing for a cool evening. The smells there wide & blue like eyes. And like kids, or the radio calling saturdays of the world of simple adventure. Made me weep with excitement. Heart pumping: not at all towards where we were. But the general sweep of my blood brought whole existences fresh and tingling into those images of romance had trapped me years ago.

*   *   *   *

The place used me. Its softness, and in a way, indirect warmth, coming from the same twisting streets we walked. (After the bus, into the main fashion of the city: Shreveport, Louisiana. And it all erected itself for whoever ... me, I supposed then, "it's here, and of course, the air, for my own weakness. Books fell by. But open yr eyes, nose, speak to whom you want to. Are you contemporary?)

And it seemed a world for aztecs lost on the bone side of mountains. A world, even strange, sat in that leavening light & we had come in raw from the elements. From the cardboard moonless world of ourselves ... to whatever. To grasp at straws. (If indeed we wd confront us with those wiser selves ... But that was blocked. The weather held. No rain. That smell wrapped me up finally & sent me off to seek its source. And men stopped us. Split our melting fingers. The sun moved till it stopped at the edge of the city. The south stretched past any eye. Outside any peculiar thot. Itself, whatever it becomes, is lost to what formal selves we have. Lust, a condition of the weather. The air, lascivious. Men die from anything ... and this portion of my life was carefully examining the rules. How to die? How to die?

*   *   *   *

The place, they told us, we'd have to go to "ball" was called by them *Bottom*. The Bottom; where the colored lived. There, in whatever wordless energies your lives cd be taken up. Step back: to the edge, soothed the wind drops. Fingers are cool. Air sweeps. Trees one hundred feet down, smoothed over, the wind sways.

they tell me there is one place/

                                                        And

                                        for me to be. Where
                                        it all
                                                comes down. &
                                        you take up
                                        your sorrowful
                                                        life. There/
                                        with us all. To
                                        whatever death

                        *   *   *   *

The Bottom lay like a man under a huge mountain. You cd see it slow in
some mist, miles off. On the bus, the other guy craned & pulled my arm from
the backseats at the mile descent we'd make to get the juice. The night had it.
Air like mild seasons and come. That simple elegance of semen on the single
buds of air. As if the night were feathers ... and they settled solid on my
speech ... and preached sinister love for the sun.
                        The day ... where had it
gone? It had moved away as we wound down into the mass of trees and
broken lives.
                        The bus stopped finally a third of the way down the slope. The
last whites had gotten off a mile back & 6 or seven negroes and we two flyers
had the bus. The driver smiled his considerate paternal smile in the mirror at
our heads as we popped off. Whole civilization considered, considered. "They
live in blackness. No thought runs out. They kill each other & hate the sun.
They have no God save who they are. Their black selves. Their lust. Their
insensible animal eyes."
                        "Hey, son, 'dyou pay for him?" He asked me be-
cause I hopped off last. He meant not my friend, the other pilot, but some
slick head coon in yellow pants cooling it at top speed into the grass. &
knowing no bus driver was running in after no 8 cents.

                                        "Man, the knives
                                        flash. Souls
                                        are spittle
                                        on black earth. Metal
                                        dug in flesh chipping
                                        at the bone."

I turned completely around to look at the bus driver. I saw a knife in him hacking chunks of bone. He stared, & smiled at the thin mob rolling down the hill. Friday night. Nigguhs is Nigguhs. I agreed. & smiled, he liked the wings, had a son who flew. "You gon pay for that ol coon?"

"No," I said, "No. Fuck, man, I hate coons." He laughed. I saw the night around his head warped with blood. The bus, moon & trees floated heavily in blood. It washed down the side of the hill & the negroes ran from it.

I turned towards my friend who was loping down the hill shouting at me & ran towards him & what we saw at the foot of the hill. The man backed the bus up & turned around / pretending he was a mystic.

* * * *

I caught Don(?) and walked beside him laughing. And the trees passed & some lights and houses sat just in front of us. We trailed the rest of the crowd & they spread out soon & disappeared into their lives.

The Bottom was like Spruce & Belmont(the ward) in Nwk. A culture of violence and foodsmells. There, for me. Again. And it stood strange when I thot finally how much irony. I had gotten so elegant (that was college / a new order of foppery). But then the army came & I was dragged into a kind of stillness. Everything I learned stacked up and the bones of love shattered in my face. And I never smiled again at anything. Everything casual in my life (except that life itself) was gone. Those naked shadows of men against the ruined walls. Penis, testicles. All there (and I sat burned like wire, w/ farmers, thinking of what I had myself. When I peed I thot that. "Look. Look what you're using to do this. A dick. And two balls, one a little lower than the other. The first thing warped & crooked when it hardened." But it meant nothing. The books meant nothing. My idea was to be loved. What I accused John of. And it meant going into that huge city melting. And the first face I saw I went to and we went home and she shoved her old empty sack of self against my frozen skin.

* * * *

Shadows, phantoms, recalled by that night. Its heavy moon. A turning slow and dug in the flesh and wet spots grew under my khaki arms. Alive to mystery. And the horror in my eyes made them large and the moon came in. The moon and the quiet southern night.

* * * *

We passed white shut houses. It seemed misty or smoky. Things settled dumbly in the fog and we passed, our lives spinning off in simple anonymous laughter.

We were walking single file because of the dirt road. Not wanting to get in the road where drunk niggers roared by in dead autos stabbing each other's laughter in some grey abandon of suffering. That they suffered and cdn't know it. Knew that somehow, forever. Each dead nigger stinking his same suffering thru us. Each word of blues some dead face melting. Some life drained off in silence. Under some grey night of smoke. They roared thru this night screaming. Heritage of hysteria and madness, the old meat smells and silent grey sidewalks of the North. Each father, smiling mother, walked thru these nights frightened of their children. Of the white sun scalding their nights. Of each hollow loud footstep in whatever abstruse hall.

* * * *

THE JOINT

(a letter was broken and I can't remember. The other guy laughed, at the name. And patted his. I took it literal and looked thru my wallet as not to get inflamed and sink on that man screaming of my new loves. My cold sin in the cities. My fear of my own death's insanity, and an actual longing for men that brooded in each finger of my memory.

He laughed at the sign. And we stood, for the moment (he made me warm with his laughing), huge white men who knew the world (our wings) and would give it to whoever showed as beautiful or in our sad lone smiles, at least willing to love us.

He pointed, like Odysseus wd. Like Virgil, the weary shade, at some circle. For Dante, me, the yng wild virgin of the universe to look. To see what terror. What illusion. What sudden shame, the world is made. Of what death and lust I fondled and thot to make beautiful or escape, at least, into some other light, where each death was abstract & intimate.

* * * *

There were, I think, 4 women standing across the street. The neon winked, and the place seemed mad to be squatted in this actual wilderness. "For Madmen Only." Mozart's Ornithology and yellow greasy fags moaning german jazz. Already, outside. The passage, I sensed in those women. And black space yawned. Damned and burning souls. What has been your sin? Your ugliness?

And they waved. Calling us natural names. "Hey, ol bigeye sweet nigger ... com'ere." "Littl ol' skeeter dick ...

don't you want none?" And to each other giggling at their centuries, "Um, that big nigger look sweet" . . . "Yeh, that little one look sweet too." The four walls of some awesome city. Once past you knew that your life had ended. That roads took up the other side, and wound into thicker dusk. Darker, more insane, nights.

And Don shouted back, convinced of his hugeness, his grace . . . my wisdom. I shuddered at their eyes and tried to draw back into the shadows. He grabbed my arm, and laughed at my dry lips.

Of the 4, the pretty one was Della and the fat one, Peaches. 17 year old whores strapped to negro weekends. To the black thick earth and smoke it made to hide their maudlin sins. I stared and was silent and they, the girls and Don, the white man, laughed at my whispering and sudden midnight world. Frightened of myself, of the night's talk, and not of them. Of myself.

The other two girls fell away hissing at their poverty. And the two who had caught us exchanged strange jokes. Told us of themselves thru the other's mouth. Don already clutching the thin beautiful Della. A small tender flower she seemed. Covered with the pollen of desire. Ignorance. Fear of what she was. At her 17th birthday she had told us she wept, in the department store, at her death. That the years wd make her old and her dresses wd get bigger. She laughed and felt my arm, and laughed, Don pulling her closer. And ugly negroes passed close to us frowning at the uniforms and my shy clipped speech which they called "norf."

So Peaches was mine. Fat with short baked hair split at the ends. Pregnant empty stomach. Thin shrieky voice like knives against a blackboard. Speeded up records. Big feet in white, shiny polished shoes. Fat tiny hands full of rings. A purple dress with wrinkles across the stomach. And perspiring flesh that made my khakis wet.

The four of us went in the joint and the girls made noise to show this world their craft. The two rich boys from the castle. (Don looked at me to know how much cash I had and shouted and shook his head and called "18, man," patting his ass.)

The place was filled with shades. Ghosts. And the huge ugly hands of actual spooks. Standing around the bar, spilling wine on greasy shirts. Yelling at a fat yellow spliv who talked about all their mothers, pulling out their drinks. Laughing with wet cigarettes and the paper stuck to fat lips. Crazy as anything in the world, and sad because of it. Yelling as not to hear the sad breathing world. Turning all music up. Screaming all lyrics. Tough black men . . . weak black men. Filthy drunk women whose perfume was cheap un-natural flowers. Quiet thin ladies whose lives had ended and whose teeth hung stupidly in their silent mouths . . . rotted by thousands of nickel wines. A smell of despair and drunkenness. Silence and laughter, and the sounds of their movement under it. Their frightening lives.

*   *   *   *

Of course the men didn't dig the two imitation white boys come in on their leisure. And when I spoke someone wd turn and stare, or laugh, and point me out. The quick new jersey speech, full of italian idiom, and the invention of the jews. Quick to describe. Quicker to condemn. And when we finally got a seat in the back of the place, where the dance floor was, the whole place had turned a little to look. And the girls ate it all up, laughing as loud as their vanity permitted. Other whores grimaced and talked almost as loud ... putting us all down.

10 feet up on the wall, in a kind of balcony, a jew sat, with thick glasses and a cap, in front of a table. He had checks and money at the table & where the winding steps went up to him a line of shouting woogies waved their pay & waited for that bogus christ to give them the currency of that place. Two tremendous muthafuckers with stale white teeth grinned in back of the jew and sat with baseball bats to protect the western world.

On the dance floor people hung on each other. Clutched their separate flesh and thought, my god, their separate thots. They stunk. They screamed. They moved hard against each other. They pushed. And wiggled to keep the music on. Two juke boxes blasting from each corner, and four guys on a bandstand who had taken off their stocking caps and come to the place with guitars. One with a saxophone. All that screaming came together with the smells and the music, the people bumped their asses and squeezed their eyes shut.

Don ordered a bottle of schenley's which cost 6 dollars for a pint after hours. And Peaches grabbed my arm and led me to the floor.

The dancing like a rite no one knew, or had use for outside their secret lives. The flesh they felt when they moved, or I felt all their flesh and was happy and drunk and looked at the black faces knowing all the world thot they were my own, and lusted at that anonymous America I broke out of, and long for it now, where I am.

We danced, this face and I, close so I had her sweat in my mouth, her flesh the only sound my brain could use. Stinking, and the music over us like a sky, choked any other movement off. I danced. And my history was there, had passed no further. Where it ended, here, the light white talking jig, died in the arms of some sentry of Africa. Some short-haired witch out of my mother's most hideous dreams. I was nobody now, mama. Nobody. Another secret nigger. No one the white world wanted or would look at. (My mother shot herself. My father killed by a white tree fell on him. The sun, now, smothered. Dead.

*   *   *   *

Don and his property had gone when we finished. 3 or 4 dances later. My uniform dripping and soggy on my skin. My hands wet. My eyes turned up to darkness. Only my nerves sat naked and my ears were stuffed with gleaming horns. No one face sat alone, just that image of myself, forever screaming. Chiding me. And the girl, Peaches, laughed louder than the crowd. And wearily I pushed her hand from my fly and looked for a chair.

We sat at the table and I looked around the room for my brother, and only shapes of black men moved by. Their noise and smell. Their narrow paths to death. I wanted to panic, but the dancing and gin had me calm, almost cruel in what I saw.

Peaches talked. She talked at what she thought she saw. I slumped on the table and we emptied another pint. My stomach turning rapidly and the room moved without me. And I slapped my hands on the table laughing at myself. Peaches laughed, peed, thinking me crazy, returned, laughed again. I was silent now, and felt the drunk and knew I'd go out soon. I got up feeling my legs, staring at the fat guard with me, and made to leave. I mumbled at her. Something ugly. She laughed and held me up. Holding me from the door. I smiled casual, said, "Well, honey, I gotta split ... I'm fucked up." She grinned the same casual, said, "You can't go now, big eye, we jist gittin into sumpum."

"Yeh, yeh, I know ... but I can't make it." My head was shaking on my chest, fingers stabbed in my pockets. I staggered like an acrobat towards the stars and trees I saw at one end of the hall. "UhUh ... baby where you going?"

"Gotta split, gotta split ... really, baby, I'm fucked ... up." And I twisted my arm away, moving faster as I knew I should towards the vague smell of air. Peaches was laughing and tugging a little at my sleeve. She came around and rubbed my tiny pecker with her fingers. And still I moved away. She had my elbow when I reached the road, head still slumped, and feet pushing for a space to go down solid on. When I got outside she moved in front of me. Her other girls had moved in too, to see what was going on. Why Peaches had to relinquish her share so soon. I saw the look she gave me and wanted some-how to protest, say, "I'm sorry. I'm fucked up. My mind, is screwy, I don't know why. I can't think. I'm sick. I've been fucked in the ass. I love books and smells and my own voice. You don't want me. Please, Please, don't want me."

But she didn't see. She heard, I guess, her own blood. Her own whore's bones telling her what to do. And I twisted away from her, headed across the road and into the dark. Out of, I hoped, Bottom, towards what I thot was light. And I could hear the girls laughing at me, at Peaches, at whatever thing I'd brought to them to see.

So the fat bitch grabbed my hat. A blue "overseas cap" they called it in the service. A cunt cap the white boys called it. Peaches had it and was laughing like kids in the playground doing the same thing to some unfortunate fag. I knew the second she got it, and stared crazily at her, and my look softened to fear and I grinned, I think. "You ain't going back without dis cap, big eye nigger," tossing it over my arms to her screaming friends. They tossed it back to her. I stood in the center staring at the lights. Listening to my own head. The things I wanted. Who I thot I was. What was it? Why was this going on? Who was involved? I screamed for the hat. And they shot up the street, 4 whores, Peaches last in her fat, shouting at them to throw the hat to her. I stood for a while and then tried to run after them. I cdn't go back to my base without that cap. Go to jail, drunken nigger! Throw him in the stockade! You're out of uniform, shine! When I got close to them, the other three ran off, and only Peaches stood at the top of the hill waving the hat at me, cackling at her wealth. And she screamed at the world, that she'd won some small niche in it. And did a dance, throwing her big hips at me, cursing and spitting . . . laughing at the drunk who had sat down on the curb and started to weep and plead at her for some cheap piece of cloth.

And I was mumbling under the tears. "My hat, please, my hat. I gott get back, please." But she came over to me and leaned on my shoulder, brushing the cap in my face. "You gonna buy me another drink . . . just one more?"

* * * *

She'd put the cap in her brassiere, and told me about the Cotton Club. Another place at the outskirts of Bottom. And we went there, she was bouncing and had my hand, like a limp cloth. She talked of her life. Her husband, in the service too. Her family. Her friends. And predicted I would be a lawyer or something else rich.

The Cotton Club was in a kind of ditch. Or valley. Or three flights down. Or someplace removed from where we stood. Like movies, or things you think up abstractly. Poles, where the moon was. Signs, for streets, beers, pancakes. Out front. No one moved outside, it was too late. Only whores and ignorant punks were out.

The place when we got in was all light. A bar. Smaller than the joint, with less people and quieter. Tables were strewn around and there was a bar with a fat white man sitting on a stool behind it. His elbows rested on the bar and he chewed a cigar spitting the flakes on the floor. He smiled at Peaches, knowing her, leaning from his talk. Four or five stood at the bar. White and black, moaning and drunk. And I wondered how it was they got in. The both colors? And I saw a white stripe up the center of the floor, and taped to the bar, going clear up, over the counter. And the black man who talked, stood at one side, the left, of the tape, furtherest from the door. And the white man, on the right, closest to the door. They talked, and were old friends, touching each other, and screaming with laughter at what they said.

We got vodka. And my head slumped, but I looked around to see, what place this was. Why they moved. Who was dead. What faces came. What moved. And they sat in their various skins and stared at me.

Empty man. Walk thru shadows. All lives the same. They give you wishes. The old people at the window. Dead man. Rised, come gory to their side, Wish to be lovely, to be some other self. Even here, without you. Some other soul, than the filth I feel. Have in me. Guilt, like something of God's. Some separate suffering self.

Locked in a lightless shaft. Light at the top, pure white sun. And shadows twist my voice. Iron clothes to suffer. To pull down, what had grown so huge. My life wrested away. The old wood. Eyes of the damned uncomprehending. Who it was. Old slack nigger. Drunk punk. Fag. Get up. Where's your home? Your mother. Rich nigger. Porch sitter. It comes down. So cute, huh? Yellow thing. Think you cute.

And suffer so slight, in the world. The world? Literate? Brown skinned. Stuck in the ass. Suffering from what? Can you read? Who is T. S. Eliot? So what? A cross. You've got to like girls. Weirdo. Break, Roi, break. Now come back, do it again. Get down, hard. Come up. Keep your legs high, crouch hard when you get the ball . . . churn, churn, churn. A blue jacket, and alone. Where? A chinese restaurant. Talk to me. Goddamnit. Say something. You never talk, just sit there, impossible to love. Say something. Alone, there, under those buildings. Your shadows. Your selfish tongue. Move. Frightened bastard. Frightened scared sissy motherfucker.

* * * *

I felt my head go down. And I moved my hand to keep it up. Peaches laughed again. The white man turned and clicked his tongue at her wagging his hand. I sucked my thin mustache, scratched my chest, held my sore head dreamily. Peaches laughed. 2 bottles more of vodka she drank (half pints at 3.00 each) & led me out the back thru some dark alley down steps and thru a dark low hall to where she lived.

She was dragging me, I tried to walk and couldn't and stuck my hands in my pockets to keep them out of her way. Her house, a room painted blue and pink with Rheingold women glued to the wall. Calendars. The Rotogravure. The picture of her husband? Who she thot was some officer, and he was grinning like watermelon photos with a big white apron on and uncle jemima white hat and should've had a skillet. I slumped on the bed, and she made me get up and sit in a chair and she took my hat out of her clothes and threw it across the room. Coffee, she said, you want coffee. She brought it anyway, and I got some in my mouth. Like winter inside me. I coughed and she laughed. I turned my head away from the bare bulb. And she went in a closet and got out a thin yellow cardboard shade and stuck it on the light trying to push the burned part away from the huge white bulb.

Willful sin. in your toilets jerking off. You refused God. All frauds, the cold mosques glitter winters. "Morsh-Americans." Infidels fat niggers at the gates. What you want. What you are now. Liar. All sins, against your God. Your own flesh. TALK. TALK.

And I still slumped and she pushed my head back against the greasy seat and sat on my lap grinning in my ear, asking me to say words that made her laugh. Orange. Probably. Girl. Newark. Peaches. Talk like a white man, she laughed. From up north (she made the "th" an "f").

And sleep seemed good to me. Something my mother would say. My grandmother, all those heads of heaven. To get me in. Roi, go to sleep, You need sleep, and eat more. You're too skinny. But this fat bitch pinched my neck and my eyes would shoot open and my hands dropped touching the linoleum and I watched roaches, trying to count them getting up to 5, and slumped again. She pinched me. And I made some move and pushed myself up standing and went to the sink and stuck my head in cold water an inch above the pile of stale egg dishes floating in brown she used to wash the eggs off.

I shook my head. Took out my handkerchief to dry my hands, leaving my face wet and cold, for a few seconds. But the heat came back, and I kept pulling my shirt away from my body and smelled under my arms, trying to laugh with Peaches, who was laughing again.

I wanted to talk now. What to say. About my life. My thots. What I'd found out, and tried to use. Who I was. For her. This lady, with me.

She pushed me backwards on the bed and said you're sleepy I'll get in with you. and I rolled on my side trying to push up on the bed and couldn't, and she pulled one of my shoes off and put it in her closet. I turned on my back and groaned at my head told her again I had to go. I was awol or something. I had to explain awol and she knew what it meant when I finished. Everybody that she knew was that. She was laughing again. O, God, I wanted to shout and it was groaned. Oh God.

She had my pants in her fingers pulling them over my one shoe. I was going to pull them back up and they slipped from my hands and I tried to raise up and she pushed me back. "Look, Ol nigger, I ain't even gonna charge you. I like you." And my head was turning, flopping straight back on the chenille, and the white ladies on the wall did tricks and grinned and pissed on the floor. "Baby, look, Baby," I was sad because I fell. From where it was I'd come to. My silence.

The streets I used for books. All come in. Lost. Burned. And soothing she rubbed her hard hair on my stomach and I meant to look to see if grease was there it was something funny I meant to say, but my head twisted to the side and I bit the chenille and figured there would be a war or the walls would collapse and I would have to take the black girl out, a hero. And my mother would grin and tell her friends and my father would call me "mcgee" and want me to tell about it.

When I had only my shorts on she pulled her purple dress over her head. It was all she had, except a grey brassiere with black wet moons where her arms went down. She kept it on.

Some light got in from a window. And one white shadow sat on a half-naked woman on the wall. Nothing else moved. I drew my legs up tight & shivered. Her hands pulled me to her.

*   *   *   *

It was Chicago. The fags & winter. Sick thin boy, come out of those els. Ask about the books. Thin mathematics and soup. Not the black Beverly, but here for the first time I'd seen it. Been pushed in. What was flesh I hadn't used till then. To go back. To sit lonely. Need to be used, touched, and see for the first time how it moved. Why the world moved on it. Not a childish sun. A secret fruit. But hard things between their legs. And lives governed under it. So here, it can sit now, as evil. As demanding, for me, to have come thru and found it again. I hate it. I hate to touch you. To feel myself go soft and want some person myself. And here, it had moved outside. Left my wet fingers and was not something I fixed. But dropped on me and sucked me inside. That I walked the streets hunting for warmth. To be pushed under a quilt, and call it love. To shit water for days and say I've been loved. Been warm. A real thing in the world. See my shadow. My reflection. I'm here, alive. Touch me. Please, Please, touch me.

*   *   *   *

She rolled on me and after my pants were off pulled me on her thick stomach. I dropped between her legs and she felt between my cheeks to touch my balls. Her fingers were warm and she grabbed everything in her palm and wanted them harder. She pulled to get them harder and it hurt me. My head hurt me. My life. And she pulled, breathing spit on my chest. "Comeon, Baby, Comeon . . . Get hard." It was like being slapped. And she did it that way, trying to laugh. "Get hard . . . Get hard." And nothing happened or the light changed and I couldn't see the paper woman.

And she slapped me now, with

her hand. A short hard punch and my head spun. She cursed. & she pulled as hard as she could. I was going to be silent but she punched again and I wanted to laugh . . . it was another groan. "Young peachtree," she had her mouth at my ear lobe. "You don't like women, huh?" "No wonder you so pretty . . . ol bigeye faggot." My head was turned from that side to the other side turned to the other side turned again and had things in it bouncing.

"How'd you ever get in them airplanes, peaches (her name she called me)? Why they let fairies in there now? (She was pulling too hard now & I thot everything would give and a hole in my stomach would let out words and tears.) Goddam punk, you gonna fuck me tonight or I'm gonna pull your fuckin dick aloose."

How to be in this world. How to be here, not a shadow, but thick bone and meat. Real flesh under real sun. And real tears falling on black sweet earth.

I was crying now. Hot hot tears and trying to sing. Or say to Peaches. "Please, you don't know me. Not what's in my head. I'm beautiful. Stephen Dedalus. A mind, here where there is only steel. Nothing else. Young pharaoh under trees. Young pharaoh, romantic, liar. Feel my face, how tender. My eyes. My soul is white, pure white, and soars. Is the God himself. This world and all others."

And I thot of a black man under the el who took me home in the cold. And I remembered telling him all these things. And how he listened and showed me his new suit. And I crawled out of bed morning and walked thru the park for my train. Loved. Afraid. Huger than any world. And the hot tears wet Peaches and her bed and she slapped me for pissing.

I rolled hard on her and stuck my soft self between her thighs. And ground until I felt it slip into her stomach. And it got harder in her spreading the meat. Her arms around my hips pulled down hard and legs locked me and she started yelling. Faggot. Faggot. Sissy Motherfucker. And I pumped myself. Straining. Threw my hips at her. And she yelled, for me to fuck her. Fuck me, you lousy fag. And I twisted, spitting tears, and hitting my hip on hers, pounding flesh in her, hearing myself weep.

* * * *

Later, I slipped out into Bottom. Without my hat or tie, shoes loose and pants wrinkled and filthy. No one was on the streets now. Not even the whores. I walked not knowing where I was or was headed for. I wanted to get out. To see my parents, or be silent for the rest of my life. Huge moon was my light. Black straight trees the moon showed. And the dirt roads and scattered wreck houses. I still had money and I.D., and a pack of cigarettes. I trotted, then stopped, then trotted, and talked out loud to myself. And laughed a few times. The place was so still, so black and full of violence. I felt myself.

At one road, there were several houses. Larger than a lot of them. Porches, yards. All of them sat on cinder blocks so the vermin would have trouble getting in. Someone called to me. I thought it was in my head and kept moving, but slower. They called again. "Hey, psst. Hey comere." A whisper, but loud. "Comere, baby." All the sides of the houses were lit up but underneath, the space the cinder blocks made was black. And the moon made a head shadow on the ground, and I could see an arm in the same light. Someone kneeling under one of the houses, or an arm and the shadow of a head. I stood straight, and stiff, and tried to see right thru the dark. The voice came back, chiding like. Something you want. Whoever wants. That we do and I wondered who it was kneeling in the dark, at the end of the world, and I heard breathing when I did move, hard and closed.

I bent towards the space to see who it was. Why they had called. And I saw it was a man. Round red-rimmed eyes, sand-colored jew hair, and teeth for a face. He had been completely under the house but when I came he crawled out and I saw his dripping smile and yellow soggy skin full of red freckles. He said, "Come on here. Comere a second." I moved to turn away. The face like a dull engine. Eyes blinking. When I turned he reached for my arm grazing my shirt and the voice could be flushed down a toilet. He grinned and wanted to panic seeing me move. "Lemme suck yo dick, honey, Huh?" I was backing away like from the hyena cage to see the rest of them. Baboons? Or stop at the hotdog stand and read a comic book. He came up off all fours and sat on his knees and toes, shaking his head and hips. "Comeon baby, comeon now." As I moved back he began to scream at me. All lust, all panic, all silence and sorrow, and finally when I had moved and was trotting down the road, I looked around and he was standing up with his hands cupped to his mouth yelling into the darkness in complete hatred of what was only some wraith. Irreligious spirit pushing thru shadows, frustrating and confusing the flesh. He screamed behind me and when the moon sunk for minutes behind the clouds or trees his scream was like some animal's, some hurt ugly thing dying alone.

*   *   *   *

It was good to run. I would jump every few steps like hurdling, and shoot my arm out straight to take it right, landing on my right heel, snapping the left leg turned and flat, bent for the next piece. 3 steps between 180 yard lows, 7 or 9 between the 220's. The 180's I thought the most beautiful. After the first one, hard on the heel and springing up. Like music; a scale. Hit, 1–23. UP (straight right leg, down low just above the wood. Left turned at the angle, flat, tucked. Head low to the knee, arms reaching for the right toe, pulling the left leg to snap it down. HIT (right foot). Snap left HIT (left). Stride. The big one. 1–23. UP. STRETCH. My stride was long enough for the 3 step move. Stretching and hopping almost but in perfect scale. And I moved ahead of Wang and held it, the jew boy pooping at the last wood. I hit hard and threw my chest out, pulling the knees high, under my chin. Arms pushing. The last ten yards I picked up 3 and won by that, head back wrong (Nap said) and galloping like a horse (wrong again Nap said) but winning in new time and leaping in the air like I saw heroes do in flicks.

* * * *

I got back to where I thought the Joint, would be, and there were city-like houses and it was there somewhere. From there, I thought I could walk out, get back to the world. It was getting blue again. Sky lightening blue and grey trees and buildings black against it. And a few lights going on in some wood houses. A few going off. There were alleys now. And high wood fences with slats missing. Dogs walked across the road. Cats sat on the fences watching. Dead cars sulked. Old newspapers torn in half pushed against fire hydrants or stoops and made tiny noises flapping if the wind came up.

I had hands in my pockets, relaxed. The anonymous seer again. Looking slowly at things. Touching wood rails so years later I would remember I had touched wood rails in Louisiana when no one watched. Swinging my leg at cans, talking to the cats, doing made up dance steps or shadow boxing. And I came to a corner & saw some big black soldier stretched in the road with blood falling out of his head and stomach. I thot first it was Don. But this guy was too big and was in the infantry. I saw a paratrooper patch on his cap which was an inch away from his chopped up face, but the blue and silver badge had been taken off his shirt.

He was groaning quiet, talking to himself. Not dead, but almost. And I bent over him to ask what happened. He couldn't open his eyes and didn't hear me anyway. Just moaned and moaned losing his life on the ground. I stood up and wondered what to do. And looked at the guy and saw myself and looked over my shoulder when I heard someone move behind me. A tall black skinny woman hustled out of the shadows and looking at me disappeared into a hallway. I shouted after her. And stepped in the street to see the door she'd gone in.

I turned to go back to the soldier and there was a car pulling up the road. A red swiveling light on top and cops inside. One had his head hung out the window and yelled towards me. "Hey, you, Nigger, What's goin on?" That would be it. AWOL. Out of uniform (with a norfern accent). Now murder too. "30 days for nigger killing." I spun and moved. Down the road & they started to turn. I hit the fence, swinging up and dove into the black yard beyond. Fell on my hands and knees & staggered, got up, tripped on garbage, got up, swinging my hands, head down and charged off in the darkness.

The crackers were yelling on the other side of the fence and I could hear one trying to scale it. There was another fence beyond, and I took it the same as the first. Swinging down into another yard. And turned right and went over another fence, ripping my shirt. Huge cats leaped out of my path and lights went on in some houses. I saw the old woman who'd been hiding near the soldier just as I got to the top of one fence. She was standing in a hallway that led out in that yard, and she ducked back laughing when she saw me. I started to go after her, but I just heaved a big rock in her direction and hit another fence.

I got back to where the city houses left off, and there were the porches and cinder blocks again. I wondered if "sweet peter eater" would show up. (He'd told me his name.) And I ran up the roads hoping it wdn't get light until I found Peaches again.

At the Cotton Club I went down the steps, thru the alley, rested in the black hall, and tapped on Peaches' door. I bounced against it with my ass, resting between bumps, and fell backwards when she opened the door to shove her greasy eyes in the hall.

"You back again? What you want, honey? Know you don't want no pussy. Doyuh?"

I told her I had to stay there. That I wanted to stay there, with her. That I'd come back and wanted to sleep. And if she wanted money I'd give her some. And she grabbed my wrist and pulled me in, still bare-assed except for the filthy brassiere.

She loved me, she said. Or liked me a lot. She wanted me to stay, with her. We could live together and she would show me how to fuck. How to do it good. And we could start as soon as she took a pee. And to undress, and get in bed and wait for her, unless I wanted some coffee, which she brought back anyway and sat on the edge of the bed reading a book about Linda Darnell.

"Oh, we can have some good times baby. Movies, all them juke joints. You live here with me and I'll be good to you. Wallace (her husband) ain't due back in two years. We can raise hell waiting for him." She put the book down and scratched the inside of her thighs, then under one arm. Her hair was standing up and she went to a round mirror over the sink and brushed it. And turned around and shook her big hips at me, then pumped the air to suggest our mission. She came back and we talked about our lives: then she pushed back the sheets, helped me undress again, got me hard and pulled me into her. I came too quick and she had to twist her hips a few minutes longer to come herself. "Uhauh, good even on a sof. But I still got to teach you."

* * * *

I woke up about 1 the next afternoon. The sun, thru that one window, full in my face. Hot, dust in it. But the smell was good. A daytime smell. And I heard daytime voices thru the window up and fat with optimism. I pulled my hands under my head and looked for Peaches, who was out of bed. She was at the kitchen end of the room cutting open a watermelon. She had on a slip, and no shoes, but her hair was down flat and greased so it made a thousand slippery waves ending in slick feathers at the top of her ears.

"Hello, sweet," she turned and had a huge slice of melon on a plate for me. It was bright in the room now & she'd swept and straightened most of the shabby furniture in her tiny room. And the door sat open so more light, and air could come in. And her radio up on a shelf above the bed was on low with heavy blues and twangy guitar. She sat the melon on the "end table" and moved it near the bed. She had another large piece, dark red and spilling seeds in her hand and had already started. "This is good. Watermelon's a good breakfast. Peps you up."

And I felt myself smiling, and it seemed that things had come to an order. Peaches sitting on the edge of the bed, just beginning to perspire around her forehead, eating the melon in both hands, and mine on a plate, with a fork (since I was "smart" and could be a lawyer, maybe). It seemed settled. That she was to talk softly in her vague american, and I was to listen and nod, or remark on the heat or the sweetness of the melon. And that the sun was to be hot on our faces and the day smell come in with dry smells of knuckles or greens or peas cooking somewhere. Thing moving naturally for us. At what bliss we took. At our words. And slumped together in anonymous houses I thought of black men sitting on their beds this saturday of my life listening quietly to their wives' soft talk. And felt the world grow together as I hadn't known it. All lies before, I thought. All fraud and sickness. This was the world. It leaned under its own suns, and people moved on it. A real world. of flesh, of smells, of soft black harmonies and color. The dead maelstrom of my head, a sickness. The sun so warm and lovely on my face, the melon sweet going down. Peaches' music and her radio's. I cursed chicago, and softened at the world. "You look so sweet," she was saying. "Like you're real rested."

* * * *

I dozed again even before I finished the melon and Peaches had taken it and put it in the icebox when I woke up. The greens were cooking in our house now. The knuckles on top simmering. And biscuits were cooking, and chicken. "How you feel, baby," she watched me stretch. I yawned loud and scratched my back getting up to look at what the stove was doing. "We gonna eat a good lunch before we go to the movies. You so skinny, you could use a good meal. Don't you eat nuthin?" And she put down her cooking fork and hugged me to her, the smell of her, heavy, traditional, secret.

"Now you get dressed, and go get me some tomatoes . . . so we can eat." And it was good that there was something I could do for her. And go out into that world too. Now I knew it was there. And flesh.

I put on the stained khakis & she gave me my hat. "You'll get picked up without yo cap. We have to get you some clothes so you can throw that stuff away. The army don't need you no way." She laughed. "Leastways not as much as I does. Old Henry at the joint'll give you a job. You kin count money as good as that ol' jew I bet."

And I put the tie on, making some joke, and went out shopping for my wife.

*   *   *   *

Into that sun. The day was bright and people walked by me smiling. And waved "Hey" (a greeting) and they all knew I was Peaches' man.

I got to the store and stood talking to the man about the weather about airplanes and a little bit about new jersey. He waved at me when I left "O.K. . . . you take it easy now." "O.K., I'll see you," I said. I had the tomatoes and some plums and peaches I bought too. I took a tomato out of the bag and bit the sweet flesh. Pushed my hat on the back of my head and strutted up the road towards the house.

It was a cloud I think came up. Something touched me. "That color which cowardice brought out in me." Fire burns around the tombs. Closed from the earth. A despair came down. Alien grace. Lost to myself, I'd come back. To that ugliness sat inside me waiting. And the mere sky greying could do it. Sky spread thin out away from this place. Over other heads. Beautiful unknowns. And my marriage a heavy iron to this tomb. "Show us your countenance." Your light.

It was a light clap of thunder. No lightning. And the sky greyed. Introitus. That word came in. And the yellow light burning in my rooms. To come to see the world, and yet lose it. And find sweet grace alone.

It was this or what I thought, made me turn and drop the tomatoes on Peaches' porch. Her window was open and I wondered what she was thinking. How my face looked in her head. I turned and looked at the sad bag of tomatoes. The peaches, some rolling down one stair. And a light rain came down. I walked away from the house. Up the road, to go out of Bottom.

* * * *

The rain wet my face and I wanted to cry because I thot of the huge black girl
watching her biscuits get cold. And her radio playing without me. The rain
was hard for a second, drenching me. And then it stopped, and just as quick
the sun came out. Heavy bright hot. I trotted for awhile then walked slow,
measuring my steps. I stank of sweat and the uniform was a joke.

I asked some
people how to get out and they pointed up the road where 10 minutes' walking
had me at the bottom of the hill the bus came down. A wet wind blew up soft
full of sun and I began to calm. To see what had happened. Who I was and
what I thought my life should be. What people called "experience." Young
male. My hands in my pockets, and the grimy silver wings still hanging
gravely on my filthy shirt. The feeling in my legs was to run up the rest of the
hill but I just took long strides and stretched myself and wondered if I'd have
K.P. or some army chastisement for being 2 days gone.

3 tall guys were com-
ing down the hill I didn't see until they got close enough to speak to me. One
laughed (at the way I looked). Tall strong black boys with plenty of teeth and
pegged rayon pants. I just looked and nodded and kept on. One guy, with an
imitation tattersall vest with no shirt, told the others I was in the Joint last
night "playin cool." Slick city nigger, one said. I was going to pass close to
them and the guy with the vest put up his hand and asked me where I was
coming from. One with suspenders and a belt asked me what the wings stood
for. I told him something. The third fellow just grinned. I moved to walk
around them and the fellow with the vest asked could he borrow fifty cents. I
only had a dollar in my pocket and told him that. There was no place to get
change. He said to give him the dollar. I couldn't do that and get back to my
base I told him and wanted to walk away. And one of the guys had gotten
around in back of me and kneeled down and the guy with the vest pushed me
backwards so I fell over the other's back. I fell backwards into the dust, and
my hat fell off, and I didn't think I was mad but I still said something stupid
like "What'd you do that for."

"I wanna borrow a dollar, Mr. Half-white muthafucka. And that's that." I
sidestepped the one with the vest and took a running step but the grinning
one tripped me, and I fell tumbling head forward back in the dust. This time
when they laughed I got up and spun around and hit the guy who tripped me
in the face. His nose was bleeding and he was cursing while the guy with the
suspenders grabbed my shoulders and held me so the hurt one could punch
me back. The guy with the vest punched too. And I got in one good kick into
his groin, and stomped hard on one of their feet. The tears were coming again
and I was cursing, now when they hit me, completely crazy. The dark one
with the suspenders punched me in my stomach and I felt sick and the guy

with the vest, the last one I saw, kicked me in my hip. The guy still held on for awhile then he pushed me at one of the others and they hit me as I fell. I got picked up and was screaming at them to let me go. "Bastards, you filthy stupid bastards, let me go." Crazy out of my head. Stars were out. And there were no fists just dull distant jolts that spun my head. It was in a cave this went on. With music and whores danced on the tables. I sat reading from a book aloud and they danced to my reading. When I finished reading I got up from the table and for some reason, fell forward weeping on the floor. The negroes danced around my body and spilled whisky on my clothes. I woke up 2 days later, with white men, screaming for God to help me.

SOUND AND IMAGE

What is hell? Your definitions.

I am and was and will be a social animal. Hell is definable only in those terms. I can get no place else; it wdn't exist.

Hell in this book which moves from sound and image ("association complexes") into fast narrative is what vision I had of it around 1960–61 and that fix on my life, and my interpretation of my earlier life.

Hell in the head.

The torture of being the unseen object, and, the constantly observed subject.

The flame of social dichotomy. Split open down the center, which is the early legacy of the black man unfocused on blackness. The dichotomy of what is seen and taught and desired opposed to what is felt. Finally, God is simply a white man, a white "idea," in this society, unless we have made some other image which is stronger, and can deliver us from the salvation of our enemies.

For instance, if we can bring back on ourselves the absolute pain our people must have felt when they came onto this shore, we are more ourselves again, and can begin to put history back in our menu, and forget the propaganda of devils that they are not devils.

*　*　*　*

Hell is actual, and people with hell in their heads. But the pastoral moments in a man's life will also mean a great deal as far as his emotional references. One thinks of home, or the other "homes" we have had. And we remember w/love those things bathed in soft black light. The struggles away or towards this peace is Hell's function. (Wars of consciousness. Antithetical definitions of feeling(s).

Once, as a child, I would weep for compassion and understanding. And Hell was the inferno of my frustration. But the world is clearer to me now, and many of its features, more easily definable.

1965

SWING—FROM VERB TO NOUN
from *Blues People*

The blues was conceived by freedmen and ex-slaves—if not as the result of a personal or intellectual experience, at least as an emotional confirmation of, and reaction to, the way in which most Negroes were still forced to exist in the United States. The blues impulse was a psychological correlative that obscured the most extreme ideas of *assimilation* for most Negroes, and made any notion of the complete abandonment of the traditional black culture an unrealizable possibility. In a sense, the middle-class spirit could not take root among most Negroes because they sensed the final fantasy involved. Besides, the pay check, which was the aspect of American society that created a modern black middle class, was, as I mentioned before, also available to what some of my mother's friends would refer to as "low-type coons." And these "coons" would always be unavailable both socially and culturally to any talk of assimilation from white man or black. The Negro middle class, always an exaggeration of its white model, could include the professional men and educators, but after the move north it also included men who worked in stores and as an added dig, "sportsmen," i.e., gamblers and numbers people. The idea of Negro "society," as E. Franklin Frazier pointed out, is based only on acquisition, which, as it turns out, makes the formation of a completely parochial meta-society impossible. Numbers bankers often make as much money as doctors and thereby are part of Negro "society." And even if the more formal ("socially responsible") Negro middle class wanted to become simply white Americans, they were during the late twenties and thirties merely a swelling minority.

The two secularities I spoke of are simply the ways in which the blues was beginning to be redistributed in black America through these years. The people who were beginning to move toward what they could think of as citizenship also moved away from the older blues. The unregenerate Northerners already had a music, the thin-willed "society" bands of Jim Europe, and the circus as well as white rag had influenced the "non-blues" bands of Will Marion Cook and Wilbur Sweatman that existed before the migration. But the huge impact the Southerners made upon the North changed that. When the city blues began to be powerful, the larger Negro dance bands hired some of the emigrants as soloists, and to some degree the blues began to be heard in most of the black cabarets, "dance schools," and theaters. The true jazz sound had moved north, and even the blackest blues could be heard in the house parties of Chicago and New York. But for most of America by the twenties, jazz (or *jass,* the noun, not the verb) meant the Original Dixieland Jazz Band (to the hip) and Paul Whiteman (to the square). Whiteman got rich; the O.D.J.B. never did.

The O.D.J.B. was a group of young white men who had been deeply influenced by the King Oliver band in New Orleans; they moved north, and became the first jazz band to record. They had a profound influence upon America, and because they, rather than the actual black innovators, were heard by the great majority of Americans *first,* the cultural lag had won again.

A Negro jazz band, Freddie Keppard's Original Creoles, turned down an invitation to record a few months before the O.D.J.B.; Keppard (myth says) didn't accept the offer because he thought such a project would merely invite imitation of his style! That is probably true, but it is doubtful that Keppard's band would have caught as much national attention as the smoother O.D.J.B. anyway, for the same reason the O.D.J.B. could never have made as much money as Whiteman.

It is significant that by 1924, when Bessie Smith was still causing riots in Chicago and when young Louis Armstrong was on his way to New York to join the Fletcher Henderson band—and by so doing, to create the first really swinging *big* jazz band, the biggest names in "jazz" were Whiteman and the Mound City Blue Blowers, another white group. Radio had come into its own by 1920, and the irony is that most Negroes probably thought of jazz, based on what they had heard, as being a white dilution of older blues forms! It was only after there had been a few recordings sufficiently distributed through the black Northern and urban Southern neighborhoods, made by Negro bands like King Oliver's (Oliver was then in Chicago with his historic Creole Jazz Band, which featured Louis Armstrong, second cornet), Fletcher Henderson's, and two Kansas City bands—Bennie Moten's and Clarence Williams', that the masses of Negroes became familiar with jazz. At Chicago's Lincoln Gardens Cafe, Oliver first set the Northern Negro neighborhoods on fire, and then bands like Moten's and Williams' in the various clubs around Kansas City; but Henderson reached his Negro audience mostly via records because even when he got his best band together (with Coleman Hawkins, Louis Armstrong, Don Redman, etc.) he was still playing at Roseland, which was a white club.

The earliest jazz bands, like Buddy Bolden's, were usually small groups. Bolden's instrumentation was supposed to have been cornet, clarinet, trombone, violin, guitar, bass (which was one of the first instrumental innovations for that particular group since most bands of that period and well after used the tuba) and drums. These groups were usually made up of musicians who had other jobs (like pre-classic blues singers) since there was really no steady work for them. And they played most of the music of the time: quadrilles, schottisches, polkas, ragtime tunes, like many of the other "cleaner" groups around New Orleans. But the difference with the Bolden band was the blues quality, the Uptown flavor, of all their music. But this music still had the flavor of the brass marching bands. Most of the musicians of that period had come through those bands; in fact, probably still marched with them when there was a significant funeral. Another quality that must have distinguished the Bolden band was the improvisational character of a good deal of their music. Charles Edward Smith remarks that "the art of group improvisation— like the blues, the life blood of jazz—was associated with this uptown section of New Orleans in particular. As in folk music, two creative forces were involved, that of the group and that of the gifted individual." [1]

Most of the Uptown bands were noted for their "sloppy ensemble styles." The Bolden band and the other early jazz groups must have sounded even sloppier. The music was a raw mixture of march, dance, blues, and early rag rhythm, with all the players improvising simultaneously. It is a wonderful concept, taking the unison tradition of European march music, but infesting it with teeming improvisations, catcalls, hollers, and the murky rhythms of the ex-slaves. The Creoles must have hated that music more than anything in life.

But by the time the music came upriver along with the fleeing masses, it had changed a great deal. Oliver's Creole Band, the first really influential Negro jazz band in the North, had a much smoother ensemble style than the Bolden band: the guitar and violin had disappeared, and a piano had been added. In New Orleans, pianists had been largely soloists in the various bawdy houses and brothels of Storyville. In fact, pianists were the only Negro musicians who worked steadily and needed no other jobs. But the early New Orleans jazz groups usually did not have pianos. Jelly Roll Morton, one of the first jazz pianists, was heavily influenced by the ragtime style, though his own rags were even more heavily influenced by blues and that rougher rag style called "barrelhouse." As Bunk Johnson is quoted as saying, Jelly played music "the whores liked." And played in a whorehouse, it is easy to under-stand how functional that music must have been. But the piano as part of a jazz ensemble was something not indigenous to earlier New Orleans music. The smoother and more clearly polyphonic style of Oliver's band, as opposed to what must have been a veritable heterophony of earlier bands like Bolden's—Kid Ory's Sunshine Orchestra, the first black jazz band to record (Los Angeles, 1921), gives us some indication—showed a discipline and for-mality that must certainly have been imposed to a large degree by ragtime and the more precise pianistic techniques that went with it.

Oliver's band caused a sensation with audiences and musicians alike and brought the authentic accent of jazz into the North. Garvin Bushell remem-

<hr>

[1] "New Orleans and Traditions in Jazz," in *Jazz*, p. 39.

bers: "We went on the road with Mamie Smith in 1921. When we got to Chicago, Bubber Miley and I went to hearing Oliver at the Dreamland every night. [This was before Armstrong joined the band and they moved to Lincoln Gardens.] It was the first time I'd heard New Orleans jazz to any advantage and I studied them every night for the entire week we were in town. I was very much impressed with their blues and their sound. The trumpets and clarinets in the East had a better 'legitimate' quality, but their [Oliver's band's] sound touched you more. It was less cultivated but more expressive of how the people felt. Bubber and I sat there with our mouths open." [2]

Louis Armstrong's arrival at twenty-two with Oliver's band had an even more electrifying effect on these Northern audiences, which many times included white jazz musicians. Hoagy Carmichael went to the Lincoln Gardens with Bix Beiderbecke in 1923 to hear that band:

"The King featured two trumpets, a piano, a bass fiddle and a clarinet . . . a big black fellow . . . slashed into *Bugle Call Rag.*

"I dropped my cigarette and gulped my drink. Bix was on his feet, his eyes popping. For taking the first chorus was that second trumpet, Louis Armstrong.

"Louis was taking it fast. Bob Gillette slid off his chair and under the table Every note Louis hit was perfection." [3]

This might seem amusing if it is noted that the first and deepest influences on most white Northern and Midwestern jazz musicians were necessarily the recordings of the O.D.J.B., who were imitating the earlier New Orleans styles, and Oliver, who had brought that style to its apex. Thus, this first hearing of the genuine article by these white musicians must have been much like tasting real eggs after having been brought up on the powdered variety. (Though, to be sure, there's no certainty that a person will like the original if he has developed a taste for the other. So it is that Carmichael can write that he still preferred Beiderbecke to Armstrong, saying, "Bix's breaks were not as wild as Armstrong's but they were hot and he selected each note with musical care." [4])

Blues as an autonomous music had been in a sense inviolable. There was no clear way into it, *i.e.,* its production, not its appreciation, except as concomitant with what seems to me to be the peculiar social, cultural, economic, and emotional experience of a black man in America. The idea of a white blues singer seems an even more violent contradiction of terms than the idea of a middle-class blues singer. The materials of blues were not available to

[2] "Garvin Bushell and New York Jazz in the 1920's," *Jazz Review* (February 1959), p. 9.
[3] *The Stardust Road* (New York, Rinehart, 1946), p. 53.
[4] As quoted in *The Story of Jazz,* p. 128.

the white American, even though some strange circumstance might prompt him to look for them. It was as if these materials were secret and obscure, and blues a kind of ethno-historic rite as basic as blood.

The classic singers brought this music as close to white America as it could ever get and still survive. W. C. Handy, with the publication of his various "blues compositions," *invented* it for a great many Americans and also showed that there was some money to be made from it. Whiteman, Wilbur Sweatman, Jim Europe, all played Handy's compositions with success. There was even what could be called a "blues craze" (of which Handy's compositions were an important part) just after the ragtime craze went on the skids. But the music that resulted from the craze had little, if anything, to do with legitimate blues. That could not be got to, except as the casual expression of a whole culture. And for this reason, blues remained, and remains in its most moving manifestations, obscure to the mainstream of American culture.

Jazz made it possible for the first time for something of the legitimate feeling of Afro-American music to be imitated successfully. (Ragtime had moved so quickly away from any pure reflection of Negro life that by the time it became popular, there was no more original source to imitate. It was, in a sense, a premature attempt at the socio-cultural merger that later produced jazz.) Or rather, jazz enabled separate and *valid* emotional expressions to be made that were based on older traditions of Afro-American music that were clearly not a part of it. The Negro middle class would not have a music if it were not for jazz. The white man would have no access to blues. It was a music capable of reflecting not only the Negro and a black America but a white America as well.

During the twenties, serious young white musicians were quick to pick up more or less authentic jazz accents as soon as they had some contact with the music. The O.D.J.B., who came out of a parallel tradition of white New Orleans marching bands, whizzed off to Chicago and stunned white musicians everywhere as well as many Negro musicians in the North who had not heard the new music before, Young white boys, like Beiderbecke, in the North and Midwest were already forming styles of their own based on the O.D.J.B.'s records and the playing of another white group, the New Orleans Rhythm Kings, before Joe Oliver's band got to Chicago. And the music these boys were making, or trying to make, had very little to do with Paul Whiteman. They had caught the accent, understood the more generalized emotional statements, and genuinely moved, set out to involve themselves in this music as completely as possible. They hung around the Negro clubs, listening to the newly employed New Orleans musicians, and went home and tried to play their tunes.

The result of this cultural "breakdown" was not always mere imitation. As I have said, jazz had a broadness of emotional meaning that allowed of many separate ways into it, not all of them dependent on the "blood ritual" of blues. Bix Beiderbecke, as a mature musician, was even an innovator. But the real point of this breakdown was that it reflected not so much the white American's increased understanding of the Negro, but rather the fact that the Negro had created a music that offered such a profound reflection of America that it could attract white Americans to want to play it or listen to it for exactly that reason. The white jazz musician was even a new *class* of white American. Unlike the earlier blackface acts and the minstrels who sought to burlesque certain facets of Negro life (and, superficially, the music associated with it), there were now growing ranks of white jazz musicians who wanted to play the music because they thought it emotionally and intellectually fulfilling. It made a common cultural ground where black and white America seemed only day and night in the same city and at their most disparate, proved only to result in different *styles,* a phenomenon I have always taken to be the whole point (and value) of divergent cultures.

It is interesting that most of these young white musicians who emerged during the early twenties were from the middle class and from the Middle West. Beiderbecke was born in Davenport, Iowa; that town, however, at the turn of the century was a river port, and many of the riverboats docked there—riverboats whose staffs sometimes included bands like Fate Marable's, Dewey Jackson's, and Albert Wynn's, and musicians like Jelly Roll Morton and Louis Armstrong. Beiderbecke's first group, the Wolverines, played almost exclusively at roadhouses and colleges in the Midwest, most notably at Indiana University.

A few years after the Wolverines had made their reputation as what George Hoefer calls "the first white band to play the genuine Negro style of jazz," another group of young white musicians began to play jazz "their own way." They were also from the Midwest, but from Chicago. Eddie Condon, Jimmy McPartland, Bud Freeman, PeeWee Russell, Dave Tough, and some others, all went to Austin High School and became associated with a style of playing known as "Chicago jazz," which took its impetus from the records of the O.D.J.B. and the New Orleans Rhythm Kings dates on the North Side of Chicago.

Chicago and nearby parts of the Midwest were logically the first places where jazz could take root in the North (although there were some parallel developments in New York). In a sense Chicago was, and to a certain extent is now, a kind of frontier town. It sits at the end of the riverboat runs, and it was the kind of industrial city that the first black emigrants were drawn to. It had many of the heavy industries that would employ Negroes, whereas New York's heaviest industry is paperwork. And in Chicago, during what was called the "Jazz Age," there was an easiness of communication on some levels between black and white that was not duplicated in New York until some time later. Chicago at this time was something like the musical capital of

America, encompassing within it black emigrants, white emigrants, country blues people, classic stylists, city house-party grinders, New Orleans musicians, and young Negro musicians and younger white musicians listening and reacting to this crush of cultures that so clearly typified America's rush into the twentieth century.

The reaction of young white musicians to jazz was not always connected directly to any *"understanding* of the Negro." In many cases, the most profound influence on young white musicians was the music of other white musicians. Certainly this is true with people like Beiderbecke and most of the Chicago-style players. But the entrance of the white man into jazz at this level of sincerity and emotional legitimacy did at least bring him, by implication, much closer to the Negro; that is, even if a white trumpet player were to learn to play "jazz" by listening to Nick LaRocca and had his style set (as was Beiderbecke's case) *before* he ever heard black musicians, surely the musical debt to Negro music (and to the black culture from which it issued) had to be understood. As in the case of LaRocca's style, it is certainly an appropriation of black New Orleans brass style, most notably King Oliver's; though the legitimacy of its deviation can in no way be questioned, the fact that it is a deviation must be acknowledged. The serious white musician was in a position to do this. And this acknowledgment, whether overt or tacit, served to place the Negro's culture and Negro society in a position of intelligent regard it had never enjoyed before.

This acknowledgment of a developed and empirical profundity to the Negro's culture (and as the result of its separation from the mainstream of American culture) also caused the people who had to make it to be separated from this mainstream themselves. Any blackness admitted within the mainstream existed only as it could be shaped by the grimness of American sociological (and political) thought. There was no life to Negroes in America that could be understood by America, except negatively or with the hopeless idealism of impossible causes. During the Black Renaissance the white liberal and sensual dilettante "understood" the Negro. During the Depression, so did the Communist Party. The young white jazz musicians at least had to face the black American head-on and with only a very literal drum to beat. And they could not help but do this with some sense of rebellion or separateness from the rest of white America, since white America could have no understanding of what they were doing, except perhaps in the terms that Whiteman and the others succeeded in doing it, which was not at all—that is, explaining a bird by comparing it with an airplane.

"Unlike New Orleans style, the style of these musicians—often and confusingly labeled 'Chicago'—sacrificed ease and relaxation for tension and drive, perhaps because they were mastering a new idiom in a more hectic environment. They had read some of the literature of the 20's—drummer Dave Tough loved Mencken and the *American Mercury*—and their revolt against their own middle-class background tended to be conscious. The role of the improvising—and usually non-reading—musician became almost heroic." [5]

Music, as paradoxical as it might seem, is the result of thought. It is the result of thought perfected at its most empirical, *i.e.,* as *attitude,* or *stance.* Thought is largely conditioned by reference; it is the result of consideration or speculation against reference, which is largely arbitrary.

There is no *one* way of thinking, since reference (hence value) is as scattered and dissimilar as men themselves. If Negro music can be seen to be the result of certain attitudes, certain specific ways of thinking about the world (and only ultimately about the *ways* in which music can be made), then the basic hypothesis of this book is understood. The Negro's music changed as he changed, reflecting shifting attitudes or (and this is equally important) *consistent attitudes within changed contexts.* And it is *why* the music changed that seems most important to me.

When jazz first began to appear during the twenties on the American scene, in one form or another, it was introduced in a great many instances into that scene by white Americans. Jazz as it was originally conceived and in most instances of its most vital development was the result of certain attitudes, or empirical ideas, attributable to the Afro-American culture. Jazz as played by white musicians was not the same as that played by black musicians, nor was there any reason for it to be. The music of the white jazz musician did not issue from the same cultural circumstance; it was, at its most profound instance, a learned art. The blues, for example, which I take to be an autonomous black music, had very little weight at all in pre-jazz white American culture. But blues is an extremely important part of jazz. However, the way in which jazz utilizes the blues "attitude" provided a musical analogy the white musician could understand and thus utilize in his music to arrive at a style of jazz music. The white musician understood the blues first as music, but seldom as an attitude, since the attitude, or world-view, the white musician was responsible to was necessarily quite a different one. And in many cases, this attitude, or world-view, was one that was not consistent with the making of jazz.

There should be no cause for wonder that the trumpets of Bix Beiderbecke and Louis Armstrong were so dissimilar. The white middle-class boy from Iowa was the product of a culture which could *place* Louis Armstrong, but could never understand him. Beiderbecke was also the product of a subculture that most nearly emulates the "official" or formal culture of North America. He was an instinctive intellectual who had a musical taste that included Stravinsky, Schoenberg, and Debussy, and had an emotional life

5 *The Story of Jazz,* p. 129.

that, as it turned out, was based on his conscious or unconscious disapproval of most of the sacraments of his culture. On the other hand, Armstrong was, in terms of emotional archetypes, an honored priest of his culture—one of the most impressive products of his society. Armstrong was not *rebelling* against anything with his music. In fact, his music was one of the most beautiful refinements of Afro-American musical tradition, and it was immediately recognized as such by those Negroes who were not busy trying to pretend that they had issued from Beiderbecke's culture. The incredible irony of the situation was that both stood in similar places in the superstructure of American society: Beiderbecke, because of the isolation any deviation from mass culture imposed upon its bearer; and Armstrong, because of the socio-historical estrangement of the Negro from the rest of America. Nevertheless, the music the two made was as dissimilar as is possible within jazz. Beiderbecke's slight, reflective tone and impressionistic lyricism was the most impressive example of "the artifact given expression" in jazz. He played "white jazz" in the sense I am trying to convey, that is, as a music that is the product of attitudes expressive of a peculiar culture. Armstrong, of course, played jazz that was securely within the traditions of Afro-American music. His tone was brassy, broad, and aggressively dramatic. He also relied heavily on the vocal blues tradition in his playing to amplify the expressiveness of his instrumental technique.

I am using these two men as examples because they were two early masters of a developing *American* music, though they expressed almost antithetical versions of it. The point is that Afro-American music did not become a completely American expression until the white man could play it! Bix Beiderbecke, more than any of the early white jazzmen, signified this development because he was the first white jazz musician, the first white musician who brought to the jazz he created any of the *ultimate concern* Negro musicians brought to it as a casual attitude of their culture. This development signified also that jazz would someday have to contend with the idea of its being an art (since that was the white man's only way into it). The emergence of the white player meant that Afro-American culture had already become the expression of a particular kind of American experience, and what is most important, that this experience was available intellectually, that it could be learned.

Louis Armstrong's departure from the Oliver Creole Jazz Band is more than an historical event; given further consideration, it may be seen as a musical and socio-cultural event of the highest significance. First, Armstrong's departure from Chicago (as well as Beiderbecke's three years later, in 1927, to join the Goldkette band and then Paul Whiteman's enterprise) was, in a sense, symbolic of the fact that the most fertile period for jazz in Chicago was finished and that the jazz capital was moving to New York. It also meant that Louis felt mature enough musically to venture out on his own without the presence of his mentor Joe Oliver. But most important, Armstrong in his tenure with Fletcher Henderson's Roseland band was not only responsible to a great degree for giving impetus to the first big jazz band, but in his capacity as one of the hot soloists in a big dance (later, jazz) band, he moved jazz into another era: the ascendancy of the soloist began.

Primitive jazz, like most Afro-American music that preceded it, was a communal, collective music. The famous primitive ensemble styles of earlier jazz allowed only of "breaks," or small solo-like statements by individual players, but the form and intent of these breaks were still dominated by the form and intent of the ensemble. They were usually just quasi-melodic punctuations at the end of the ensemble chorus. Jazz, even at the time of Oliver's Creole Band, was still a matter of *collective improvisation,* though the Creole Band did bring a smoother and more complex polyphonic technique to the ensemble style. As Larry Gushee remarked in a review of a recent LP of the Creole Band (Riverside 12-122) ". . . the Creole Jazz Band . . . sets the standard (possibly, who knows, only because of an historical accident) for all kinds of jazz that do not base their excellence on individual expressiveness, but on form and *shape* achieved through control and balance." [6]

The emergence of this "individual expressiveness" in jazz was signaled impressively by Armstrong's recordings with a small group known as the Hot Five. The musicians on these recordings, made in 1925 and 1926, were Kid Ory, trombone; Johnny Dodds, clarinet and *alto saxophone;* Lil Hardin, now Mrs. Armstrong, piano; and Johnny St. Cyr, banjo. On these sides, Armstrong clearly dominates the group, not so much because he is the superior instrumentalist, but because rhythmically and harmonically the rest of the musicians followed where Louis led, sometimes without a really clear knowledge of where that would be. The music made by the Hot Five is Louis Armstrong music: it has little to do with collective improvisation.

"The 1926 Hot Five's playing is much less purely collective than King Oliver's. In a sense, the improvised ensembles are cornet solos accompanied by *impromptu countermelodies* [my italics], rather than true collective improvisation. This judgment is based on the very essence of the works, and not merely on the cornet's closeness to the microphone. Listen to them carefully. Isn't it obvious that Armstrong's personality absorbs the others? Isn't your attention spontaneously concentrated on Louis? With King Oliver, you listen to the *band,* here, you listen first to *Louis.*" [7]

The development of the soloist is probably connected to the fact that about

[6] *Jazz Review* (November 1958), p. 37.
[7] André Hodeir, *Jazz: Its Evolution and Essence* (New York, Grove Press, 1956), pp. 50–51.

this time in the development of jazz, many of the "hot" musicians had to seek employment with larger dance bands of usually dubious quality. The communal, collective improvisatory style of early jazz was impossible in this context, though later the important big jazz bands and big "blues bands" of the Southwest solved this problem by "uniting on a higher level the individual contribution with the entire group." [8]

The isolation that had nurtured Afro-American musical tradition before the coming of jazz had largely disappeared by the mid-twenties, and many foreign, even debilitating, elements drifted into this broader instrumental music. The instrumentation of the Henderson Roseland band was not chosen initially for its jazz possibilities, but in order to imitate the popular white dance bands of the day. The Henderson band became a jazz band because of the collective personality of the individual instrumentalists in the band, who were stronger than any superficial forms that might be imposed upon them. The saxophone trio, which was a clichéed novelty in the large white dance bands, became something of remarkable beauty when transformed by Henderson's three reeds, Buster Bailey, Don Redman, and Coleman Hawkins. And just as earlier those singular hollers must have pierced lonely Southern nights after the communal aspect of the slave society had broken down and had been replaced by a pseudoautonomous existence on many tiny Southern plots (which represented, however absurd it might seem, the widest breadth of this country for those Negroes, and their most exalted position in it), so the changed society in which the large Negro dance bands existed represented, in a sense, another post-communal black society. The move north, for instance, had broken down the old communities (the house parties were one manifestation of a regrouping of the newer communities: the Harlems and South Chicagos). Classic blues, the public face of a changed Afro-American culture, was the solo. The blues that developed at the house parties was the collective, communal music. So the jam sessions of the late twenties and thirties became the musicians' collective communal expression, and the solo in the large dance bands, that expression as it had to exist to remain vital outside its communal origins. The dance bands or society orchestras of the North replaced the plot of land, for they were the musician's only means of existence, and the solo, like the holler, was the only link with an earlier, more intense sense of the self in its most vital relationship to the world. The solo spoke singly of a collective music, and because of the emergence of the great soloists (Armstrong, Hawkins, Hines, Harrison), even forced the great bands (Henderson's, Ellington's, and later Basie's) into wonderfully extended versions of that communal expression.

The transformation of the large dance bands into jazz bands was in good

[8] *Jazz: A People's Music*, p. 206.

measure the work of the Fletcher Henderson orchestra, aided largely by the arrangments of Don Redman, especially his writing for the reed section which gave the saxophones in the Henderson band a fluency that was never heard before. The reeds became the fiery harmonic and melodic imagination of the big jazz bands. And it was the growing prominence of the saxophone in the big band and the later elevation of that instrument to its fullest expressiveness by Coleman Hawkins that planted the seed for the kind of jazz that is played even today. However, it was not until the emergence of Lester Young that jazz became a saxophone or reed music, as opposed to the brass music it had been since the early half-march, half-blues bands of New Orleans.

Louis Armstrong had brought *brass jazz* to its fullest flowering and influenced every major innovation in jazz right up until the forties, and bebop. Earl Hines, whose innovations as a pianist began a new, single-note line approach to the jazz piano, was merely utilizing Armstrong's trumpet style on a different instrument, thereby breaking out of the ragtime-boogie-stride approach to piano that had been predominant since that instrument was first used in jazz bands. Coleman Hawkins' saxophone style is still close to the Armstrong-perfected brass style, and of course, all Hawkins' imitators reflect that style as well. Jimmy Harrison, the greatest innovator on the trombone, was also profoundly influenced by Armstrong's brass style.

With the emergence of many good "hot" musicians from all over the country during the mid-twenties, the big jazz bands continued to develop. By the late twenties there were quite a few very good jazz bands all over the country. And competent musicians "appeared from everywhere, from 1920 on: by 1930 every city outside the Deep South with a Negro population (1920 census) above sixty thousand except Philadelphia had produced an important band: Washington, Duke Ellington; Baltimore, Chick Webb; Memphis, Jimmie Lunceford; St. Louis, the Missourians; Chicago, Luis Russell and Armstrong; New York, Henderson, Charlie Johnson, and half a dozen more." [9]

So an important evolution in Afro-American musical form had occurred again and in much the same manner that characterized the many other changes within the tradition of Negro music. The form can be called basically a Euro-American one—the large (sweet) dance band, changed by the contact with Afro-American musical tradition into another vehicle for that tradition. Just as the Euro-American religious song and ballad had been used, so with the transformation of the large dance band into the jazz band and the adaptation of the thirty-two-bar popular song to jazz purposes, the music itself was broadened and extended even further, and even more complex expressions of older musical traditions were made possible.

[9] Hsio Wen Shih, "The Spread of Jazz and the Big Bands," in *Jazz*, p. 161.

By the late twenties a great many more Negroes were going to high school and college, and the experience of an American "liberal" education was bound to leave traces. The most expressive big bands of the late twenties and thirties were largely middle-class Negro enterprises. The world of the professional man had opened up, and many scions of the new Negro middle class who had not gotten through professional school went into jazz "to make money." Men like Fletcher Henderson (who had a chemistry degree), Benny Carter, Duke Ellington, Coleman Hawkins, Jimmie Lunceford, Sy Oliver, and Don Redman, for example, all went to college: "They were a remarkable group of men. Between 1925 and 1935 they created, in competition, a musical tradition that required fine technique and musicianship (several of them were among the earliest virtuosi in jazz); they began to change the basis of the jazz repertory from blues to the wider harmonic possibilities of the thirty-two-bar popular song; they created and perfected the new ensemble-style big-band jazz; they kept their groups together for years, working until they achieved a real unity. They showed that jazz could absorb new, foreign elements without losing its identity, that it was in fact capable of evolution." [10]

These men were all "citizens," and they had all, to a great extent, moved away from the older *lowdown* forms of blues. Blues was not so *direct* to them, it had to be utilized in other contexts. Big show-band jazz was a music of their own, a music that still relied on older Afro-American musical tradition, but one that had begun to utilize still greater amounts of popular American music as well as certain formal European traditions. Also, the concept of making music as a means of making a living that had developed with the coming of classic blues singers was now thoroughly a part of the constantly evolving Afro-American culture. One did not expect to hear Bessie Smith at a rent party, one went to the theater to hear her. She was, at all levels, a *performer*. The young middle-class Negroes who came into jazz during the development of the show bands and dance bands all thought of themselves as performers as well. No matter how deeply the music they played was felt, they still thought of it as a public expression.

"If so many musicians came to jazz after training in one of the professions, it was because jazz was both more profitable and safer for a Negro in the 1920's; it was a survival of this attitude that decided Ellington to keep his son out of M.I.T. and aeronautical engineering in the 1930's." [11]

Just as Bessie Smith perfected vocal blues style almost as a Western artifact, and Louis Armstrong perfected the blues-influenced brass style in jazz (which was a great influence on all kinds of instrumental jazz for more than two decades), so Duke Ellington perfected the big jazz band, transforming it into a highly expressive instrument. Ellington, after the Depression had killed off the big theater-band "show-biz" style of the large jazz bands, began to

[10] *Ibid.*, p. 164.
[11] *Ibid.*, p. 164.

create a personal style of jazz expression as impressive as Armstrong's innovation as a soloist (if not more so). Ellington replaced a "spontaneous collective music by a worked-out orchestral language." [12]

Ellington's music (even the "jungle" bits of his twenties show-band period, which were utilized in those uptown "black and tan" clubs that catered largely to sensual white liberals) was a thoroughly American music. It was the product of a native American mind, but more than that, it was a music that *could* for the first time exist within the formal boundaries of American culture. A freedman could not have created it, just as Duke could never have played like Peatie Wheatstraw. Ellington began in much the same way as a great many of the significant Northern Negro musicians of the era had begun, by playing in the ragtime, show-business style that was so prevalent. But under the influence of the Southern styles of jazz and with the growth of Duke as an orchestra leader, composer, and musician, the music he came to make was as "moving" in terms of the older Afro-American musical tradition as it was a completely American expression. Duke's sophistication was to a great extent the very quality that enabled him to integrate so perfectly the older blues traditions with the "whiter" styles of big-band music. But Ellington was a "citizen," and his music, as Vic Bellerby has suggested, was "the detached impressionism of a sophisticated Negro city dweller."

Even though many of Ellington's compositions were "hailed as uninhibited jungle music," the very fact that the music was so much an American music made it cause the stir it did: "Ellington used musical materials that were familiar to concert-trained ears, making jazz music more listenable to them. These, however, do not account for his real quality.... In his work all the elements of the old music may be found, but each completely changed because it had to be changed.... Ellington's accomplishment was to solve the problem of form and content for the large band. He did it not by trying to play pure New Orleans blues and stomp music rearranged for large bands, as Henderson did, but by re-creating all the elements of New Orleans music in new instrumental and harmonic terms. What emerged was a music that could be traced back to the old roots and yet sounded fresh and new." [13]

For these reasons, by the thirties the "race" category could be dropped from Ellington's records. Though he would quite often go into his jungle things, faking the resurrection of "African music," the extreme irony here is that Ellington was making "African sounds," but as a sophisticated American. The "African" music he made had much less to do with Africa than his best music, which, in the sense I have used throughout this book, can be seen as a truly Afro-American music, though understandable only in the context of a completely American experience. This music could, and did, find a place

[12] *Jazz:* Its *Evolution and Essence,* p. 33.
[13] *Jazz: A People's Music,* p. 192.

within the main culture. Jazz became more "popular" than ever. The big colored dance bands of the thirties were a national entertainment and played in many white night clubs as well as the black clubs that had been set up especially for white Americans. These bands were also the strongest influence on American popular music and entertainment for twenty years.

The path of jazz and the further development of the Afro-American musical tradition paradoxically had been taken over at this level to a remarkable degree by elements of the Negro middle class. Jazz was their remaining connection with blues; a connection they could make, at many points, within the mainstream of American life.

The music had moved so far into the mainstream that soon white "swing" bands developed that could play with some of the authentic accent of the great Negro bands, though the deciding factor here was the fact that there were never enough good white jazz musicians to go around in those big bands, and most of the bands then were packed with a great many studio and section men, and perhaps one or two "hot" soloists. By the thirties quite a few white bands had mastered the swing idiom of big-band jazz with varying degrees of authenticity. One of the most successful of these bands, the Benny Goodman orchestra, even began to buy arrangements from Negro arrangers so that it would have more of an authentic tone. The arranger became one of the most important men in big-band jazz, demonstrating how far jazz had gotten from earlier Afro-American musical tradition. (Fletcher Henderson, however, was paid only $37.50 per arrangement by Goodman before Goodman actually hired him as the band's chief arranger.)

The prominence of radio had also created a new medium for this new music, and the growing numbers of white swing bands automatically qualified for these fairly well paying jobs: "The studio work was monopolized by a small group of musicians who turn up on hundreds of records by orchestras of every kind. One of the least admirable characteristics of the entire arrangement was that it was almost completely restricted to white musicians and it was the men from the white orchestras who were getting the work. The Negro musicians complained bitterly about the discrimination, but the white musicians never attempted to help them, and the contractors hired the men they wanted. At the Nest Club or the Lenox Club the musicians were on close terms, but the relationship ended when the white musicians went back to their Times Square hotels. A few of them, notably Goodman, were to use a few of the Harlem musicians, but in the first Depression years the studio orchestras were white." [14]

So the widespread development of the swing style produced yet another

[14] Samuel Charters and Leonard Kunstadt, *Jazz: A History of the New York Scene* (New York, Doubleday, 1962), p. 262.

irony—when the "obscurity" of the Negro's music was lessened with the coming of arranged big-band jazz, and the music, in effect, did pass into the mainstream of American culture, in fact, could be seen as an integral part of that culture, it not only ceased to have meaning for a great many Negroes but also those Negroes who were most closely involved with the music were not even allowed to play it at the highest salaries that could be gotten. The spectacle of Benny Goodman hiring Teddy Wilson and later Lionel Hampton, Charlie Christian, and Cootie Williams into his outrageously popular bands and thereby making them "big names" in the swing world seems to me as fantastically amusing as the fact that in the jazz polls during the late thirties and early forties run by popular jazz magazines, almost no Negro musicians won. Swing music, which was the result of arranged big-band jazz, as it developed to a music that had almost nothing to do with blues, had very little to do with black America, though that is certainly where it had come from. But there were now more and more Negroes like that, too.

DUTCHMAN

DUTCHMAN was first presented at The Cherry Lane Theatre,
New York City, on March 24, 1964.

Original Cast

Jennifer West   Robert Hooks

Produced by Theater 1964
(Richard Barr, Clinton Wilder, Edward Albee)
Directed by Edward Parone

Characters

CLAY, twenty-year-old Negro

LULA, thirty-year-old white woman

RIDERS OF COACH, white and black

YOUNG NEGRO

CONDUCTOR

In the flying underbelly of the city. Steaming hot, and summer on top, outside. Underground. The subway heaped in modern myth.

Opening scene is a man sitting in a subway seat, holding a magazine but looking vacantly just above its wilting pages. Occasionally he looks blankly toward the window on his right. Dim lights and darkness whistling by against the glass. (Or paste the lights, as admitted props, right on the subway windows. Have them move, even dim and flicker. But give the sense of speed. Also stations, whether the train is stopped or the glitter and activity of these stations merely flashes by the windows.)

The man is sitting alone. That is, only his seat is visible, though the rest of the car is outfitted as a complete subway car. But only his seat is shown. There might be, for a time, as the play begins, a loud scream of the actual train. And it can recur throughout the play, or continue on a lower key once the dialogue starts.

The train slows after a time, pulling to a brief stop at one of the stations. The man looks idly up, until he sees a woman's face staring at him through the window; when it realizes that the man has noticed the face, it begins very premeditatedly to smile. The man smiles too, for a moment, without a trace of self-consciousness. Almost an instinctive though undesirable response. Then a kind of awkwardness or embarrassment sets in, and the man makes to look away, is further embarrassed, so he brings back his eyes to where the face was, but by now the train is moving again, and the face would seem to be left behind by the way the man turns his head to look back through the other windows at the slowly fading platform. He smiles then; more comfortably confident, hoping perhaps that his memory of this brief encounter will be pleasant. And then he is idle again.

Scene I

Train roars. Lights flash outside the windows.

LULA *enters from the rear of the car in bright, skimpy summer clothes and sandals. She carries a net bag full of paper books, fruit, and other anonymous articles. She is wearing sunglasses, which she pushes up on her forehead from time to time.* LULA *is a tall, slender, beautiful woman with long red hair hanging straight down her back, wearing only loud lipstick in somebody's good taste. She is eating an apple, very daintily. Coming down the car toward* CLAY.

She stops beside CLAY'S *seat and hangs languidly from the strap, still managing to eat the apple. It is apparent that she is going to sit in the seat next to* CLAY, *and that she is only waiting for him to notice her before she sits.*

CLAY *sits as before, looking just beyond his magazine, now and again pulling the magazine slowly back and forth in front of his face in a hopeless effort to fan himself. Then he sees the woman hanging there beside him and he looks up into her face, smiling quizzically.*

LULA. Hello.

CLAY. Uh, hi're you?

LULA. I'm going to sit down. . . . O.K.?

CLAY. Sure.

LULA.
      [*Swings down onto the seat, pushing her legs straight out as if she is very weary*]
Oooof! Too much weight.

CLAY. Ha, doesn't look like much to me.

[*Leaning back against the window, a little surprised and maybe stiff*]

LULA. It's so anyway.

[*And she moves her toes in the sandals, then pulls her right leg up on the left knee, better to inspect the bottoms of the sandals and the back of her heel. She appears for a second not to notice that* CLAY *is sitting next to her or that she has spoken to him just a second before.* CLAY *looks at the magazine, then out the black window. As he does this, she turns very quickly toward him*]
Weren't you staring at me through the window?

CLAY.

[*Wheeling around and very much stiffened*]
What?

LULA. Weren't you staring at me through the window? At the last stop?

CLAY. Staring at you? What do you mean?

LULA. Don't you know what staring means?

CLAY. I saw you through the window . . . if that's what it means. I don't know if I was staring. Seems to me you were staring through the window at me.

LULA. I was. But only after I'd turned around and saw you staring through that window down in the vicinity of my ass and legs.

CLAY. Really?

LULA. Really. I guess you were just taking those idle potshots. Nothing else to do. Run your mind over people's flesh.

CLAY. Oh boy. Wow, now I admit I was looking in your direction. But the rest of that weight is yours.

LULA. I suppose.

CLAY. Staring through train windows is weird business. Much weirder than staring very sedately at abstract asses.

LULA. That's why I came looking through the window . . . so you'd have more than that to go on. I even smiled at you.

CLAY. That's right.

LULA. I even got into this train, going some other way than mine. Walked down the aisle . . . searching you out.

CLAY. Really? That's pretty funny.

LULA. That's pretty funny. . . . God, you're dull.

CLAY. Well, I'm sorry, lady, but I really wasn't prepared for party talk.

LULA. No, you're not. What are you prepared for?
[*Wrapping the apple core in a Kleenex and dropping it on the floor*]

CLAY.
[*Takes her conversation as pure sex talk. He turns to confront her squarely with this idea*]
I'm prepared for anything. How about you?

LULA.
[*Laughing loudly and cutting it off abruptly*]
What do you think you're doing?

CLAY. What?

LULA. You think I want to pick you up, get you to take me somewhere and screw me, huh?

CLAY. Is that the way I look?

LULA. You look like you been trying to grow a beard. That's exactly what you look like. You look like you live in New Jersey with your parents and are trying to grow a beard. That's what. You look like you've been reading Chinese poetry and drinking lukewarm sugarless tea.
[*Laughs, uncrossing and recrossing her legs*]
You look like death eating a soda cracker.

CLAY.
[*Cocking his head from one side to the other, embarrassed and trying to make some comeback, but also intrigued by what the woman is saying . . . even the sharp city coarseness of her voice, which is still a kind of gentle sidewalk throb*]
Really? I look like all that?

LULA. Not all of it.

[*She feigns a seriousness to cover an actual somber tone*]

I lie a lot.

[*Smiling*]

It helps me control the world.

CLAY.

[*Relieved and laughing louder than the humor*]

Yeah, I bet.

LULA. But it's true, most of it, right? Jersey? Your bumpy neck?

CLAY. How'd you know all that? Huh? Really, I mean about Jersey . . . and even the beard. I met you before? You know Warren Enright?

LULA. You tried to make it with your sister when you were ten.

[CLAY *leans back hard against the back of the seat, his eyes opening now, still trying to look amused*]

But I succeeded a few weeks ago.

[*She starts to laugh again*]

CLAY. What're you talking about? Warren tell you that? You're a friend of Georgia's?

LULA. I told you I lie. I don't know your sister. I don't know Warren Enright.

CLAY. You mean you're just picking these things out of the air?

LULA. Is Warren Enright a tall skinny black black boy with a phony English accent?

CLAY. I figured you knew him.

LULA. But I don't. I just figured you would know somebody like that.

[*Laughs*]

CLAY. Yeah, yeah.

LULA. You're probably on your way to his house now.

CLAY. That's right.

LULA.

[*Putting her hand on Clay's closer knee, drawing it from the knee up to the thigh's hinge, then removing it, watching his face very closely, and continuing to laugh, perhaps more gently than before*]
Dull, dull, dull. I bet you think I'm exciting.

CLAY. You're O.K.

LULA. Am I exciting you now?

CLAY. Right. That's not what's supposed to happen?

LULA. How do I know?
[*She returns her hand, without moving it, then takes it away and plunges it in her bag to draw out an apple*]
You want this?

CLAY. Sure.

LULA.
[*She gets one out of the bag for herself*]
Eating apples together is always the first step. Or walking up uninhabited Seventh Avenue in the twenties on weekends.
[*Bites and giggles, glancing at Clay and speaking in loose singsong*]
Can get you involved ... boy! Get us involved. Um-huh.
[*Mock seriousness*]
Would you like to get involved with me, Mister Man?

CLAY.
[*Trying to be a flippant as Lula, whacking happily at the apple*]
Sure. Why not? A beautiful woman like you. Huh, I'd be a fool not to.

LULA. And I bet you're sure you know what you're talking about.
[*Taking him a little roughly by the wrist, so he cannot eat the apple, then shaking the wrist*]
I bet you're sure of almost everything anybody ever asked you about ... right?
[*Shakes his wrist harder*]
Right?

CLAY. Yeah, right. .... Wow, you're pretty strong, you know? Whatta you, a lady wrestler or something?

LULA. What's wrong with lady wrestlers? And don't answer because you never knew any. Huh.

[*Cynically*]

That's for sure. They don't have any lady wrestlers in that part of Jersey. That's for sure.

CLAY. Hey, you still haven't tole me how you know so much about me.

LULA. I told you I didn't know anything about *you* . . . you're a well-known type.

CLAY. Really?

LULA. Or at least I know the type very well. And your skinny English friend too.

CLAY. Anonymously?

LULA.

[*Settles back in seat, single-mindedly finishing her apple and humming snatches of rhythm and blues song*]

What?

CLAY. Without knowing us specifically?

LULA. Oh boy.

[*Looking quickly at Clay*]

What a face. You know, you could be a handsome man.

CLAY. I can't argue with you.

LULA.

[*Vague, off-center response*]

What?

CLAY.

[*Raising his voice, thinking the train noise has drowned part of his sentence*]

I can't argue with you.

LULA. My hair is turning gray. A gray hair for each year and type I've come through.

CLAY. Why do you want to sound so old?

LULA. But it's always gentle when it starts.
　　　[*Attention drifting*]
Hugged against tenements, day or night.

CLAY. What?

LULA.
　　　[*Refocusing*]
Hey, why don't you take me to that party you're going to?

CLAY. You must be a friend of Warren's to know about the party.

LULA. Wouldn't you like to take me to the party?
　　　[*Imitates clinging vine*]
Oh, come on, ask me to your party.

CLAY. Of course I'll ask you to come with me to the party. And I'll bet you're a friend of Warren's.

LULA. Why not be a friend of Warren's? Why not?
　　　[*Taking his arm*]
Have you asked me yet?

CLAY. How can I ask you when I don't know your name?

LULA. Are you talking to my name?

CLAY. What is it, a secret?

LULA. I'm Lena the Hyena.

CLAY. The famous woman poet?

LULA. Poetess! The same!

CLAY. Well, you know so much about me . . . what's my name?

LULA. Morris the Hyena.

CLAY. The famous woman poet?

LULA. The same.
   [*Laughing and going into her bag*]
You want another apple?

CLAY. Can't make it, lady. I only have to keep one doctor away a day.

LULA. I bet your name is . . . something like . . . uh, Gerald or Walter. Huh?

CLAY. God, no.

LULA. Lloyd, Norman? One of those hopeless colored names creeping out of New Jersey. Leonard? Gag. . . .

CLAY. Like Warren?

LULA. Definitely, Just exactly like Warren. Or Everett.

CLAY. Gag. . . .

LULA. Well, for sure, it's not Willie.

CLAY. It's Clay.

LULA. Clay? Really? Clay what?

CLAY. Take your pick. Jackson, Johnson, or Williams.

LULA. Oh, really? Good for you. But it's got to be Williams. You're too pretentious to be a Jackson or Johnson.

CLAY. Thass right.

LULA. But Clay's O.K.

CLAY. So's Lena.

LULA. It's Lula.

CLAY. Oh?

LULA. Lula the Hyena.

CLAY. Very good.

LULA.

    [*Starts laughing again*]
Now you say to me, "Lula, Lula, why don't you go to this party with me tonight?" It's your turn, and let those be your lines.

CLAY. Lula, why don't you go to this party with me tonight, Huh?

LULA. Say my name twice before you ask, and no huh's.

CLAY. Lula, Lula, why don't you go to this party with me tonight?

LULA. I'd like to go, Clay, but how can you ask me to go when you barely know me?

CLAY. That is strange, isn't it?

LULA. What kind of reaction is that? You're supposed to say, "Aw, come on, we'll get to know each other better at the party."

CLAY. That's pretty corny.

LULA. What are you into anyway?
    [*Looking at him half sullenly but still amused*]
What thing are you playing at, Mister? Mister Clay Williams?
    [*Grabs his thigh, up near the crotch*]
What are *you* thinking about?

CLAY. Watch it now, you're gonna excite me for real.

LULA.

    [*Taking her hand away and throwing her apple core through the window*]
I bet.

    [*She slumps in the seat and is heavily silent*]

CLAY. I thought you knew everything about me? What happened?
    [LULA *looks at him, then looks slowly away, then over where the other aisle would be. Noise of the train. She reaches in her bag and pulls out one of the paper books. She puts it on her leg and thumbs the pages listlessly.* CLAY *cocks his head to see the title of the book. Noise of the train.* LULA *flips pages and her eyes drift. Both remain silent*]
Are you going to the party with me, Lula?

LULA.
[*Bored and not even looking*]
I don't even know you.

CLAY. You said you know my type.

[*Strangely irritated*]

Don't get smart with me, Buster. I know you like the palm of my hand.

CLAY. The one you eat the apples with?

LULA. Yeh. And the one I open doors late Saturday evening with. That's my door. Up at the top of the stairs. Five flights. Above a lot of Italians and lying Americans. And scrape carrots with. Also . . .
[*looks at him*]
the same hand I unbutton my dress with, or let my skirt fall down. Same hand. Lover.

CLAY. Are you angry about anything? Did I say something wrong?

LULA. Everything you say is wrong.
[*Mock smile*]
That's what makes you so attractive. Ha. In that funnybook jacket with all the buttons.
[*More animate, taking hold of his jacket*]
What've you got the jacket and tie on in all this heat for? And why're you wearing a jacket and tie like that? Did your people ever burn witches or start revolutions over the price of tea? Boy, those narrow-shoulder clothes come from a tradition you ought to feel oppressed by. A three-button suit. What right do you have to be wearing a three-button suit and striped tie? Your grandfather was a slave, he didn't go to Harvard.

CLAY. My grandfather was a night watchman.

LULA. And you went to a colored college where everybody thought they were Averell Harriman.

CLAY. All except me.

LULA. And who did you think you were? Who do you think you are now?

CLAY.

[*Laughs as if to make light of the whole trend of the conversation*]
Well, in college I thought I was Baudelaire. But I've slowed down since.

LULA. I bet you never once thought you were a black nigger.
[*Mock serious, then she howls with laughter.* CLAY *is stunned but after initial reaction, he quickly tries to appreciate the humor.* LULA *almost shrieks*]
A black Baudelaire.

CLAY. That's right.

LULA. Boy, are you corny. I take back what I said before. Everything you say is not wrong. It's perfect. You should be on television.

CLAY. You act like you're on television already.

LULA. That's because I'm an actress.

CLAY. I thought so.

LULA. Well, you're wrong. I'm no actress. I told you I always lie. I'm nothing, honey, and don't you ever forget it.
[*Lighter*]
Although my mother was a Communist. The only person in my family ever to amount to anything.

CLAY. My mother was a Republican.

LULA. And your father voted for the man rather than the party.

CLAY. Right!

LULA. Yea for him. Yea, yea for him.

CLAY. Yea!

LULA. And yea for America where he is free to vote for the mediocrity of his choice! Yea!

CLAY Yea!

LULA. And yea for both your parents who even though they differ about so crucial a matter as the body politic still forged a union of love and sacrifice that was destined to flower at the birth of the noble Clay ... what's your middle name?

CLAY. Clay.

LULA. A union of love and sacrifice that was destined to flower at the birth of the noble Clay Clay Williams. Yea! And most of all yea yea for you, Clay Clay. The Black Baudelaire! Yes!
[*And with knifelike cynicism*]
My Christ. My Christ.

CLAY. Thank you, ma'am.

LULA. May the people accept you as a ghost of the future. And love you, that you might not kill them when you can.

CLAY. What?

LULA. You're a murderer, Clay, and you know it.
[*Her voice darkening with significance*]
You know goddamn well what I mean.

CLAY. I do?

LULA. So we'll pretend the air is light and full of perfume.

CLAY.
[*Sniffing at her blouse*]
It is.

LULA. And we'll pretend the people cannot see you. That is, the citizens. And that you are free of your own history. And I am free of my history. We'll pretend that we are both anonymous beauties smashing along through the city's entrails.
[*She yells as loud as she can*]
GROOVE!

Black

SCENE II

Scene is the same as before, though now there are other seats visible in the car. And throughout the scene other people get on the subway. There are maybe one or two seated in the car as the scene opens, though neither CLAY nor LULA notices them. CLAY's tie is open. LULA is hugging his arm.

CLAY. The party!

LULA. I know it'll be something good. You can come in with me, looking casual and significant. I'll be strange, haughty, and silent, and walk with long slow strides.

CLAY. Right.

LULA. When you get drunk, pat me once, very lovingly on the flanks, and I'll look at you cryptically, licking my lips.

CLAY. It sounds like something we can do.

LULA. You'll go around talking to young men about your mind, and to old men about your plans. If you meet a very close friend who is also with someone like me, we can stand together, sipping our drinks and exchanging codes of lust. The atmosphere will be slithering in love and half-love and very open moral decision.

CLAY. Great. Great.

LULA. And everyone will pretend they don't know your name, and then . . .
    [*She pauses heavily*]
later, when they have to, they'll claim a friendship that denies your sterling character.

CLAY.
    [Kissing her neck and fingers]
And then what?

LULA. Then? Well, then we'll go down the street, late night, eating apples and winding very deliberately toward my house.

CLAY. Deliberately?

LULA. I mean, we'll look in all the shopwindows, and make fun of the queers. Maybe we'll meet a Jewish Buddhist and flatten his conceits over some pretentious coffee.

CLAY. In honor of whose God?

LULA. Mine.

CLAY. Who is . . . ?

LULA. Me . . . and you?

CLAY. A corporate Godhead.

LULA. Exactly. Exactly.
    [Notices one of the other people entering]

CLAY. Go on with the chronicle. Then what happens to us?

LULA.
    [A mild depression, but she still makes her description triumphant and increasingly direct]
To my house, of course.

CLAY. Of course.

LULA. And up the narrow steps of the tenement.

CLAY. You live in a tenement?

LULA. Wouldn't live anywhere else. Reminds me specifically of my novel form of insanity.

CLAY. Up the tenement stairs.

LULA. And with my apple-eating hand I push open the door and lead you, my tender big-eyed prey, into my . . . God, what can I call it . . . into my hovel.

CLAY. Then what happens?

LULA. After the dancing and games, after the long drinks and long walks, the real fun begins.

CLAY. Ah, the real fun.
[*Embarrassed, in spite of himself*]
Which is . . .?

LULA.
[*Laughs at him*]
Real fun in the dark house. Hah! Real fun in the dark house, high up above the street and the ignorant cowboys. I lead you in, holding your wet hand gently in my hand . . .

CLAY. Which is not wet?

LULA. Which is dry as ashes.

CLAY. And cold?

LULA. Don't think you'll get out of your responsibility that way. It's not cold at all. You Fascist! Into my dark living room. Where we'll sit and talk endlessly, endlessly.

CLAY. About what?

LULA. About what? About your manhood, what do you think? What do you think we've been talking about all this time?

CLAY. Well, I didn't know it was that. That's for sure. Every other thing in the world but that.
[*Notices another person entering, looks quickly, almost involuntarily, up and down the car, seeing the other people in the car*]
Hey, I didn't even notice when those people got on.

LULA.Yeah, I know.

CLAY. Man, this subway is slow.

LULA. Yeah, I know.

CLAY. Well, go on. We were talking about my manhood.

LULA. We still are. All the time.

CLAY. We were in your living room.

LULA. My dark living room. Talking endlessly.

CLAY. About my manhood.

LULA. I'll make you a map of it. Just as soon as we get to my house.

CLAY. Well, that's great.

LULA. One of the things we do while we talk. And screw.

CLAY.
        [*Trying to make his smile broader and less shaky*]
We finally got there.

LULA. And you'll call my rooms black as a grave. You'll say, "This place is like Juliet's tomb."

CLAY.
        [*Laughs*]
I might.
LULA. I know. You've probably said it before.

CLAY. And is that all? The whole grand tour?

LULA. Not all. You'll say to me very close to my face, many, many times, you'll say, even whisper, that you love me.

CLAY. Maybe I will.

LULA. And you'll be lying.

CLAY. I wouldn't lie about something like that.

LULA. Hah. It's the only kind of thing you will lie about. Especially if you think it'll keep me alive.

CLAY. Keep you alive? I don't understand.

LULA.

> [*Bursting out laughing, but too shrilly*]

Don't understand? Well, don't look at me. It's the path I take, that's all. Where both feet take me when I set them down. One in front of the other.

CLAY. Morbid. Morbid. You sure you're not an actress? All that self-aggrandizement.

LULA. Well, I told you I wasn't an actress ... but I also told you I lie all the time. Draw your own conclusions.

CLAY. And is that all of our lives together you've described? There's no more?

LULA. I've told you all I know. Or almost all.

CLAY. There's no funny parts?

LULA. I thought it was all funny.

CLAY. But you mean peculiar, not ha-ha.

LULA. You don't know what I mean.

CLAY. Well, tell me the almost part then. You said almost all. What else? I want the whole story.

LULA.

> [*Searching aimlessly through her bag. She beings to talk breathlessly, with a light and silly tone*]

All stories are whole stories. All of 'em. Our whole story ... nothing but change. How could things go on like that forever? Huh?

> [*Slaps him on the shoulder, begins finding things in her bag, taking them out and throwing them over her shoulder into the aisle*]

Except I do go on as I do. Apples and long walks with deathless intelligent lovers. But you mix it up. Look out the window, all the time. Turning pages. Change change change. Till, shit, I don't know you. Wouldn't, for that matter. You're too serious. I bet you're even too serious to be psychoanalyzed. Like all those Jewish poets from Yonkers, who leave their mothers looking for other mothers, or others' mothers, on whose baggy tits they lay their fumbling heads. Their poems are always funny, and all about sex.

CLAY. They sound great. Like movies.

LULA. But you change.
[*Blankly*]
And things work on you till you hate them.
[*More people come into the train. They come closer to the couple, some of them not sitting, but swinging drearily on the straps, staring at the two with uncertain interest*]

CLAY. Wow. All these people, so suddenly. They must all come from the same place.

LULA. Right. That they do.

CLAY. Oh? You know about them too?

LULA. Oh yeah. About them more than I know about you. Do they frighten you?

CLAY. Frighten me? Why should they frighten me?

LULA. 'Cause you're an escaped nigger.

CLAY. Yeah?

LULA. 'Cause you crawled through the wire and made tracks to my side.

CLAY. Wire?

LULA. Don't they have wire around plantations?

CLAY. You must be Jewish. All you can think about is wire. Plantations didn't have any wire. Plantations were big open whitewashed places like heaven, and everybody on 'em was grooved to be there. Just strummin' and hummin' all day.

LULA. Yes, yes.

CLAY. And that's how the blues was born.

LULA. Yes, yes. And that's how the blues was born.
[*Begins to make up a song that becomes quickly hysterical. As she sings she rises from her seat, still throwing things out of her bag into*

the aisle, beginning a rhythmical shudder and twistlike wiggle, which she continues up and down the aisle, bumping into many of the standing people and tripping over the feet of those sitting. Each time she runs into a person she lets out a very vicious piece of profanity, wiggling and stepping all the time]

And that's how the blues was born. Yes. Yes. Son of a bitch, get out of the way. Yes. Quack. Yes. Yes. And that's how the blues was born. Ten little niggers sitting on a limb, but none of them ever looked like him.

[Points to CLAY, *returns toward the seat, with her hands extended for him to rise and dance with her]*

And that's how blues was born. Yes. Come on, Clay. Let's do the nasty. Rub bellies. Rub bellies.

CLAY.

[Waves his hands to refuse. He is embarrassed, but determined to get a kick out of the proceedings]

Hey, what was in those apples? Mirror, mirror on the wall, who's the fairest one of all? Snow White, baby, and don't you forget it.

LULA.

[Grabbing for his hands, which he draws away]

Come on, Clay. Let's rub bellies on the train. The nasty. The nasty. Do the gritty grind, like your ol' rag-head mammy. Grind till you lose your mind. Shake it, shake it, shake it, shake it! OOOOweeee! Come on, Clay. Let's do the choo-choo train shuffle, the navel scratcher.

CLAY. Hey, you coming on like the lady who smoked up her grass skirt.

LULA.

[Becoming annoyed that he will not dance, and becoming more animated as if to embarrass him still further]

Come on, Clay . . . let's do the thing. Uhh! Uhh! Clay! Clay! You middle-class black bastard. Forget your social-working mother for a few seconds and let's knock stomachs. Clay, you liver-lipped white man. You would-be Christian. You ain't no nigger, you're just a dirty white man. Get up, Clay. Dance with me, Clay.

CLAY. Lula! Sit down, now. Be cool.

LULA.

[Mocking him, in wild dance]

Be cool. Be cool. That's all you know . . . shaking that wildroot cream-oil on your knotty head, jackets buttoning up to your chin, so full of white man's words. Christ! God! Get up and scream at these people. Like scream meaningless shit in these hopeless faces.

[*She screams at people in train, still dancing*]
Red trains cough Jewish underwear for keeps! Expanding smells of silence. Gravy snot whistling like sea birds. Clay. Clay, you got to break out. Don't sit there dying the way they want you to die. Get up.

CLAY. Oh, sit the fuck down.
[*He moves to restrain her*]
Sit down, goddamn it.

LULA.
[Twisting out of his reach]
Screw yourself, Uncle Tom. Thomas Woolly-Head.
[*Begins to dance a kind of jig, mocking Clay with loud forced humor*]
There is Uncle Tom . . . I mean, Uncle Thomas Woolly-Head. With old white matted mane. He hobbles on his wooden cane. Old Tom. Old Tom. Let the white man hump his ol' mama, and he jes' shuffle off in the woods and hide his gentle gray head. Ol' Thomas Woolly-Head.
[*Some of the other riders are laughing now. A drunk gets up and joins* LULA *in her dance, singing, as best he can, her "song."* CLAY *gets up out of his seat and visibly scans the faces of the other riders*]

CLAY. Lula! Lula!
[*She is dancing and turning, still shouting as loud as she can. The drunk too is shouting, and waving his hands wildly*]
Lula . . . you dumb bitch. Why don't you stop it?
[*He rushes half stumbling from his seat, and grabs one of her flailing arms*]

LULA. Let me go! You black son of a bitch.
[*She struggles against him*]
Let me go! Help!
[CLAY *is dragging her towards her seat, and the drunk seeks to interfere. He grabs* CLAY *around the shoulders and begins wrestling with him.* CLAY *clubs the drunk to the floor without releasing* LULA, *who is still screaming.* CLAY *finally gets her to the seat and throws her into it*]

CLAY. Now you shut the hell up.
[*Grabbing her shoulders*]
Just shut up. You don't know what you're talking about. You don't know anything. So just keep your stupid mouth closed.

LULA. You're afraid of white people. And your father was. Uncle Tom Big Lip!

CLAY.
[*Slaps her as hard as he can, across the mouth.* LULA*'s head bangs against the back of the seat. When she raises it again,* CLAY *slaps her again*]
Now shut up and let me talk.
[*He turns toward the other riders, some of whom are sitting on the edge of their seats. The drunk is on one knee, rubbing his head, and singing softly the same song. He shuts up too when he sees* CLAY *watching him. The others go back to newspapers or stare out the windows*]
Shit, you don't have any sense, Lula, nor feelings either. I could murder you now. Such a tiny ugly throat. I could squeeze it flat, and watch you turn blue, on a humble. For dull kicks. And all these weak-faced ofays squatting around here, staring over their papers at me. Murder them too. Even if they expected it. That man there . . .
[*Points to well-dressed man*]
I could rip that *Times* right out of his hand, as skinny and middle-classed as I am, I could rip that paper out of his hand and just as easily rip out his throat. It takes no great effort. For what? To kill you soft idiots? You don't understand anything but luxury.

LULA. You fool!

CLAY.
[*Pushing her against the seat*]
I'm not telling you again, Tallulah Bankhead! Luxury. In your face and your fingers. You telling me what I ought to do.
[*Sudden scream frightening the whole coach*]
Well, don't! Don't you tell me anything! If I'm a middle-class fake white man . . . let me be. And let me be in the way I want.
[*Through his teeth*]
I'll rip your lousy breasts off! Let me be who I feel like being. Uncle Tom. Thomas. Whoever. It's none of your business. You don't know anything except what's there for you to see. An act. Lies. Device. Not the pure heart, the pumping black heart. You don't ever know that. And I sit here, in this buttoned-up suit, to keep myself from cutting all your throats. I mean wantonly. You great liberated whore! You fuck some black man, and right away you're an expert on black people. What a lotta shit that is. The only thing you know is that you come if he bangs you hard enough. And that's all. The belly rub? You wanted to do the belly rub? Shit, you don't even know how. You

don't know how. That ol' dipty-dip shit you do, rolling your ass like an elephant. That's not my kind of belly rub. Belly rub is not Queens. Belly rub is dark places, with big hats and overcoats held up with one arm. Belly rub hates you. Old bald-headed four-eyed ofays popping their fingers . . . and don't know yet what they're doing. They say, "I love Bessie Smith." And don't even understand that Bessie Smith is saying, "Kiss my ass, kiss my black unruly ass." Before love, suffering, desire, anything you can explain, she's saying, and very plainly, "Kiss my black ass." And if you don't know that, it's you that's doing the kissing.

Charlie Parker? Charlie Parker. All the hip white boys scream for Bird. And Bird saying, "Up your ass, feebleminded ofay! Up your ass." And they sit there talking about the tortured genius of Charlie Parker. Bird would've played not a note of music if he just walked up to East Sixty-seventh Street and killed the first ten white people he saw. Not a note! And I'm the great would-be poet. Yes. That's right! Poet. Some kind of bastard literature . . . all it needs is a simple knife thrust. Just let me bleed you, you loud whore, and one poem vanished. A whole people of neurotics, struggling to keep from being sane. And the only thing that would cure the neurosis would be your murder. Simple as that. I mean if I murdered you, then other white people would begin to understand me. You understand? No. I guess not. If Bessie Smith had killed some white people she wouldn't have needed that music. She could have talked very straight and plain about the world. No metaphors. No grunts. No wiggles in the dark of her soul. Just straight two and two are four. Money. Power. Luxury. Like that. All of them. Crazy niggers turning their backs on sanity. When all it needs is that simple act. Murder. Just murder! Would make us all sane.

    [Suddenly weary]

Ahhh. Shit. But who needs it? I'd rather be a fool. Insane. Safe with my words, and no deaths, and clean, hard thoughts, urging me to new conquests. My people's madness. Hah! That's a laugh. My people. They don't need me to claim them. They got legs and arms of their own. Personal insanities. Mirrors. They don't need all those words. They don't need any defense. But listen, though, one more thing. And you tell this to your father, who's probably the kind of man who needs to know at once. So he can plan ahead. Tell him not to preach so much rationalism and cold logic to these niggers. Let them alone. Let them sing curses at you in code and see your filth as simple lack of style. Don't make the mistake, through some irresponsible surge of Christian charity, of talking too much about the advantages of Western rationalism, or the great intellectual legacy of the white man, or maybe they'll begin to listen. And then, maybe one day, you'll find they actually do understand exactly what you are talking about, all these fantasy people. All these blues people. And on that day, as sure as shit, when you really believe you can "accept" them into your fold, as half-white trusties late of the subject peoples. With no more blues, except the very old ones, and not a watermelon in sight, the great missionary heart will have triumphed, and all of those ex-coons will be stand-up Western men, with eyes for clean hard useful lives, sober, pious and sane, and they'll murder you. They'll murder you, and have very rational explanations. Very much like your own. They'll cut your throats, and drag you out to the edge of your cities so the flesh can fall away from your bones, in sanitary isolation.

LULA.

> [*Her voice takes on a different, more businesslike quality*]

I've heard enough.

CLAY.

> [*Reaching for his books*]

I bet you have. I guess I better collect my stuff and get off this train. Looks like we won't be acting out that little pageant you outlined before.

LULA. No. We won't. You're right about that, at least.

> [*She turns to look quickly around the rest of the car*]

All right!

> [*The others respond*]

CLAY.

> [*Bending across the girl to retrieve his belongings*]

Sorry, baby, I don't think we could make it.

> [*As he is bending over her, the girl brings up a small knife and plunges it into CLAY's chest. Twice. He slumps across her knees, his mouth working stupidly*]

LULA. Sorry is right.

> [*Turning to the others in the car who have already gotten up from their seats*]

Sorry is the rightest thing you've said. Get this man off me! Hurry, now!

> [*The others come and drag CLAY's body down the aisle*]

Open the door and throw his body out.

> [*They throw him off*]

And all of you get off at the next stop.

> [LULA *busies herself straightening her things. Getting everything in order. She takes out a notebook and makes a quick scribbling note. Drops it in her bag. The train apparently stops and all the others get off, leaving her alone in the coach.*]

Very soon a young Negro of about twenty comes into the coach, with a couple of books under his arm. He sits a few seats in back of LULA. *When he is seated she turns and gives him a long slow look. He looks up from his book and drops the book on his lap. Then an old Negro conductor comes into the car, doing a sort of restrained soft shoe, and half mumbling the words of some song. He looks at the young man, briefly, with a quick greeting*]

CONDUCTOR. Hey, brother!

YOUNG MAN. Hey.
[*The conductor continues down the aisle with his little dance and the mumbled song.* LULA *turns to stare at him and follows his movements down the aisle. The conductor tips his hat when he reaches her seat, and continues out the car*]

Curtain

THE SLAVE

A Fable in a Prologue and Two Acts

THE SLAVE was first presented at the St. Mark's Playhouse, New York City, in December 1964.

Original Cast

GRACE	Nan Martin
WALKER	Al Freeman, Jr.
EASLEY	Jerome Raphel

Produced by Leo Garen and Stan Swerdlow in association with Gene Persson

Directed by Leo Garen
Designed by Larry Rivers

Characters

WALKER VESSELS, tall, thin Negro about forty.

GRACE, blond woman about the same age. Small, thin, beautiful.

BRADFORD EASLEY, tall, broad white man, with thinning hair, about forty-five.

The action takes place in a large living room, tastefully furnished the way an intelligent university professor and his wife would furnish it.

Room is dark at the beginning of the play, except for light from explosions, which continue, sometimes close, sometimes very far away, throughout both acts, and well after curtain of each act.

PROLOGUE

WALKER.

[*Coming out dressed as an old field slave, balding, with white hair, and an old ragged vest. (Perhaps he is sitting, sleeping, initially-nodding and is awakened by faint cries, like a child's.) He comes to the center of the stage slowly, and very deliberately, puffing on a pipe, and seemingly uncertain of the reaction any audience will give his speech*]

Whatever the core of our lives. Whatever the deceit. We live where we are, and seek nothing but ourselves. We are liars, and we are murderers. We invent death for others. Stop their pulses publicly. Stone possible lovers with heavy worlds we think are ideas . . . and we know, even before these shapes are realized, that these worlds, these depths or heights we fly to smoothly, as in a dream, or slighter, when we stare dumbly into space, leaning our eyes just behind a last quick moving bird, then sometimes the place and twist of what we are will push and sting, and what the crust of our stance has become will ring in our ears and shatter that piece of our eyes that is never closed. An ignorance. A stupidity. A stupid longing not to know ... which is automatically fulfilled. Automatically triumphs. Automatically makes us killers or foot-dragging celebrities at the core of any filth. And it is a deadly filth that passes as whatever thing we feel is too righteous to question, too deeply felt to deny.

[*Pause to relight pipe*]

I am much older than I look ... or maybe much younger. Whatever I am or seem ...

[*Significant pause*]

to you, then let that rest. But figure, still, that you might not be right. Figure, still, that you might be lying ... to save yourself. Or myself's image, which might set you crawling like a thirsty dog, for the meanest of drying streams. The meanest of ideas.

[*Gentle, mocking laugh*]

Yeah. Ideas. Let that settle! Ideas. Where they form. Or whose they finally seem to be. Yours? The other's? Mine?

[*Shifts uneasily, pondering the last*]

No, no more. Not mine. I served my slow apprenticeship ... and maybe came up lacking. Maybe. Ha. Who's to say, really? Huh? But figure, still, ideas are still in the world. They need judging. I mean, they don't come in that singular or wild, that whatever they are, just because they're beautiful and brilliant, just because they strike us full in the center of the heart. ... My God!

[*Softer*]

My God, just because, and even this, believe me, even if, that is, just because they're *right* ... doesn't mean anything. The very rightness stinks a lotta times. The very rightness.

[*Looks down and speaks softer and quicker*]

I am an old man. An old man.

[*Blankly*]

The waters and wars. Time's a dead thing really ... and keeps nobody whole. An old man, full of filed rhythms. Terrific, eh? That I hoarded so much dignity? An old man full of great ideas. Let's say theories. As: Love is an instrument of knowledge. Oh, not my own. Not my own ... is right. But listen now. ... Brown is not brown except when used as an intimate description of personal phenomenological fields. As your brown is not my brown, et cetera, that is, we need, ahem, a meta-language. We need some thing not included here.

[*Spreads arms*]

Your ideas? An old man can't be expected to be right. If I'm old. If I really claim that embarrassment.

[*Saddens ... brightens*]

A poem? Lastly, that, to distort my position? To divert you ... in your hour of need. Before the thing goes on. Before you get your lousy chance. Discovering racially the funds of the universe. Discovering the last image of the thing. As the sky when the moon is broken. Or old, old blues people moaning in their sleep, singing, man, oh, nigger, nigger, you still here, as hard as nails, and takin' no shit from nobody. He say, yeah, yeah, he say yeah, yeah. He say, yeah, yeah ... goin' down slow, man. Goin' down slow. He say ... yeah, heh ...

> [*Running down, growing anxiously less articulate, more "field hand" sounding, blankly lyrical, shuffles slowly around, across the stage as the lights dim and he enters the set proper and assumes the position he will have when the play starts ... still moaning ...*]

Act I

THE SCENE: *A light from an explosion lights the room dimly for a second and the outline of a figure is seen half sprawled on a couch. Every once in a while another blast shows the figure in silhouette. He stands from time to time, sits, walks nervously around the room examining books and paintings. Finally, he climbs a flight of stairs, stays for a few minutes, then returns. He sits smoking in the dark, until some sound is heard outside the door. He rises quickly and takes a position behind the door, a gun held out stiffly.* GRACE *and* EASLEY *open the door, turn on the light, agitated and breathing heavily.* GRACE *quiet and weary.* EASLEY *talking in harsh angry spurts.*

EASLEY. Son of a bitch. Those black son of a bitches. Why don't they at least stop and have their goddamned dinners? Goddamn son of a bitches. They're probably gonna keep that horseshit up all goddamn night. Goddamnit. Goddamn it!
[*He takes off a white metal hat and slings it across the room. It bangs loudly against the brick of the fireplace*]

GRACE. Brad! You're going to wake up the children!

EASLEY. Oh, Christ! ... But if they don't wake up under all that blasting, I don't think that tin hat will do it.
[*He unbuttons his shirt, moves wearily across the room, still mumbling under his breath about the source of the explosions*]
Hey, Grace ... you want a drink? That'll fix us up.
[*He moves to get the drink and spots* WALKER *leaning back against the wall, half smiling, also very weary, but still holding the gun, stomach-high, and very stiffly.* EASLEY *freezes, staring at* WALKER's *face and then the gun, and then back to* WALKER's *face. He makes no sound. The two men stand confronting each other until* GRACE *turns and sees them*]

GRACE. Sure, I'll take a drink ... one of the few real pleasures left in the Western world.

> [*She turns and drops her helmet to the floor, staring unbelievingly*]

Ohh!

WALKER.

> [*Looks over slowly at* GRACE *and waves as from a passing train. Then he looks back at* EASLEY; *the two men's eyes are locked in the same ugly intensity.* WALKER *beckons to* GRACE]

The blinds.

GRACE. Walker!

> [*She gets the name out quietly, as if she is trying to hold so many other words in*]

Walker ... the gun!

WALKER.

> [*Half turning to look at her. He looks back at* EASLEY, *then lets the gun swing down easily toward the foor. He looks back at* GRACE, *and tries to smile*]

Hey, momma. How're you?

EASLEY.

> [*At* WALKER, *and whatever else is raging in his own head*]

Son of a bitch!

GRACE. What're you doing here, Walker? What do you want?

WALKER.

> [*Looking at* EASLEY *from time to time*]

Nothing. Not really. Just visiting.

> [*Grins*]

I was in the neighborhood; thought I'd stop by and see how the other half lives.

GRACE. Isn't this dangerous?

> [*She seems relieved by* WALKER'*s relative good spirits and she begins to look for a cigarette.* EASLEY *has not yet moved. He is still staring at* WALKER]

WALKER. Oh, it's dangerous as a bitch. But don't you remember how heroic I am?

EASLEY.

[*Handing* GRACE *a cigarette, then waiting to light it*]
Well, what the hell do you want, hero?

[*Drawn out and challenging*]

WALKER.

[*With same challenge*]
Nothing you have, fellah, not one thing.

EASLEY. Oh?

[*Cynically*]
Is *that* why you and your noble black brothers are killing what's left of this city?

[*Suddenly broken*]
I should say ... what's left of this country ... or world.

WALKER. Oh, fuck you

[*Hotly*]
fuck you ... just fuck you, that's all. Just fuck you!

[*Keeps voice stiffly contained, but then it rises sharply*]
I mean really, just fuck you. Don't, goddamnit, don't tell me about any goddamn killing of anything. If that's what's happening. I mean if this shitty town is being flattened ... let it. It needs it.

GRACE. Walker, shut up, will you?

[*Furious from memory*]
I had enough of your twisted logic in my day ... you remember? I mean like your heroism. The same kind of memory. Or Lie. Do you remember which? Huh?

[*Starting to weep*]

WALKER.

[*Starts to comfort her*]
Grace ... look ... there's probably nothing I can say to make you understand me ... now.

EASLEY.

[*Steps in front of* WALKER *as he moves toward* GRACE ... *feigning a cold sophistication*]
Uh ... no, now come, Jefe, you're not goig to make one of those embrace the weeping ex-wife dramas, are you? Well, once a bad poet always a bad poet ... even in the disguise of a racist murderer!

/ 103

WALKER.
[*Not quite humbled*]
Yeah.

[*Bends head, then he brings it up quickly, forcing the joke*]
Even disguised as a racist murderer ... I remain a bad poet. Didn't St.
Thomas say that? Once a bad poet always a bad poet ... or was it Carl
Sandburg, as some kind of confession?

EASLEY. You're not still writing ... now, are you? I should think the political,
now military estates would be sufficient. And you always used to speak of the
Renaissance as an evil time.
[*Begins making two drinks*]
And now you're certainly the gaudiest example of Renaissance man I've
heard of.
[*Finishes making drinks and brings one to* GRACE. WALKER *watches
him and then as he starts to speak he walks to the cabinet, picks up the
bottle, and empties a good deal of it*]

GRACE.
[*Looking toward* WALKER *even while* EASLEY *extends the drink toward
her*]
Walker ... you are still writing, aren't you?

WALKER. Oh, God, yes. Want to hear the first lines of my newest work?
[*Drinks, does a theatrical shiver*]
Uh, how's it go ... ? Oh, "Straddling each dolphin's back/And steadied by a
fin,/Those innocents relive their death,/Their wounds open again."

GRACE.
[*Staring at him closely*]
It's changed quite a bit.

WALKER. Yeah ... it's changed to Yeats.
[*Laughs very loudly*]

Yeah, Yeats ... Hey, professor, anthologist, lecturer, loyal opposition, et
cetera, et cetera, didn't you recognize those words as being Yeats's? Goddamn, I mean if you didn't recognize them ... who the hell would? I thought
you knew all kinds of shit.

EASLEY.
[*Calmly*]
I knew they were Yeats'.

WALKER.
> [*Tilting the bottle again quickly*]

Oh, yeah? What poem?

EASLEY. The second part of "News for the Delphic Oracle."

WALKER.
> [*Hurt*]

"News for the Delphic Oracle." Yeah. That's right.
> [*To* GRACE]

You know that, Grace? Your husband knows all about everything. The second part of "News for the Delphic Oracle."
> [*Rhetorically*]

Intolerable music falls. Nymphs and satyrs copulate in the foam.
> [*Tilts bottle again, some liquor splashes on the floor*]

EASLEY.
> [*Suddenly straightening and stopping close to* WALKER]

Look ... LOOK! You arrogant maniac, if you get drunk or fall out here, so help me, I'll call the soldiers or somebody ... and turn you over to them. I swear I'll do that.

GRACE. Brad!

WALKER. Yeah, yeah, I know. That's your job. A liberal education, and a long history of concern for minorities and charitable organizations can do that for you.

EASLEY.
> [*Almost taking hold of* WALKER's *clothes*]

No! I mean this, friend! Really! If I get the slightest advantage, some cracker soldier will be bayonetting you before the night is finished.

WALKER.
> [*Slaps* EASLEY *across the face with the back of his left hand, pulling the gun out with his right and shoving it as hard as he can against* EASLEY's *stomach.* EASLEY *slumps, and the cruelty in* WALKER's *face at this moment also frightens* GRACE]

"My country, 'tis of thee. Sweet land of liber-ty."
> [*Screams off key like drunken opera singer*]

Well, let's say liberty and ignorant vomiting faggot professors.
> [*To* GRACE]

Right, lady? Isn't that right? I mean you ought to know, 'cause you went out of your way to marry one.

[*Turns to* GRACE *and she takes an involuntary step backward. And in a cracked ghostlike voice that he wants to be loud . . .*]

Huh? Huh? And then fed the thing my children.

[*He reaches stiffly out and pushes her shoulder, intending it to be strictly a burlesque, but there is quite a bit of force in the gesture.* GRACE *falls back, just short of panic, but* WALKER *hunches his shoulders and begins to jerk his finger at the ceiling; one eye closed and one leg raised, jerking his finger absurdly at the ceiling, as if to indicate something upstairs that was to be kept secret*]

Ah, yes, the children . . .

[*Affecting an imprecise "Irish" accent*]

sure and they looked well enough . . .

[*Grins*]

and white enough, roosting in that kennel. Hah, I hope you didn't tell Faggy, there, about those two lovely ladies.

[EASLEY *is kneeling on the floor holding his stomach and shaking his head*]

Ahh, no, lady, let's keep that strictly in the family. I mean among those of us who screw.

[*He takes another long drink from the bottle, and "threatens"* EASLEY'S *head in a kind of burlesque*]

For Lawrence, and all the cocksmen of my underprivileged youth. When we used to chase that kind of frail little sissy-punk down Raymond Boulevard and compromise his sister-in-laws in the cloak room . . . It's so simple to work from the bottom up. To always strike, and know, from the blood's noise that you're right, and what you're doing is right, and even *pretty*.

[*Suddenly more tender toward* GRACE]

I swear to you, Grace, I did come into the world pointed in the right direction. Oh, shit, I learned so many words for what I've wanted to say. They all come down on me at once. But almost none of them are mine.

[*He straightens up, turning quickly toward the still kneeling* EASLEY, *and slaps him as hard as he can across the face, sending his head twisting around*]

Bastard! A poem for your mother!

GRACE.

[*Lets out a short pleading cry*]

Ohh! Get away from him, Walker! Get away from him,

[*Hysterically*]

you nigger murderer!

WALKER.

> [*Has started to tilt the bottle again, after he slaps* EASLEY, *and when* GRACE *shouts at him, he chokes on the liquor, spitting it out, and begins laughing with a kind of hysterical amusement*]

Oh! Ha, ha, ha . . . you mean . . .Wow!

> [*Trying to control laughter, but it is an extreme kind of release*]

No kidding? Grace, Gracie! Wow! I wonder how long you had that stored up.

GRACE.

> [*Crying now, going over to* EASLEY, *trying to help him up*]

Brad. Brad. Walker, why'd you come here? Why'd you come here? Brad?

WALKER.

> [*Still laughing and wobbling clumsily around*]

Nigger murderer? Wowee. Gracie, are you just repeating your faggot husband, or did you have that in you a long time? I mean . . . for all the years we were together? Hooo! Yeah.

> [*Mock seriously*]

Christ, it could get to be a weight after a time, huh? When you taught the little girls to pray . . . you'd have to whisper, "And God bless Mommy, and God bless Daddy, the nigger murderer." Wow, that's some weight.

GRACE. Shut up, Walker. Just shut up, and get out of here, away from us, please. I don't want to hear you . . . I don't need to hear you, again. Remember, I heard it all before, baby . . . you don't get me again.

> [*She is weeping and twisting her head, trying at the same time to fully revive* EASLEY, *who is still on the floor with legs sprawled apart, both hands held to the pit of his stomach, his head nodding back and forth in pain*]

Why'd you come here . . . just to do this? Why don't you leave before you kill somebody?

> [*Trying to hold back a scream*]

Before you kill another white person?

WALKER.

> [*Sobering, but still forcing a cynical hilarity*]

Ah . . . the party line. Stop him before he kills another white person! Heh. Yeah. Yeah. And that's not such a bad idea, really. . . . I mean, after all, only you and your husband there are white in this house. Those two lovely little girls upstairs are niggers. You know, circa 1800, one drop makes you whole?

GRACE. Shut up, Walker!

> [*She leaps to her feet and rushes toward him*]

Shut your ugly head!
[*He pushes her away*]

EASLEY.
[*Raising his head and shouting as loud as he can manage*]
You're filth, boy. Just filth. Can you understand that anything and everything
you do is stupid, filthy, or meaningless! Your inept formless poetry. Hah.
Poetry? A flashy doggerel for inducing all those unfortunate troops of yours
to spill their blood in your behalf. But I guess that's something! Ritual drama,
we used to call it at the university. The poetry of ritual drama.
[*Pulls himself up*]
And even that's giving that crap the benefit of the doubt. Ritual filth would
have been the right name for it.

WALKER. Ritual drama . . .
[*Half musing*]
yeah, I remember seeing that phrase in an old review by one of your queer
academic friends. . . .
[*Noticing* EASLEY *getting up*]
Oh well, look at him coming up by his bootstraps. I didn't mean to hit you
that hard, Professor Easley, sir . . . I just don't know my own strent'.
[*Laughs and finishes the bottle . . . starts as if he is going to throw it
over his shoulder, then he places it very carefully on the table. He
starts dancing around and whooping like an "Indian"*]
More! Bwana, me want more fire water!

EASLEY. As I said, Vessels, you're just filth. Pretentious filth.

WALKER.
[*Dances around a bit more, then stops abruptly in front of* EASLEY; *so
close they are almost touching. He speaks in a quiet menacing tone*]
The liquor, turkey. The liquor. No opinions right now. Run off and get more
liquor, *sabe?*

GRACE.
[*Has stopped crying and managed to regain a cynical composure*]
I'll get it, Brad. Mr. Vessels is playing the mad scene from *Native Son*.
[*Turns to go*]
A second-rate Bigger Thomas.

WALKER.
[*Laughs*]
Yeah. But remember when I used to play a second-rate Othello? Oh, wow . . .

you remember that, don't you, Professor No-Dick? You remember when I used to walk around wondering what that fair sister was thinking?

[*Hunches* EASLEY]

Oh, come on now, you remember that. . . . I was Othello . . . Grace there was Desdemona . . . and you were Iago . . .

[*Laughs*]

or at least between classes, you were Iago. Hey, who were you during classes? I forgot to find that out. Ha, the key to my downfall. I knew you were Iago between classes, when I saw you, but I never knew who you were during classes. Ah ah, that's the basis of an incredibly profound social axiom. I quote: . . . and you better write this down, Bradford, so you can pass it on to your hipper colleagues at the university . . .

[*Laughs*]

I mean if they ever rebuild the university. What was I saying to you, enemy? Oh yeah . . . the axiom. Oh . . .

GRACE.

[*Returning with a bottle*]

You still at it, huh, Bigger?

WALKER. Yeah, yeah . . .

[*Reaches for bottle*]

lemme see. I get it. . . . If a white man is Iago when you see him . . . uhh . . . chances are he's eviler when you don't.

[*Laughs*]

EASLEY. Yes, that was worthy of you.

WALKER. It *was* lousy, wasn't it?

GRACE. Look

[*Trying to be earnest*]

Walker, pour yourself a drink . . . as many drinks as you need . . . and then leave, will you? I don't see what you think you're accomplishing by hanging around us.

EASLEY. Yes . . . I was wondering who's taking care of your mighty army while you're here in the enemy camp? How can the black liberation movement spare its illustrious leader for such a long stretch?

WALKER.

[*Sits abruptly on couch and stretches both legs out, drinking big glass of bourbon. Begins speaking in pidgin "Japanese"*]

Oh, don't worry about that, doomed American dog. Ha. You see and hear those shells beating this town flat, don't you? In fact, we'll probably be here en masse in about a week. Why don't I just camp here and wait for my brothers to get here and liberate the whole place? Huh?
[*Laughs*]

GRACE. Walker, you're crazy!

EASLEY. I think he's got more sense than that.

WALKER.
[*Starting to make up a song*]
Ohhh! I'll stay here and rape your wife . . . as I so often used to do . . . as I so often used . . .

GRACE. Your mind is gone, Walker . . . completely gone.
[*She turns to go upstairs. A bright blast rocks the house and she falls against the wall*]

WALKER.
[*Thrown forward to the floor, rises quickly to see how* GRACE *is*]
Hey, you all right, lady?

EASLEY. Grace!
[*He has also been rocked, but he gets to* GRACE *first*]
Don't worry about my wife, Vessels. That's my business.

GRACE. I'm O.K., Brad. I was on my way upstairs to look in on the girls. It's a wonder they're not screaming now.

WALKER. They were fine when I looked in earlier. Sleeping very soundly.

EASLEY. You were upstairs?

WALKER.
[*Returning to his seat, with another full glass*]
Of course I went upstairs, to see my children. In fact, I started to take them away with me, while you patriots were out.
[*Another close blast*]
But I thought I'd wait to say hello to the mommy and stepdaddy.

EASLEY. You low bastard.
[*Turning toward* WALKER *and looking at* GRACE *at the same time*]

GRACE. No . . . you're not telling the truth now, Walker.
[*Voice quavering and rising*]
You came here just to say that. Just to see what your saying that would do to me.
[*Turns away from him*]
You're a bad liar, Walker. As always . . . a very bad liar.

WALKER. You know I'm not lying. I want those children. You know that, Grace.

EASLEY. I know you're drunk!

GRACE. You're lying. You don't want those children. You just want to think you want them for the moment . . . to excite one of those obscure pathological instruments you've got growing in your head. Today, you want to feel like you want the girls. Just like you wanted to feel hurt and martyred by your misdirected cause, when you first drove us away.

WALKER. Drove you away? You knew what I was into. You could have stayed. You said you wanted to pay whatever thing it cost to stay.

EASLEY. How can you lie like this, Vessels? Even I know you pushed Grace until she couldn't retain her sanity and stay with you in that madness. All the bigoted racist imbeciles you started to cultivate. Every white friend you had knows that story.

WALKER. You shut up. . . . I don't want to hear anything you've got to say.

GRACE. There are so many bulbs and screams shooting off inside you, Walker. So many lies you have to pump full of yourself. You're split so many ways . . . your feelings are cut up into skinny horrible strips . . . like umbrella struts . . . holding up whatever bizarre black cloth you're using this performance as your self's image. I don't even think you know who you are any more. No, I don't think you *ever* knew.

WALKER. I know what I can use.

GRACE. No, you never even found out who you were until you sold the last of your loves and emotions down the river . . . until you killed your last old friend . . . and found out *what* you were. My God, it must be hard being you, Walker Vessels. It must be a sick task keeping so many lying separate uglinesses together . . . and pretending they're something you've made and understand.

WALKER. What I can use, madam . . . what I can use. I move now trying to be certain of that.

EASLEY. You're talking strangely. What is this, the pragmatics of war? What are you saying . . . use? I thought you meant yourself to be a fantastic idealist? All those speeches and essays and poems . . . the rebirth of idealism. That the Western white man had forfeited the most impressive characteristic of his culture . . . the idealism of rational liberalism . . . and that only the black man in the West could restore that quality to Western culture, because he still understood the necessity for it. Et cetera, et cetera. Oh, look, I remember your horseshit theories, friend. I remember. And now the great black Western idealist is talking about use.

WALKER. Yeah, yeah. Now you can call me the hypocritical idealist nigger murderer. You see, what I want is more titles.

GRACE. And saying you want the children is another title . . . right? Every time you say it, one of those bulbs goes off in your head and you think you can focus on still another attribute, another beautiful quality in the total beautiful structure of the beautiful soul of Walker Vessels, sensitive Negro poet, savior of his people, deliverer of Western idealism . . . commander-in-chief of the forces of righteousness . . . Oh, God, et cetera, et cetera.

WALKER. Grace Locke Vessels Easley . . . whore of the middle classes.

EASLEY.
    [*Turning suddenly as if to offer combat*]
Go and fuck yourself.

GRACE. Yes, Walker, by all means . . . go and fuck yourself.
    [*And softer*]
Yes, do anything . . . but don't drag my children into your scheme for martyrdom and immortality, or whatever else it is makes you like you are . . . just don't . . . don't even mention it.

EASLEY.
    [*Moving to comfort her*]
Oh, don't get so worried, Grace . . . you know he just likes to hear himself talk . . . more than anything . . . he just wants to hear himself talk, so he can find out what he's supposed to have on his mind.
    [*To* WALKER]
He knows there's no way in the world he could have those children. No way in the world.

WALKER.

[*Feigning casual matter-of-fact tone*]

Mr. Easley, Mrs. Easley, those girls' last name is Vessels. Whatever you think is all right. I mean I don't care what you think about me or what I'm doing . . . the whole mess. But those beautiful girls you have upstairs there are my daughters. They even look like me. I've loved them all their lives. Before this there was too much to do, so I left them with you.

[*Gets up, pours another drink*]

But now . . . things are changed. . . . I want them with me.

[*Sprawls on couch again*]

I want them with me very much.

GRACE. You're lying. Liar, you don't give a shit about those children. You're a liar if you say otherwise. You never never never cared at all for those children. My friend, you have never cared for anything in the world that I know of but what's in there behind your eyes. And God knows what ugliness that is . . . though there are thousands of people dead or homeless all over this country who begin to understand a little. And not just white people . . . you've killed so many of your own people too. It's a wonder they haven't killed you.

EASLEY.

[*Walks over to* WALKER]

Get up and get out of here! So help me . . . if you don't leave here now . . . I'll call the soldiers. They'd just love to find you.

[WALKER *doesn't move*]

Really, Vessels, I'll personally put a big hole in that foul liberation movement right now . . . I swear it.

[*He turns to go to the phone*]

WALKER.

[*At first as if he is good-natured*]

Hey, hey . . . Professor Easley, I've got this gun here, remember? Now don't do that . . . in fact, if you take another step, I'll blow your goddamn head off. And I mean that, Brad, turn around and get back here in the center of the room.

GRACE.

[*Moves for the stairs*]

Ohhh!

WALKER. Hey, Grace, stop . . . you want me to shoot this fairy, or what? Come back here!

GRACE. I was only going to see about the kids.

WALKER. I'm their father . . . I'm thinking about their welfare, too. Just come back here. Both of you sit on this couch where I'm sitting, and I'll sit in that chair over there near the ice tray.

EASLEY. So now we get a taste of Vessels the hoodlum.

WALKER. Uh, yeah. Another title, boss man. But just sit the fuck down for now.
    [Goes to the window. Looks at his watch]
I got about an hour.

GRACE. Walker, what are you going to do?

WALKER. Do? Well, right now I'm going to have another drink.

EASLEY. You know what she means.

GRACE. You're not going to take the children, are you? You wouldn't just take them, would you? You wouldn't do that. You can't hate me so much that you'd do that.

WALKER. I don't hate you at all, Grace. I hated you when I wanted you. I haven't wanted you for a long time. But I do want those children.

GRACE. You're lying!

WALKER. No, I'm not lying . . . and I guess that's what's cutting you up . . . because you probably know I'm not lying, and you can't understand that. But I tell you now that I'm not lying, and that in spite of all the things I've done that have helped kill love in me, I still love those girls.

EASLEY. You mean, in spite of all the people you've killed.

WALKER. O.K., O.K., however you want it . . . however you want it, let it go at that. In spite of all the people I've killed. No, better, in spite of the fact that I, Walker Vessels, single-handedly, and with no other adviser except my own ego, promoted a bloody situation where white and black people are killing each other; despite the fact that I know that this is at best a war that will only change, ha, the complexion of tyranny . . .
    [Laughs sullenly]
in spite of the fact that I have killed for all times any creative impulse I will

ever have by the depravity of my murderous philosophies . . . despite the fact that I am being killed in my head each day and by now have no soul or heart or warmth, even in my long killer fingers, despite the fact that I have no other thing in the universe that I love or trust, but myself . . . despite or in spite, the respite, my dears, my dears, hear me, O Olympus, O Mercury, God of thieves, O Damballah, chief of all the dead religions of pseudo-nigger patriots hoping to open big restaurants after de wah . . . har har . . . in spite, despite, the resistance in the large cities and the small towns, where we have taken, yes, dragged piles of darkies out of their beds and shot them for being in Rheingold ads, despite the fact that all of my officers are ignorant mother-fuckers who have never read any book in their lives, despite the fact that I would rather argue politics, or literature, or boxing, or anything, with you, dear Easley, with you . . .

[*Head slumps, weeping*]
despite all these things and in spite of all the drunken noises I'm making, despite . . . in spite of . . . I want those girls, very, very much. And I will take them out of here with me.

EASLEY. No you won't . . . not if I can help it.

WALKER. Well, you can't help it.

GRACE.
[*Jumps up*]
What? Is no one to reason with you? Isn't there any way something can exist without you having the final judgment on it? Is the whole world yours . . . to deal with or destroy? You're right! You feel! You have the only real vision of the world. You love! No one else exists in the world except you, and those who can help you. Everyone else is nothing or else they're something to be destroyed. I'm your enemy now . . . right? I'm wrong. You are the children's father . . . but I'm no longer their mother. Every one of your yesses or nos is intended by you to reshape the world after the image you have of it. They *are* my children! I am their mother! But because somehow I've become your enemy, I suddenly no longer qualify. Forget you're their mother, Grace. Walker has decided that you're no longer to perform that function. So the whole business is erased as if it never existed. I'm *not* in your head, Walker. Neither are those kids. We are all flesh and blood and deserve to live . . . even unabstracted by what you think we ought to be in the general scheme of things. Even alien to it. I left you . . . and took the girls because you'd gone crazy. You're crazy now. This stupid ugly killing you've started will never do anything, for anybody. And you and all your people will be wiped out, you know that. And you'll have accomplished nothing. Do you want those two babies to be with you when you're killed so they can witness the death of a

great man? So they can grow up and write articles for a magazine sponsored by the Walker Vessels Society?

WALKER. Which is still better than being freakish mulattoes in a world where your father is some evil black thing you can't remember. Look, I was going to wait until the fighting was over . . .
      [*Reflective*]
until we had won, before I took them. But something occurred to me for the first time, last night. It was the idea that we might not win. Somehow it only got through to me last night. I'd sort've taken it for granted . . . as a solved problem, that the fighting was the most academic of our problems, and that the real work would come necessarily after the fighting was done. But . . .

EASLEY. Things are not going as well for you as you figured.

WALKER. No. It will take a little longer, that's all. But this city will fall soon. We should be here within a week. You see, I could have waited until then. Then just marched in, at the head of the triumphant army, and seized the children as a matter of course. In fact I don't know why I didn't, except I did want to see you all in what you might call your natural habitats. I thought maybe I might be able to sneak in just as you and my ex-wife were making love, or just as you were lining the girls up against the wall to beat them or make them repeat after you, "Your daddy is a racist murderer." And then I thought I could murder both of you on the spot, and be completely justified.

GRACE. You've convinced yourself that you're rescuing the children, haven't you?

WALKER. Just as you convinced yourself you were rescuing them when you took them away from me.

EASLEY. She was!

WALKER. Now so am I.

GRACE. Yes,
      [*Wearily*]
I begin to get some of your thinking now. When you mentioned killing us. I'm sure you thought the whole thing up in quite heroic terms. How you'd come through the white lines, murder us, and *rescue* the girls. You probably went over that . . . or had it go through your head on that gray film, a thousand times until it was some kind of obligatory reality.
      [WALKER *laughs*]

EASLEY. The kind of insane reality that brought about all the killing.

WALKER. Christ, the worst thing that ever happened to the West was the psychological novel . . . believe me.

EASLEY. When the Nazis were confronted with Freud, they claimed his work was of dubious value.

WALKER. Bravo!

GRACE. It's a wonder you *didn't* murder us!

WALKER.
[*Looking suddenly less amused*]
Oh . . . have I forfeited my opportunity?

EASLEY.
[*Startled reaction*]
You're not serious? What reason . . . what possible reason would there be for killing us? I mean I could readily conceive of your killing me, but the two of us, as some kind of psychological unit. I don't understand that. You said you didn't hate Grace.

GRACE.
[*To press* WALKER]
He's lying again, Brad. Really, most times he's not to be taken seriously. He was making a metaphor before . . . one of those ritual-drama metaphors . . .
[*Laughs, as does* BRAD]
You said it before . . . just to hear what's going on in his head. Really, he's not to be taken seriously.
[*She hesitates, and there is a silence*]
Unless there's some way you can kill him.

WALKER.
[*Laughs, then sobers, but begins to show the effects of the alcohol*]
Oh, Grace, Grace. Now you're trying to incite your husbean . . . which I swear is hardly Christian. I'm really surprised at you. But more so because you completely misunderstand me now . . . or maybe I'm not so surprised. I guess you never did know what was going on. That's why you left. You thought I betrayed you or something. Which really knocked me on my ass, you know? I was preaching hate the white man . . . get the white man off our backs . . . if necessary, kill the white man for our rights . . . whatever the hell that finally came to mean. And don't, now, for God's sake start thinking he's disillu-

sioned, he's cynical, or any of the rest of these horseshit liberal definitions of the impossibility or romanticism of idealism. But those things I said . . . and would say now, pushed you away from me. I couldn't understand that.

GRACE. You couldn't understand it? What are you saying?

WALKER. No, I couldn't understand it. We'd been together a long time, before all that happened. What I said . . . what I thought I had to do . . . I knew you, if any white person in the world could, I knew you would understand. And then you didn't.

GRACE. You began to align yourself with the worst kind of racists and second-rate hack political thinkers.

WALKER. I've never aligned myself with anything or anyone I hadn't thought up first.

GRACE. You stopped telling me everything!

WALKER. I never stopped telling you I loved you . . . or that you were my wife!

GRACE.
        [*Almost broken*]
It wasn't enough, Walker. It wasn't enough.

WALKER. God, it should have been.

GRACE. Walker, you were preaching the murder of all white people. Walker, I was, am, white. What do you think was going through my mind every time you were at some rally or meeting whose sole purpose was to bring about the destruction of white people?

WALKER. Oh, goddamn it, Grace, are you so stupid? You were my wife . . . I loved you. You mean because I loved you and was married to you . . . had had children by you, I wasn't supposed to say the things I felt. I was crying out against three hundred years of oppression; not against individuals.

EASLEY. But it's individuals who are dying.

WALKER. It was individuals who were doing the oppressing. It was individuals who were being oppressed. The horror is that oppression is not a concept that can be specifically transferable. From the oppressed, down on the oppressor. To keep the horror where it belongs . . . on those people who we can speak of, even in this last part of the twentieth century, as evil.

EASLEY. You're so wrong about everything. So terribly, sickeningly wrong. What can you change? What do you hope to change? Do you think Negroes are better people than whites ... that they can govern a society *better* than whites? That they'll be more judicious or more tolerant? Do you think they'll make fewer mistakes? I mean really, if the Western white man has proved one thing ... it's the futility of modern society. So the have-not peoples become the haves. Even so, will that change the essential functions of the world? Will there be more love or beauty in the world ... more knowledge ... because of it?

WALKER. Probably. Probably there will be more ... if more people have a chance to understand what it is. But that's not even the point. It comes down to baser human endeavor than any social-political thinking. What does it matter if there's more love or beauty? Who the fuck cares? Is that what the Western ofay thought while he was ruling ... that his rule somehow brought more love and beauty into the world? Oh, he might have thought that concomitantly, while sipping a gin rickey and scratching his ass ... but that was not ever the point. Not even on the Crusades. The point is that you had your chance, darling, now these other folks have theirs.
  [*Quietly*]
Now they have theirs.

EASLEY. God, what an ugly idea.

WALKER.
  [*Head in hands*]
I know. I know.
  [*His head is sagging, but he brings it up quickly. While it is down,* EASLEY *crosses* GRACE *with a significant look*]
But what else you got, champ? What else you got? I remember too much horseshit from the other side for you to make much sense. Too much horseshit. The cruelty of it, don't you understand, now? The complete ugly horseshit cruelty of it is that there doesn't have to be a change. It'll be up to individuals on that side, just as it was supposed to be up to individuals on this side. Ha! ... Who failed! Just like you failed, Easley. Just like you failed.

EASLEY. Failed? What are you talking about?

WALKER.
  [*Nodding*]
Well, what do you think? You never did anything concrete to avoid what's

going on now. Your sick liberal lip service to whatever was the least filth. Your high aesthetic disapproval of the political. Letting the sick ghosts of the thirties strangle whatever chance we had.

EASLEY. What are you talking about?

WALKER. What we argued about so many times . . . befo' de wah.

EASLEY. And you see . . . what I predicted has happened. Now, in whatever cruel, and you said it, cruel political synapse you're taken with, or anyone else is taken with, with sufficient power I, any individual, any person who thinks of life as a purely anarchic relationship between man and God . . . or man and his work . . . any consciousness like that is destroyed . . . along with your *enemies*. And you, for whatever right or freedom or sickening cause you represent, kill me. Kill what does not follow.

WALKER. Perhaps you're right. But I have always found it hard to be neutral when faced with ugliness. Especially an ugliness that has worked all my life to twist me.

GRACE. And so you let it succeed!

WALKER. The aesthete came long after all the things that really formed me. It was the easiest weight to shed. And I couldn't be merely a journalist . . . a social critic. No social protest . . . right is in the act! And the act itself has some place in the world . . . it makes some place for itself. Right? But you all accuse me, not understanding that what you represent, you, my wife, all our old intellectual cutthroats, was something that was going to die anyway. One way or another. You'd been used too often, backed off from reality too many times. Remember the time, remember that time long time ago, in the old bar when you and Louie Rino were arguing with me, and Louie said then that he hated people who wanted to change the world. You remember that?

EASLEY. I remember the fight.

WALKER. Yeah, well, I know I thought then that none of you would write any poetry either. I knew that you had moved too far away from the actual meanings of life . . . into some lifeless cocoon of pretended intellectual and emotional achievement, to really be able to see the world again. What was Rino writing before he got killed? Tired elliptical little descriptions of what he could see out the window.

EASLEY. And how did he die?

WALKER. An explosion in the school where he was teaching.
[*Nodding*]

EASLEY. One of your terrorists did it.

WALKER. Yeah, yeah.

EASLEY. He was supposed to be one of your closest friends.

WALKER. Yeah, yeah.

GRACE. Yeah, yeah, yeah, yeah.

WALKER. [*With face still covered*] We called for a strike to show the government we had all the white intellectuals backing us.
[*Nodding*]

Hah, and the only people who went out were those tired political hacks. No one wanted to be intellectually compromised.

EASLEY. I didn't go either.
[*Hunches* GRACE, *starts to ease out of his chair*]
And it was an intellectual compromise. No one in their right mind could have backed your program completely.

WALKER. No one but Negroes.

EASLEY. Well, then, they weren't in their right minds. You'd twisted them.

WALKER. The country twisted 'em.
[*Still nodding*]
The country had twisted them for so long.
[*Head almost touching his chest*]

EASLEY.
[*Taking very cautious step toward* WALKER, *still talking*]
The politics of self-pity.
[*Indicates to* GRACE *that she is to talk*]

WALKER.
[*Head down*]
Yeah. Yeah.

EASLEY. The politics of self-pity.

GRACE.
[*Raising her head slowly to watch, almost petrified*]
A murderous self-pity. An extraordinarily murderous self-pity.
[*There is another explosion close to the house. The lights go out for a few seconds. They come on, and* EASLEY *is trying to return to his seat, but* WALKER'*s head is still on his chest*]

WALKER.
[*Mumbles*]
What'd they do, hit the lights? Goddamn lousy marksmen.
[EASLEY *starts again*]
Lousy marksmen . . . and none of 'em worth shit.
[*Now, another close explosion. The lights go out again. They come on;* EASLEY *is standing almost halfway between the couch and* WALKER. WALKER'*s head is still down on his chest.* EASLEY *crouches to move closer. The lights go out again*]

Black

[*More explosions*]

Act II

Explosions are heard before the curtain goes up. When curtain rises, room is still in darkness, but the explosion does throw some light. Figures are still as they were at the end of first act; light from explosions outlines them briefly.

WALKER. Shit.
>[*Lights come up.* WALKER's *head is still down, but he is nodding from side to side, cursing something very drunkenly.* EASLEY *stands very stiffly in the center of the room, waiting to take another step.* GRACE *sits very stiffly, breathing heavily, on the couch, trying to make some kind of conversation, but not succeeding.* WALKER *has his hand in his jacket pocket, on the gun*]

GRACE. It is self-pity, and some weird ambition, Walker.
>[*Strained silence*]

But there's no reason . . . the girls should suffer. There's . . . no reason.
>[EASLEY *takes a long stride, and is about to throw himself at* WALKER, *when there is another explosion, and the lights go out again, very briefly. When they come up,* EASLEY *is set to leap, but* WALKER's *head comes abruptly up. He stares drunkenly at* EASLEY, *not moving his hand. For some awkward duration of time the two men stare at each other, in almost the same way as they had at the beginning of the play. Then* GRACE *screams*]

GRACE. Walker!
>[WALKER *looks at her slightly, and* EASLEY *throws himself on him. The chair falls backward and the two men roll on the floor.* EASLEY *trying to choke* WALKER. WALKER *trying to get the gun out of his pocket*]

GRACE. Walker! Walker!
>[*Suddenly,* WALKER *shoves one hand in* EASLEY's *face, shooting him*

without taking the gun from his pocket. EASLEY *slumps backward, his face twisted, his mouth open and working.* WALKER *rolls back off* EASLEY, *pulling the gun from his pocket. He props himself against the chair, staring at the man's face*]

GRACE. Walker.
[*Her shouts have become whimpers, and she is moving stiffly toward* EASLEY]
Walker. Walker.

EASLEY.
[*Mouth is still working ... and he is managing to get a few sounds, words, out*]

WALKER.
[*Still staring at him, pulling himself up on the chair*]
Shut up, you!
[*To* EASLEY]
You shut up. I don't want to hear anything else from you. You just die, quietly. No more talk.

GRACE. Walker!
[*She is screaming again*]
Walker!
[*She rushes toward* EASLEY, *but* WALKER *catches her arm and pushes her away*]
You're an insane man. You hear me, Walker?
[*He is not looking at her, he is still staring down at* EASLEY]
Walker, you're an insane man.
[*She screams*]
You're an insane man.
[*She slumps to the couch, crying*]
An insane man . . .

WALKER. No profound statements, Easley. No horseshit like that. No elegance. You just die quietly and stupidly. Like niggers do. Like they are now.
[*Quieter*]
Like I will. The only thing I'll let you say is, "I only regret that I have but one life to lose for my country." You can say that.
[*Looks over at* GRACE]
Grace! Tell Bradford that he can say, "I only regret that I have but one life to lose for my country." You can say that, Easley, but that's all.

EASLEY.
[*Straining to talk*]
Ritual drama. Like I said, ritual drama . . .
[*He dies.*

> WALKER *stands staring at him. The only sounds are an occasional explosion, and* GRACE'*s heavy brittle weeping*]

WALKER. He could have said, "I only regret that I have but one life to lose for my country." I would have let him say that . . . but no more. No more. There is no reason he should go out with any kind of dignity. I couldn't allow that.

GRACE. You're out of your mind.
[*Slow, matter-of-fact*]

WALKER. Meaning?

GRACE. You're out of your mind.

WALKER.
[*Wearily*]
Turn to another station.

GRACE. You're out of your mind.

WALKER. I said, turn to another station . . . will you? Another station! Out of my mind is not the point. You ought to know that.
[*Brooding*]
The way things are, being out of your mind is the only thing that qualifies you to stay alive. The only thing. Easley was in his right mind. Pitiful as he was. That's the reason he's dead.

GRACE. He's dead because you killed him.

WALKER. Yeah. He's dead because I killed him. Also, because he thought he ought to kill me.
[*Looking over at the dead man*]
You want me to cover him up?

GRACE. I don't want you to do anything, Walker . . . but leave here.
[*Raising her voice*]
Will you do that for me . . . or do you want to kill me too?

WALKER. Are you being ironic? Huh?

[*He grabs her arm, jerking her head up so she has to look at him*]

Do you think you're being ironic? Or do you want to kill me, too? . . .

[*Shouting*]

You're mighty right I want to kill you. You're mighty goddamn right. Believe me, self-righteous little bitch, I want to kill you.

GRACE.

[*Startled, but trying not to show it*]

The cause demands it, huh? The cause demands it.

WALKER. Yeah, the cause demands it.

GRACE.

[*She gets up and goes to* EASLEY, *kneeling beside the body*]

The cause demands it, Brad. That's why Walker shot you . . . because the cause demands it.

[*Her head droops but she doesn't cry. She sits on her knees, holding the dead man's hand*]

I guess the point is that now when you take the children I'll be alone.

[*She looks up at* WALKER]

I guess that's the point, now. Is that the point, Walker? Me being alone . . . as you have been now for so long? I'll bet that's the point, huh? I'll bet you came here to do exactly what you did . . . kill Brad, then take the kids, and leave me alone . . . to suffocate in the stink of my memories.

[*She is trying not to cry*]

Just like I did to you. I'm sure that's the point. Right?

[*She leaps up suddenly at* WALKER]

You scum! You murdering scum.

[*They grapple for a second, then* WALKER *slaps her to the floor. She kneels a little way off from* EASLEY'*s body*]

WALKER. Yeh, Grace. That's the point. For sure, that's the point.

GRACE. You were going to kill Brad from the first. You knew that before you even got here.

WALKER. I'd thought about it.

GRACE.

[*Weeping, but then she stops and is quiet for a minute*]

So what's supposed to happen then . . . I mean after you take the kids and leave me here alone? Huh? I know you've thought about that, too.

WALKER. I have. But you know what'll happen much better than I do. But maybe you don't. What do you think happened to me when you left? Did you ever think about that? You must have.

GRACE. You had your cause, friend. Your cause, remember. And thousands of people following you, hoping that shit you preached was right. I pitied you.

WALKER. I know that. It took me a while, but then I finally understood that you did pity me. And that you were somewhere, going through whatever mediocre routine you and Easley called your lives . . . pitying me. I figured that, finally, you weren't really even shocked by what was happening . . . what had happened. You were so secure in the knowledge that you were good, and compassionate . . . and right, that most of all . . . you were certain, my God, so certain . . . emotionally and intellectually, that you were right, until the only idea you had about me was to pity me.
[*He wheels around to face her squarely*]
God, that pissed me off. You don't really know how furious that made me. You and that closet queen, respected, weak-as-water intellectual, pitying me. God. God!
[*Forcing the humor*]
Miss Easley, honey, I could have killed both of you every night of my life.

GRACE. Will you kill me now if I say right here that I still pity you?

WALKER.
[*A breathless half-broken little laugh*]
No. No, I won't kill you.

GRACE. Well, I pity you, Walker. I really do.

WALKER. Only until you start pitying yourself.

GRACE. I wish I could call you something that would hurt you.

WALKER. So do I.

GRACE.
[*Wearily*]
Nigger.

WALKER. So do I.
[*Looks at his watch*]
I've got to go soon.

GRACE. You're still taking the girls.

[*She is starting to push herself up from the floor.*

WALKER *stares at her, then quickly over his shoulder at the stairway. He puts his hand in the pocket where the gun is, then shakes his head slowly*]

GRACE.
[*Not seeing this gesture*]
You're still taking the children?
[WALKER *shakes his head slowly. An explosion shakes the house a little*]

GRACE. Walker. Walker.
[*She staggers to her feet, shaking with the next explosion*]
Walker? You shook your head?
[WALKER *stands very stiffly looking at the floor.*

GRACE *starts to come to him, and the next explosion hits very close or actually hits the house. Beams come down; some of the furniture is thrown around.* GRACE *falls to the floor.* WALKER *is toppled backward. A beam hits* GRACE *across the chest. Debris falls on* WALKER. *There are more explosions, and then silence*]

GRACE. Walker! Walker!
[*She is hurt very badly and is barely able to move the debris that is covering her*]
Walker! The girls! Walker! Catherine! Elizabeth! Walker, the girls!
[WALKER *finally starts to move. He is also hurt badly, but he is able to move much more freely than* GRACE. *He starts to clear away the debris and make his way to his knees*]

GRACE. Walker?

WALKER. Yeah? Grace?

GRACE. Walker, the children . . . the girls . . . see about the girls.
[*She is barely able to raise one of her arms*]
The girls, Walker, see about them.

WALKER.
[*He is finally able to crawl over to* GRACE, *and pushes himself unsteadily up on his hands*]

You're hurt pretty badly? Can you move?

GRACE. The girls, Walker, see about the girls.

WALKER. Can you move?

GRACE. The girls, Walker . . .
[*She is losing strength*]
Our children!

WALKER.
[*He is silent for a while*]
They're dead, Grace. Catherine and Elizabeth are dead.
[*He starts up stairs as if to verify his statement. Stops, midway, shakes his head; retreats*]

GRACE.
[*Looking up at him frantically, but she is dying*]
Dead? Dead?
[*She starts to weep and shake her head*]
Dead?
[*Then she stops suddenly, tightening her face*]
How . . . how do you know, Walker? How do you know they're dead?
[WALKER*'s head is drooping slightly*]
How do you know they're dead, Walker? How do you . . .
[*Her eyes try to continue what she is saying, but she slumps, and dies in a short choking spasm.*
WALKER *looks to see that she is dead, then resumes his efforts to get up. He looks at his watch. Listens to see if it is running. Wipes his face. Pushes the floor to get up. Another explosion sounds very close and he crouches quickly, covering his head. Another explosion. He pushes himself up, brushing sloppily at his clothes. He looks at his watch again, then starts to drag himself toward the door*]
They're dead, Grace!
[*He is almost shouting*]
They're dead.
[*He leaves, stumbling unsteadily through the door. He is now the old man at the beginning of the play. There are more explosions. Another one very close to the house. A sudden aggravated silence, and then there is a child heard crying and screaming as loud as it can. More explosions*]

Black

[*More explosions, after curtain for some time*]

THE REVOLUTIONARY THEATRE
from *Home, Social Essays*

The Revolutionary Theatre should force change; it should be change. (All their faces turned into the lights and you work on them black nigger magic, and cleanse them at having seen the ugliness. And if the beautiful see themselves, they will love themselves.) We are preaching virtue again, but by that to mean NOW, toward what seems the most constructive use of the world.

The Revolutionary Theatre must EXPOSE! Show up the insides of these humans, look into black skulls. White men will cower before this theatre because it hates them. Because they themselves have been trained to hate. The Revolutionary Theatre must hate them for hating. For presuming with their technology to deny the supremacy of the Spirit. They will all die because of this.

The Revolutionary Theatre must teach them their deaths. It must crack their faces open to the mad cries of the poor. It must teach them about silence and the truths lodged there. It must kill any God anyone names except Common Sense. The Revolutionary Theatre should flush the fags and murders out of Lincoln's face.

It should stagger through our universe correcting, insulting, preaching, spitting craziness—but a craziness taught to us in our most rational moments. People must be taught to trust true scientists (knowers, diggers, oddballs) and that the holiness of life is the constant possibility of widening the consciousness. And they must be incited to strike back against *any* agency that attempts to prevent this widening.

The Revolutionary Theatre must Accuse and Attack anything that can be accused and attacked. It must Accuse and Attack because it is a theatre of Victims. It looks at the sky with the victims' eyes, and moves the victims to look at the strength in their minds and their bodies.

Clay in *Dutchman*, Ray in *The Toilet*, Walker in *The Slave*, are all victims. In the Western sense they could be heroes. But the Revolutionary Theatre, even if it is Western, must be anti-Western. It must show horrible coming attractions of *The Crumbling of the West*. Even as Artaud designed *The Conquest of Mexico*, so we must design *The Conquest of White Eye*, and show the missionaries and wiggly Liberals dying under blasts of concrete. For sound effects, wild screams of joy, from all the peoples of the world.

The Revolutionary Theatre must take dreams and give them a reality. It must isolate the ritual and historical cycles of reality. But it must be food for all those who need food, and daring propaganda for the beauty of the Human Mind. It is a political theatre, a weapon to help in the slaughter of these dim-witted fatbellied white guys who somehow believe that the rest of the world is here for them to slobber on.

This should be a theatre of World Spirit. Where the spirit can be shown to be the most competent force in the world. Force. Spirit. Feeling. The language will be anybody's, but tightened by the poet's backbone. And even the language must show what the facts are in this consciousness epic, what's happening. We will talk about the world, and the preciseness with which we are able to summon the world will be our art. Art is method. And art, "like any ashtray or senator," remains in the world. Wittgenstein said ethics and aesthetics are one. I believe this. So the Broadway theatre is a theatre of reaction whose ethics, like its aesthetics, reflect the spiritual values of this unholy society, which sends young crackers all over the world blowing off colored people's heads. (In some of these flippy Southern towns they even shoot up the immigrants' Favorite Son, be it Michael Schwerner or JFKennedy.)

The Revolutionary Theatre is shaped by the world, and moves to reshape the world, using as its force the natural force and perpetual vibrations of the mind in the world. We are history and desire, what we are, and what any experience can make us.

It is a social theatre, but all theatre is social theatre. But we will change the drawing rooms into places where real things can be said about a real world, or into smoky rooms where the destruction of Washington can be plotted. The Revolutionary Theatre must function like an incendiary pencil planted in Curtis Lemay's cap. So that when the final curtain goes down brains are splattered over the seats and the floor, and bleeding nuns must wire SOS's to Belgians with gold teeth.

Our theatre will show victims so that their brothers in the audience will be better able to understand that they are the brothers of victims, and that they themselves are victims if they are blood brothers. And what we show must cause the blood to rush, so that pre-revolutionary temperaments will be bathed in this blood, and it will cause their deepest souls to move, and they will find themselves tensed and clenched, even ready to die, at what the soul has been taught. We will scream and cry, murder, run through the streets in agony, if it means some soul will be moved, moved to actual life understanding of what the world is, and what it ought to be. We are preaching virtue and feeling, and a natural sense of the self in the world. All men live in the world, and the world ought to be a place for them to live.

What is called the imagination (from image, magi, magic, magician, etc.) is a practical vector from the soul. It stores all data, and can be called on to solve all our "problems." The imagination is the projection of ourselves past our sense of ourselves as "things." Imagination (Image) is all possibility, because from the image, the initial circumscribed energy, any use (idea) is possible. And so begins that image's use in the world. Possibility is what moves us.

The popular white man's theatre like the popular white man's novel shows tired white lives, and the problems of eating white sugar, or else it herds bigcaboosed blondes onto huge stages in rhinestones and makes believe they are dancing or singing. WHITE BUSINESSMEN OF THE WORLD, DO YOU WANT TO SEE PEOPLE REALLY DANCING AND SINGING??? ALL OF YOU GO UP TO HARLEM AND GET YOURSELF KILLED. THERE WILL BE DANCING AND SINGING, THEN, FOR REAL!! (In *The Slave,* Walker Vessels, the black revolutionary, wears an armband, which is the insignia of the attacking army—a big red-lipped minstrel, grinning like crazy.)

The liberal white man's objection to the theatre of the revolution (if he is "hip" enough) will be on aesthetic grounds. Most white Western artists do not need to be "political," since usually, whether they know it or not, they are in complete sympathy with the most repressive social forces in the world today. There are more junior birdmen fascists running around the West today disguised as Artists than there are disguised as fascists. (But then, that word, *Fascist,* and with it, *Fascism,* has been made obsolete by the words *America,* and *Americanism.)* The American Artist usually turns out to be just a super-Bourgeois, because, finally, all he has to show for his sojourn through the world is "better taste" than the Bourgeois—many times not even that.

Americans will hate the Revolutionary Theatre because it will be out to destroy them and whatever they believe is real. American cops will try to close the theatres where such nakedness of the human spirit is paraded. American producers will say the revolutionary plays are filth, usually because they will treat human life as if it were actually happening. American directors will say that the white guys in the plays are too abstract and cowardly ("don't get me wrong . . . I mean aesthetically . . .") and they will be right.

The force we want is of twenty million spooks storming America with furious cries and unstoppable weapons. We want actual explosions and actual brutality: AN EPIC IS CRUMBLING and we must give it the space and hugeness of its actual demise. The Revolutionary Theatre, which is now peopled with victims, will soon begin to be peopled with new kinds of heroes—not the weak Hamlets debating whether or not they are ready to die for what's on their minds, but men and women (and minds) digging out from under a thousand years of "high art" and weak-faced dalliance. We must make an art that will function so as to call down the actual wrath of world spirit. We are witch doctors and assassins, but we will open a place for the true scientists to expand our consciousness. This is a theatre of assault. The play that will split the heavens for us will be called THE DESTRUCTION

OF AMERICA. The heroes will be Crazy Horse, Denmark Vesey, Patrice Lumumba, and not history, not memory, not sad sentimental groping for a warmth in our despair; these will be new men, new heroes, and their enemies most of you who are reading this.

WORDS

from *Tales*

Now that the old world has crashed around me, and it's raining in early summer. I live in Harlem with a baby shrew and suffer for my decadence which kept me away so long. When I walk in the streets, the streets don't yet claim me, and people look at me, knowing the strangeness of my manner, and the objective stance from which I attempt to "love" them. It was always predicted this way. This is what my body told me always. When the child leaves, and the window goes on looking out on empty walls, you will sit and dream of old things, and things that could never happen. You will be alone, and ponder on your learning. You will think of old facts, and sudden seeings which made you more than you had bargained for, yet a coward on the earth, unless you claim it, unless you step upon it with your heavy feet, and feel actual hardness.

Last night in a bar a plump black girl sd, "O.K., be intellectual, go write some more of them jivey books," and it could have been anywhere, a thousand years ago, she sd "Why're you so cold," and I wasn't even thinking coldness. Just tired and a little weary of myself. Not even wanting to hear me thinking up things to say.

But the attention. To be always looking, and thinking. To be always under so many things' gaze, the pressure of such attention. I wanted something, want it now. But don't know what it is, except words. I cd say anything. But what would be left, what would I have made? Who would love me for it? Nothing. No one. Alone, I will sit and watch the sun die, the moon fly out in space, the earth wither, and dead men stand in line, to rot away and never exist.

Finally, to have passed away, and be an old hermit in love with silence. To have the thing I left, and found. To be older than I am, and with the young animals marching through the trees. To want what is natural, and strong.

Today is more of the same. In the closed circle I have fashioned. In the alien language of another tribe. I make these documents for some heart who will recognize me truthfully. Who will know what I am and what I wanted beneath the maze of meanings and attitudes that shape the reality of everything. Beneath the necessity of talking or the necessity for being angry or beneath the actual core of life we make reference to digging deep into some young woman, and listening to her come.

Selves fly away in madness. Liquid self shoots out of the joint. Lives which are salty and sticky. Why does everyone live in a closet, and hope no one will understand how badly they need to grow? How many errors they canonize or justify, or kill behind? I need to be an old monk and not feel sorry or happy for people. I need to be a billion years old with a white beard and all of ASIA to walk around.

The purpose of myself has not yet been fulfilled. Perhaps it will never be. Just these stammerings and poses. Just this need to reach into myself, and feel something wince and love to be touched.

The dialogue exists. Magic and ghosts are a dialogue, and the body bodies of material, invisible sound vibrations, humming in emptyness, and ideas less than humming, humming, images collide in empty ness, and we build our emotions into blank invisible structures which never exist, and are not there, and are illusion and pain and madness. Dead whiteness.

We turn white when we are afraid.

We are going to try to be happy.

We do not need to be fucked with.

We can be quiet and think and love the silence.

We need to look at trees more closely.

We need to listen.

Harlem, 1965

ANSWERS IN PROGRESS
from *Tales*

Can you die in airraid jiggle
torn arms flung through candystores
Touch the edge of answer. The waves of nausea
as change sweeps the frame of breath and meat.

"Stick a knife through his throat,"
he slid
in the blood
got up running toward
the blind newsdealer. He screamed
about "Cassius Clay," and slain there in the
street, the whipped figure of jesus, head opened
eyes flailing against his nose. They beat him to
pulpy answers. We wrote Muhammad Ali across his
face and chest, like a newspaper of bleeding meat.

The next day the spaceships landed. Art Blakey records was what they were looking for. We gave them Buttercorn Lady and they threw it back at us. They wanted to know what happened to The Jazz Messengers. And right in the middle, playing the Sun-Ra tape, the blanks staggered out of the department store. Omar had missed finishing the job, and they staggered out, falling in the snow, red all over the face chest, the stab wounds in one in the top of a Adam hat.

The space men thought that's what was really happening. One beeped (Ali mentioned this in the newspapers) that this was evolution. Could we dig it? Shit, yeh. We were laughing. Some blanks rounded one corner, Yaa and Dodua were behind them, to take them to the Center. Nationalized on the spot.

The space men could dig everything. They wanted to take one of us to a spot and lay for a minute, to dig what they were in to. Their culture and shit. Whistles Newark was broke up in one section. The dead mayor and other wops carried by in black trucks. Wingo, Rodney and them waving at us. They stopped the first truck and Cyril wanted to know about them thin cats hopping around us. He's always very fast finger.

Space men wanted to know what happened after Blakey. They'd watched but couldn't get close enough to dig exactly what was happening. Albert Ayler they dug immediately from Russell's mouth imitation. That's later. Red spam cans in their throats with the voices, and one of them started to scat. It wigged me. Bamberger's burning down, dead blancos all over and a cat from Sigma Veda, and his brothers, hopping up and down asking us what was happening.

We left Rachel and Lefty there to keep explaining. Me and Pinball had to go back to headquarters, and report Market Street Broad Street rundown. But we told them we'd talk to them. I swear one of those cats had a hip walk. Even thought they was hoppin and bopadoppin up and down, like they had to pee. Still this one cat had a stiff tentacle, when he walked. Yeh; long blue winggly cats, with soft liquid sounds out of their throats for voices. Like, "You know where Art Blakey, Buhainia, is working?" We fell out.

*   *   *   *

Walk through life
beautiful more than anything
stand in the sunlight
walk through life
love all the things
that make you strong, be lovers, be anything
for all the poeple of
earth.

You have brothers
you love each other, change up
and look at the world
now, it's
ours, take it slow
we've long time, a long way
to go,

we have
each other, and the
world,
dont be sorry
walk on out through sunlight life, and know
we're on the go
for love
to open
our lives
to walk
tasting the sunshine
of life.

Boulevards played songs like that and we rounded up blanks where we had to. Space men were on the South Side laying in some of the open houses. Some brothers came in from the west, Chicago, they had a bad thing going out there. Fires were still high as the buildings, but Ram sent a couple of them out to us, to dig what was happening. One of them we sent to the blue cats, to take that message, back. Could W dig what was happening with them? We sent our own evaluation back, and when I finished the report me and Pinball started weaving through the dead cars and furniture. Waving at the brothers, listening to the sounds, we had piped through the streets.

Smokey Robinson was on now. But straight up fast and winging. No more unrequited love. Damn Smokey got his thing together too. No more tracks or mirages. Just the beauty of the whole. I hope they play Sun-Ra for them blue cats, so they can dig where we at.

Magic City played later. By time we got to the courthouse. The whole top of that was out. Like you could look inside from fourth or fifth floor of the Hall of Records. Cats were all over that joint. Ogun wanted the records intact.

Past the playgrounds and all them blanks in the cold standing out there or laying on the ground crying. The rich ones really were funny. This ol cat me an Pinball recognized still had a fag thing going for him. In a fur coat, he was some kind of magistrate. Bobby and Moosie were questioning him about some silver he was supposed to have stashed. He was a silver freak. The dude was actually weeping. Crying big sobs; the women crowded away from him. I guess they really couldn't feel sorry for him because he was crying about money.

By the time we got to Weequahic Avenue where the space men and out-of-town brothers were laying I was tired as a dog. We went in there and wanted to smoke some bush, but these blue dudes had something better. Taste like carrots. It was a cool that took you. You thought something was mildly amusing and everything seemed interesting.

I talked with Pinball and the blue leader about Ben Caldwell's paintings ... the one where the guy is smoking the reefer. We thought about the changing reference, of our new world. As it stood already in the old ruins. And we all felt like Bird. The old altosaxophonist ... but the limits opened out into the pure lyric tone of powerful beings. But when the Sun-Ra tape came on this blue dude really opened up. He dug the hell out of it. Perfect harmony these cats had too. Boooooo—Iiiiiiiiioooooooooooooo ... daaaaa ahhhhhhhh aaaaahhhhhh ... booooo OOOOOOOOOOOOO oooooooooaaaaaaaaaoooaaaaa

Claude McKay I started quoting. Four o'clock in the morning to a blue dude gettin cooled out on carrots. We didn't have no duty until ten o'clock the next day, and me and Lorenzo and Ish had to question a bunch of prisoners and stuff for the TV news. Chazee had a play to put on that next afternoon about the Chicago stuff. Ray talked to him. And the name of the play was Big Fat Fire.

Man I was tired. We had taped the Sigma. They were already infested with Buddhas there, and we spoke very quietly about how we knew it was our turn. I had burned my hand somewhere and this blue cat looked at it hard and cooled it out. White came in with the design for a flag he'd been working on. Black heads, black hearts, and blue fiery space in the background. Love was heavy in the atmosphere. Ball wanted to know what the blue chicks looked like. But I didn't. Cause I knew after tomorrow's duty, I had a day off, and I knew somebody waitin for me at my house, and some kids, and some fried fish, and those carrots, and wow.

That's the way the fifth day ended.

March 1967

GREAT GOODNESS OF LIFE
from *Four Black Revolutionary Plays*

A Coon Show

For my father with love and respect

GREAT GOODNESS OF LIFE was first performed at Spirit House, Newark, by the Spirit House Movers, in November 1967. The cast was as follows:

VOICE OF THE JUDGE	David Shakes
COURT ROYAL,	
A MIDDLE AGED NEGRO MAN,	
GRAY-HAIRED, SLIGHT	Mubarak Mahmoud
ATTORNEY BRECK,	
middle aged Negro man	Yusef Iman
HOODS 1 & 2*	Damu
	Larry Miller
YOUNG WOMAN,	
around 25 years old, colored	Elaine Jones
HOODS 3 & 4	Jenga Choma
YOUNG VICTIM	Damu

The production was directed by LeRoi Jones, with lighting designed by Aminifu.

    * HOODS 1 & 2 are KKK-like figures, HOODS 3 & 4 are more refined than the first two, wear business suits.

SCENE
(Outside an old log cabin, with morning frost letting up a little.)

VOICE

Court.

(A man, COURT ROYAL, comes out, grey but still young-looking. He is around fifty. He walks straight, though he is nervous. He comes uncertainly. Pauses.)

Come on.

(He walks right up to the center of the lights.)

Come on.

COURT ROYAL
I don't quite understand.

VOICE
Shutup, nigger.

COURT ROYAL
What? *(Meekly, then trying to get some force up)* Now what's going on? I don't
see why I should . . .

VOICE
I told you to
shutup,
nigger.

COURT ROYAL
I don't understand. What's going on?

VOICE
Black lunatic. I
said shutup. I'm
not going to tell
you again!

COURT ROYAL
But . . . Yes.

VOICE
You are Court Royal,
are you not?

COURT ROYAL
Yes. I am. But I don't understand.

VOICE
You are charged
with shielding a

wanted criminal.

A murderer.

COURT ROYAL

What? Now I know you have the wrong man. I've done no such thing. I work
in the Post Office. I'm Court Royal. I've done nothing wrong. I work in the
Post Office and have done nothing wrong.

VOICE

Shutup.

COURT ROYAL

But I'm Court Royal. Everybody knows me. I've always done everything . . .

VOICE

Court Royal you
are charged with harboring
a murderer. How do you
plead?

COURT ROYAL

Plead? There's a mistake being made. I've never done anything.

VOICE

How do you plead?

COURT ROYAL

I'm not a criminal. I've done nothing . . .

VOICE

Then you plead
not guilty?

COURT ROYAL

Of course I'm not guilty. I work in the Post Office. *(Tries to work up a little
humor)* You know me, probably. Didn't you ever see me in the Post Office?
I'm a supervisor; you know me. I work at the Post Office. I'm no criminal. I've
worked at the Post Office for thirty-five years. I'm a supervisor. There must be
some mistake. I've worked at the Post Office for thirty-five years.

VOICE

Do you have an
attorney?

COURT ROYAL
Attorney? Look you'd better check you got the right man. You're making a mistake. I'll sue. That's what I'll do.

> **VOICE**
> *(The VOICE laughs long and cruelly.)*

COURT ROYAL
I'll call my attorney right now. We'll find out just what's going on here.

> **VOICE**
> If you don't have an attorney, the court will assign you one.

COURT ROYAL
Don't bother. I have an attorney. John Breck's my attorney. He'll be down here in a few minutes—the minute I call.

> **VOICE**
> The court will assign you an attorney.

COURT ROYAL
But I have an attorney. John Breck. See, it's on this card.

> **VOICE**
> Will the Legal Aid man please step forward.

COURT ROYAL
No. I have an attorney. If you'll just call, or adjourn the case until my attorney gets here.

> **VOICE**
> We have an attorney for you.
> Where is the Legal Aid man?

COURT ROYAL
But I have an attorney. I want my attorney. I don't need any Legal Aid man. I have money, I have an attorney. I work in the Post Office. I'm a supervisor; here, look at my badge. *(A bald-headed smiling house slave in a wrinkled dirty tuxedo crawls across the stage; he has a wire attached to his back leading offstage. A huge key in the side of his head. We hear the motors "animating" his body groaning like tremendous weights. He grins, and slobbers, turning his head slowly from side to side. He grins. He makes little quivering sounds.)*

VOICE
Your attorney.

COURT ROYAL
What kind of foolishness is this? *(He looks at the man.)* What's going on? What's your name? *(His "voice" begins some time after the question: the wheels churn out his answer, and the deliberating motors sound throughout the scene.)*

ATTORNEY BRECK
Pul ... lead ... errrr ... *(As if the motors are having trouble starting)* Pul ... pul ... lead ... er ... err ... Guilty! *(Motors get it together and move in proper synchronization.)* Pul ... Plead guilty, it's your only chance. Just plead guilty, brother. Just plead guilty. It's your only chance. Your only chance.

COURT ROYAL
Guilty? Of what? What are you talking about? What kind of defense atty are you? I don't even know what I'm being charged with, and you say plead guilty. What's happening here? *(At* VOICE*)* Can't I even know the charge?

VOICE
We told you the charge.
Harboring a murderer.

COURT ROYAL
But that's an obvious mistake.

ATTORNEY BRECK
There's no mistake. Plead guilty. Get off easy. Otherwise *thrrrrit.* *(Makes throat-cutting gesture, then chuckles)* Plead guilty, brother, it's your only chance. *(Laughs)*

VOICE
Plea changed to
guilty?

COURT ROYAL
What? No. I'm not pleading guilty. And I want my lawyer.

                                                    VOICE
                                        You have yr law-
                                        yer

COURT ROYAL
No, my lawyer is John Breck.

ATTORNEY BRECK
Mr. Royal, look at me. *(Grabs him by the shoulders)* I am John Breck. *(Laughs)* Your attorney and friend. And I say plead guilty.

COURT ROYAL
John Bre . . . what? *(He looks at* ATTORNEY *closely.)* Breck. Great God, what's happened to you? Why do you look like this?

ATTORNEY BRECK
Why? Haha, I've always looked like this, Mr. Royal. Always. *(Now another voice, strong, young, begins to shout in the darkness at* COURT.)

YOUNG VICTIM
Now will you believe me stupid fool? Will you believe what I tell you or your eyes? Even your eyes. You're here with me, with us, all of us, and you can't understand. Plead guilty you are guilty stupid nigger. You'll die they'll kill you and you don't know why now will you believe me? Believe me, half-white coward. Will you believe reality?

                                                    VOICE
                                        Get that criminal out
                                        of here. Beat him. Shut him
                                        up. Get him.
(Now sounds of scuffling come out of darkness. Screams. Of a group of men subduing another man.)

YOUNG VICTIM
You bastard. And you Court Royal you let them take me. You liar. You weakling, you woman in the face of degenerates. You let me be taken. How can you walk the earttttt . . . *(He is apparently taken away.)*

COURT ROYAL
Who's that? *(Peers into darkness)* Who's that talking to me?

VOICE
Shutup, Royal.
Fix your plea. Let's
get on with it.

COURT ROYAL

That voice sounded very familiar. *(Caught in thought momentarily)* I almost
thought it was . . .

VOICE
Since you keep
your plea of not
guilty you won't need a
lawyer. We can proceed without
your services, Counselor.

ATTORNEY BRECK

As you wish, your honor. Goodbye, Mr. Royal. *(He begins to crawl off.)*
Goodbye, dead sucker! Hahahaha. *(Waving hands as he crawls off and laughing)* Hahahaha, ain't I a bitch . . . I mean ain't I? *(Exits)*

COURT ROYAL

John, John. You're my attorney, you can't leave me here like this. *(Starts after him, shouts)* JOHN! *(A siren begins to scream, like in jailbreak pictures . . . "Arrrrrrrerrrrr." The lights beat off, on, in time with the metallic siren shriek.* COURT *is stopped in his tracks, bent in anticipation; the siren continues. Machine guns begin to bang bang as if very close to him, cell doors slamming, whistles, yells: "Break . . . Break!" The machine guns chatter,* COURT *stands frozen, half-bent arms held away from his body, balancing him in his terror. As the noise, din, continues, his eyes grow until he is almost going to faint.)*

Ahhhhhhgggg. Please . . . Please . . . don't kill me. Don't shoot me, I didn't do
anything, I'm not trying to escape. Please . . . Please PLEEEEEAS . . .

(The VOICE *begins to shriek almost as loud with laughter as all the other sounds and jumping lights stop as* VOICE *starts to laugh. The* VOICE *just laughs and laughs, laughs until you think it will explode or spit up blood; it laughs long and eerily out of the darkness.)*

(Still dazed and staggered, he looks around quickly, trying to get himself together. He speaks now very quietly, and shaken.) Please. Please. *(The other* VOICE *begins to subside, the laughs coming in sharp cut-off bursts of hysteria.)*

146 /

VOICE
You donkey, *(Laughs)*
You piece of wood. You
shiny shuffling piece
of black vomit.

(The laughter quits like the tide rolling softly back to silence. Now there is no sound, except for COURT ROYAL'S *breathing, and shivering clothes. He whispers . . .)*

COURT ROYAL
Please? *(He is completely shaken and defeated, frightened like a small animal, eyes barely rolling.)* Please. I won't escape. *(His words sound corny tinny stupid dropped in such silence.)* Please I won't try again. Just tell me where I am. *(The silence again. For a while no movement.* COURT *is frozen, stiff, with only eyes sneaking; now they stop, he's frozen, cannot move staring off into the cold darkness.*

(A chain, slightly, more, now heavier, dragged bent, wiggled slowly, light now heavily in the darkness, from another direction. Chains. They're dragged, like things are pulling them across the earth. The chains. And now low chanting voices, moaning, with incredible pain and despair, the voices press just softly behind the chains, for a few seconds, so very very briefly then gone. And silence.

*(*COURT *does not move. His eyes roll a little back and around. He bends his knees, dipping his head, bending. He moans.)*

COURT ROYAL
Just tell me where I am.

VOICE
HEAVEN.

(The VOICE *is cool and businesslike.* COURT'S *eyes and head raise an imperceptible trifle. He begins to pull his arms slowly to his sides, and claps them together. The lights dim, and only* COURT *is seen in dimmer illumination. The* VOICE *again . . .)*

VOICE
HEAVEN.
(Pause)
WELCOME.

COURT ROYAL

(Mumbling) I never understood . . . these things are so confusing. *(His head jerks like he's suddenly heard Albert Ayler. It raises, his whole body jerks around like suddenly animate ragdoll. He does a weird dance like a marionette jiggling and waggling.)* You'll wonder what the devil-meant. A jiggedy bob-bidy fool. You'll wonder what the devil-sent. Diggedy dobbidy cool. Ah man. *(Singing)* Ah man, you'll wonder who the devil-sent. And what was heaven heaven heaven. *(This is like a funny joke-dance, with sudden funniness from* COURT*; then suddenly as before he stops frozen again, eyes rolling, no other sound heard. . . .*

(Now a scream, and white hooded men push a greasy-head nigger lady across in front of COURT. *They are pulling her hair, and feeling her ass. One whispers from time to time in her ear. She screams and bites occasionally, occasionally kicking.)*

HOOD 1

(To the VOICE*)* She's drunk. *(Now to* COURT*)* You want to smell her breath?

COURT ROYAL

(Frightened, also sickened at the sight, embarrassed) N-no. I don't want to. I smell it from here. She drinks and stinks and brings our whole race down.

HOOD 2
Ain't it the truth!

> **VOICE**
> Grind her into
> poison jelly.
> Smear it on her
> daughter's head.

HOOD 1
Right, yr honor. You got a break, sister. *(They go off.)* Hey, uncle, you sure you don't want to smell her breath?

COURT ROYAL
(Shivers) No.

> **VOICE**
> Royal, you have
> concealed a murderer,

and we have your punish-
ment ready for you. Are you
ready?

COURT ROYAL
What? No. I want a trial. Please a trial. I deserve that. I'm a good man.

VOICE
Royal, you're not a
man!

COURT ROYAL
Please ... *(Voice breaking)* your honor, a trial. A simple one, very quick,
nothing fancy ... I'm very conservative ... no frills or loud colors, a simple
concrete black toilet paper trial.

VOICE
And funeral.

*(Now two men in hoods, white work gloves, business suits, very sporty, come in
with a stretcher. A black man is dead on it. There is long very piped applause.
"Yea. Yea.")*

HOOD 1
It's *tʰ* Prince, yr honor. We banged him down.

VOICE
He's dead?

HOOD 2
Yes. A nigger did it for us.

VOICE
Conceal the body
in a stone. And sink the stone
deep under the ocean. Call the
newspapers and give the official history.
Make sure his voice is in that stone too, or ...
(Heavy nervous pause) Just go ahead.

HOOD 1
Of course, your honor. *(Looks to* COURT, *almost as an afterthought)* You want
to smell his breath? *(They go out.)*

COURT ROYAL
(Mumbling, still very frightened) No . . . no . . . I have nothing to do with any
of this. I'm a good man. I have a car. A home. *(Running down)* A club. *(Looks
up, pleading)* Please, there's some mistake. Isn't there? I've done nothing
wrong. I have a family. I work in the Post Office, I'm a supervisor. I've
worked for thirty-five years. I've done nothing wrong.

           VOICE
        Shutup, whimpering
        pig. Shutup and
        get ready for sen-
      tencing. It'll be hard on
    you, you can bet that.

COURT ROYAL
(A little life; he sees he's faced with danger.) But tell me what I've done. I can
remember no criminal, no murderer I've housed. I work eight hours, then
home, and television, dinner, then bowling. I've harbored no murderers. I
don't know any. I'm a good man.

           VOICE
      Shutup, liar. Do you know
      this man?

*(An image is flashed on the screen behind him. It is a rapidly shifting series of
faces. Malcolm. Patrice. Rev. King. Garvey. Dead nigger kids killed by the
police. Medgar Evers)*

COURT ROYAL
What?

           VOICE
      I asked you do you know
      this man? I'm asking again,
     for the last time. There's no
    need to lie.

COURT ROYAL
But this is many men, many faces. They shift so fast I cannot tell who they are
. . . or what is meant. It's so confusing.

           VOICE
     Don't lie, Royal. We know

> all about you. You are guilty.
> Look at that face. You know this man.

COURT ROYAL

I do? *(In rising terror)* No. No. I don't I never saw that man, it's so many faces, I've never seen those faces . . . never . . .

> VOICE
> Look closer, Royal. You cannot
> get away with what you've done. Look
> more closely. You recognize
> that face . . . don't you? The face
> of the murderer you've sheltered all
> these years. Look, you liar, look at
> that face.

COURT ROYAL

No, no, no . . . I don't know them. I can't be forced into admitting something I never did. Uhhh . . . I have worked. My God, I've worked. I've meant to do the right thing. I've tried to be a . . .

(The faces shift, a long slow wail, like moan, like secret screaming, has underscored the flashing faces. Now it rises sharply to screaming point thrusts. COURT *wheels around to face the image on the screen, directly. He begins shouting loud as the voices.)*

No, I've tried . . . please I never wanted anything but peace . . . please, I tried to be a man. I did. I lost my . . . heart . . . please, it was so deep, I wanted to do the right thing, just to do the right thing. I wanted . . . everything to be . . . all right. Oh, please . . . please.

> VOICE
> Now tell me, whether you
> know that murderer's face or not.
> Tell me before you die!

COURT ROYAL

No, no. I don't know him. I don't. I want to do the right thing. I don't know them. *(Raises his hands in his agony)* Oh, son . . . son . . . dear God, my flesh, forgive me . . . *(Begins to weep and shake)* My sons. *(He clutches his body, shaken throughout by his ugly sobs.)*

Dear god . . .

                                        VOICE
                            Just as we thought. You are
                    the one. And you must be sentenced.

COURT ROYAL
I must be sentenced. I am the one. *(Almost trance-like)* I must be sentenced.
With the murderer. I am the one.

                                        VOICE
                            The murderer is dead. You
                    must be sentenced alone.

COURT ROYAL
(As first realization) The murderer . . . is . . . dead?

                                        VOICE
                            And you must be sentenced.
                    Now. Alone.

COURT ROYAL
(Voice rising, in panic, but catching it up short) The murderer . . . is dead.

                                        VOICE
                            Yes. And your sentence is . . .

COURT ROYAL
I must be sentenced . . . alone. Where is the murderer? Where is his corpse?

                                        VOICE
                            You will see it presently.

COURT ROYAL
(Head bowed) God. And I am now to die like the murderer died?

                                        VOICE
                            No. *(Long pause)* We have
                    decided to spare you. We admire
                your spirit. It is a compliment to
            know you can see the clearness of your
        fate, and the rightness of it. That you
    love the beauty of the way of life you've
chosen here in the anonymous world. No one
beautiful is guilty. So how can you be? All the

152   /

guilty have been punished. Or are being punished. You
are absolved of your crime, at this moment, because
of your infinite understanding of the compassionate
God Of The Cross. Whose head was cut off for you, to
absolve you of your weakness. The murderer is dead.
The murderer is dead.

(Applause from the darkness)

COURT ROYAL
And I am not guilty now?

                                                    VOICE
                              No, you are free. Forever.
                              It is asked only that you give the final
                    instruction.

COURT ROYAL
Final instruction ... I don't understand ...

                                                    VOICE
                              Heroes! bring the last issue in.

(The last two hooded men, HOODS *3 and 4, return with a young black man of
about twenty. The boy does not look up. He walks stiff-legged to the center in
front of* COURT. *He wears a large ankh around his neck. His head comes up
slowly. He looks into* COURT's *face.)*

YOUNG VICTIM
Peace.

COURT ROYAL
*(Looks at his face, begins to draw back. The hooded man comes and places his
arms around* COURT's *shoulders.)*

                                                    VOICE
                              Give him the instruction
                              instrument.

(Hooded man takes a pistol out of his pocket and gives it with great show to
COURT.)

HOOD 3

The silver bullet is in the chamber. The gun is made of diamonds and gold.

HOOD 4

You get to keep it after the ceremony.

> **VOICE**
>
> And now, with the rite of instruction, the last bit of guilt falls from you as if it was never there, Court Royal. Now, at last, you can go free. Perform the rite, Court Royal, the final instruction.

COURT ROYAL

What? No. I don't understand.

> **VOICE**
>
> The final instruction is the death of the murderer. The murderer is dead and must die, with each gift of our God. This gift is the cleansing of guilt, and the bestowal of freedom.

COURT ROYAL

But you told me the murderer was dead already.

> **VOICE**
>
> It *is* already. The murderer has been sentenced. You have only to carry out the rite.

COURT ROYAL

But you told me the murderer was dead. *(Starts to back away)* You told me ... you said I would be sentenced alone.

> **VOICE**
>
> The murderer *is dead.* This is his shadow. This one is not real. This is the myth of the murderer. His last fleeting astral projection. It is the murderer's myth that we ask you to instruct. To bind it forever ... with death.

COURT ROYAL

I don't ... Why do ... you said I was not guilty. That my guilt had fallen away.

                                        VOICE
                        The rite must be finished. This
                        ghost must be lost in cold space.
                        Court Royal, this is your destiny.
                        This act was done by you a million
                        years ago. This is only the memory of it.
                        This is only a rite. You cannot kill a shadow,
                        a fleeting bit of light and memory. This is only
            a rite, to show that you would be guilty but for
        the cleansing rite. The shadow is killed in place of the
        killer. The shadow for reality. So reality can exist
        beautiful like it is. This is your destiny, and your already
        lived-out life. Instruct, Court Royal, as the centuries
        pass, and bring you back to your natural reality. Without
        guilt. Without shame. Pure and blameless, your soul
        washed *(Pause)* white as snow.

    COURT ROYAL
    *(Falling to his knees, arms extended as in loving prayer, to a bright light falling
    on him, racing around the space)* Oh, yes . . . I hear you. And I have waited, for
    this promise to be fulfilled.

                                        VOICE
                        This is the fulfillment.
                        You must, at this moment, enter
                        into the covenant of guiltless si-
                        lence. Perform the rite, Court Royal.

    COURT ROYAL
    Oh, yes, yes . . . I want so much to be happy . . . and relaxed.

                                        VOICE
                        Then carry out your destiny . . .

    COURT ROYAL
    Yes, yes . . . I will . . . I will be happy . . . *(He rises, pointing the gun straight up
    at the young man's face.)* I must be . . . fulfilled . . . I will. *(He fires the weapon
    into the boy's face. One short sound comes from the boy's mouth.)*

    YOUNG VICTIM
    Papa. *(He falls.)*

    COURT ROYAL
    (Stands looking at the dead boy with the gun still up. He is motionless.)

VOICE

Case dismissed, Court Royal . . . you
are free.

COURT ROYAL

(Now suddenly to life, the lights go up full, he has the gun in his hand. He drops, flings it away from him.) My soul is as white as snow. *(He wanders up to the body.)* My soul is as white as snow. *(He starts to wander off the stage.)* White as snow. I'm free. I'm free. My life is a beautiful thing.

(He mopes slowly toward the edge of the stage, then suddenly a brighter mood strikes him. Raising his hand as if calling someone) Hey, Louise, have you seen my bowling bag? I'm going down to the alley for a minute. *(He is frozen, the lights dim to BLACK.)*

THE CHANGING SAME (R&B AND NEW BLACK MUSIC)
from *Black Music*

The blues impulse transferred ... containing a race, and its expression. *Primal* (mixtures ... transfers and imitations). Through its many changes, it remained the exact replication of The Black Man In The West.

An expression of the culture at its most unself- (therefore showing the larger consciousness of a *one self,* immune to bullshit) conscious. The direct expression of a place ... jazz seeks another place as it weakens, a middle-class place. Except the consciously separate from those aspirations. Hence the so-called avant-garde or new music, the new Black Music, is separate because it seeks to be equally separate, equally unself-conscious ... meaning more conscious of the real weights of existence as the straightest R&B. There are simply more temptations for the middle-class Negro because he can make believe in America more, cop out easier, become whiter and slighter with less trouble, than most R&B people. Simply because he is closer to begin with.

Jazz, too often, becomes a music of special, not necessarily emotional, occasion. But R&B now, with the same help from white America in its exploitation of energy for profit, the same as if it was a gold mine, strings that music out along a similar weakening line. Beginning with their own vacuous "understanding" of what Black music is, or how it acts upon you, they believe, from the Beatles on down, that it is about white life.

The Blues, its "kinds" and diversity, its identifying parent styles. The phenomenon of jazz is another way of specifying cultural influences. The jazz that is most European, popular or avant, or the jazz that is Blackest, still makes reference to a central body of cultural experience. The impulse, the force that pushes you to sing ... all up in there ... is one thing ... what it produces is another. It can be expressive of the entire force, or make it the occasion of some special pleading. Or it is all equal ... we simply identify the part of the world in which we are most responsive. It is all there. We are exact (even in our lies). The elements that turn our singing into direction reflections of our selves are heavy and palpable as weather.

We are moved and directed by our total response to the possibility of all effects.

We are bodies responding differently, a (total) force, like against you. You react to push it, re-create it, resist it. It is the opposite pressure producing (in this case) the sound, the music.

The City Blues tradition is called that by me only to recognize different elements active in its creation. The slick city people we become after the exodus, the unleashing of an energy into the Northern urban situation. Wholesale.

The line we could trace, as musical "tradition," is what we as a people dig and pass on, as best we can. The call and response form of Africa (lead and chorus) has never left us, as a mode of (musical) expression. It has come down both as vocal and instrumental form.

The rhythm quartet of the last thirty years is a very obvious continuation of Black vocal tradition, and a condensation in the form from the larger tribal singing units . . . through the form of the large religious choirs (chorus) which were initially *dancers and singers,* of religious and/or ritual purpose.

Indeed, to go back in any historical (or emotional) line of ascent in Black music leads us inevitably to religion, i.e., spirit worship. This phenomenon is always at the root in Black art, the worship of spirit—or at least the summoning of or by such force. As even the music itself was that, a reflection of, or the no thing itself.

The slave ship destroyed a great many formal art traditions of the Black man. The white man enforced such cultural rape. A "cultureless" people is a people without a memory. No history. This is the best state for slaves; to be objects, just like the rest of massa's possessions.

The breakdown of Black cultural tradition meant finally the destruction of most formal art and social tradition. Including the breakdown of the Black pre-American religious forms. Forcibly so. Christianity replaced African religions as the outlet for spirit worship. And Christian forms were traded, consciously and unconsciously, for their own. Christian forms were emphasized under threat of death. What resulted were Afro-Christian forms. These are forms which persist today.

The stripping away, gradual erosion, of the pure African form as means of expression by Black people, and the gradual embracing of mixed Afro-Christian, Afro-American forms is an initial reference to the cultural philosophy of Black People, Black Art.

Another such reference, or such stripping, is an American phenomenon, i.e., it is something that affected all of America, in fact the entire West. This, of course, is the loss of religiosity in the West, in general.

Black Music is African in origin, African-American in its totality, and its various forms (especially the vocal) show just how the African impulses were redistributed in its expression, and the expression itself became Christianized and post-Christianized.

Even today a great many of the best-known R&B groups, quartets, etc., have church backgrounds, and the music itself is as churchified as it has ever been ... in varying degrees of its complete emotional identification with the Black African-American culture (Sam and Dave, etc. at one end ... Dionne Warwick in the middle ... Leslie Uggams, the other end ... and fading).

The church continues, but not the devotion (at no level of its existence is it as large, though in the poorest, most abstractly altruistic levels of churchgoing, the emotion is the devotion, and the God, the God of that feeling and movement, remains as powerful though "redistributed" somewhat).

But the kind of church Black people belonged to usually connected them with the society as a whole ... identified them, their aspirations, their culture: because the church was one of the few places complete fullness of expression by the Black was not constantly censored by the white man. Even the asking of freedom, though in terms veiled with the biblical references of "The Jews," went down in church.

It was only those arts and cultural practices that were less obviously capable of "alien" social statement that could survive during slavery. (And even today in contemporary America, it is much the same ... though instead of out and out murder there are hardly more merciful ways of limiting Black protest or simple statement ... in the arts just as in any other aspect of American life.)

Blues (Lyric) its song quality is, it seems, the deepest expression of memory. Experience re/feeling. It is the racial memory. It is the "abstract" design of racial character that is evident, would be evident, in creation carrying the force of that racial memory.

Just as the God spoken about in the Black songs is not the same one in the white songs. Though the words might look the same. (They are not even pronounced alike.) But it is a different quality of energy they summon. It is the simple tone of varying evolution by which we distinguish the races. The peoples. The body is directly figured in it. "The life of the organs."

But evolution is not merely physical: yet if you can understand what the physical alludes to, is reflect of, then it will be understood that each process in "life" is duplicated at all levels.

The Blues (impulse) lyric (song) is even descriptive of a plane of evolution, a direction ... coming and going ... through whatever worlds. Environment, as the social workers say ... but Total Environment (including at all levels, the spiritual).

Identification is Sound Identification is Sight Identification is Touch, Feeling, Smell, Movement. (For instance, I can tell, even in the shadows, halfway across the field, whether it is a white man or Black man running. Though Whitney Young would like to see us all run the same.)

For instance, a white man could box like Muhammad Ali, only *after* seeing Muhammad Ali box. He could not initiate that style. It is no description, it *is* the culture. (AD 1966)

The Spirituals . . . The Camp Meeting Songs at backwoods churches . . . or Slave Songs talking about deliverance.

The God the slaves worshipped (for the most part, except maybe the "pure white" God of the toms) had to be willing to free them, somehow, someway . . . one sweet day.

The God, the perfection of what the spiritual delivery and world are said to be, is what the worshippers sang. That perfect Black land. The land changed with the God in charge. The churches the slaves and freedmen went to identified these Gods, and their will in heaven, as well as earth.

The closer the church was to Africa, the Blacker the God. (The Blacker the spirit.) The closer to the will (and meaning) of the West, the whiter the God, the whiter the spirit worshipped. The whiter the worshippers. This is still so. And the hard Black core of America is African.

From the different churches, the different Gods, the different versions of Earth. The different weights and "classic" versions of reality. And the different singing. Different expressions (of a whole). A whole people . . . a nation, in captivity.

Rhythm and Blues is part of "the national genius," of the Black man, of the Black nation. It is the direct, no monkey business expression of urban and rural (in its various stylistic variations) Black America.

The hard, driving shouting of James Brown identifies a place and image in America. A people and an energy, harnessed and not harnessed by America. JB is straight out, open, and speaking from the most deeply religious people on this continent.

The energy is harnessed because what JB does has to go down in a system governed by "aliens," and he will probably never become, say, as wealthy, etc., that is he will never reap the *material* benefits that several bunches of white folks will, from his own efforts. But the will of the expression transcends the physical-mental "material," finally alien system-world it has to go through to allow any "benefits" in it. Because the will of the expression is spiritual, and as such it must transcend its mineral, vegetable, animal, environment.

Form and content are both mutually expressive of the whole. And they are both equally expressive . . . each have an identifying motif and function. In Black music, both identify place and direction. We want different contents and different forms because we have different feelings. We are different peoples.

James Brown's form and content identify an entire group of people in America. However these may be transmuted and reused, reappear in other areas, in other musics for different purposes in the society, the initial energy and image are about a specific grouping of people, Black People.

Music makes an image. What image? What environment (in that word's most extended meaning, i.e., total, external and internal, environment)? I mean there is a world powered by that image. The world James Brown's images power is the lowest placement (the most alien) in the white American social order. Therefore, it is the Blackest and potentially the strongest.

It is not simply "the strongest" because of the transmutation and harnessing I spoke of earlier. This is social, but it is total. The world is a total. (And in this sense, the total function of "free music" can be understood. See, especially, H. Dumas' story in *Negro Digest* "Will the Circle Be Unbroken?" and understand the implications of music as an autonomous *judge* of civilizations, etc. Wow!)

By image, I mean that music (art for that matter . . . or any thing else if analyzed) summons and describes where its energies were gotten. The blinking lights and shiny heads, or the gray concrete and endless dreams. But the description is of a total environment. The content speaks of this environment, as does the form.

The "whitened" Negro and white man want a different content from the people James Brown "describes." They are different peoples. The softness and so-called "well being" of the white man's environment is described in his music (art) . . . in all expressions of his self. All people's are.

If you play James Brown (say, "Money Won't Change You . . . but time will take you out") in a bank, the total environment is changed. Not only the sardonic comment of the lyrics, but the total emotional placement of the rhythm, instrumentation and sound. An energy is released in the bank, a summoning of images that take the bank, and everybody in it, on a trip. That is, they visit another place. A place where Black People live.

But dig, not only is it a place where Black People live, it is a place, in the spiritual precincts of its emotional telling, where Black People move in almost absolute openness and strength. (For instance, what is a white person who walks into a James Brown or Sam and Dave song? How would he function? What would be the social metaphor for his existence in that world? What would he be doing?)

This is as true, finally, with the John Coltrane world or the Sun-Ra world. In the Albert Ayler world, or Ornette Coleman world, you would say, "well, they might just be playing away furiously at some stringed instrument." You understand?

In the Leslie Uggams world? They would be marrying a half-white singer and directing the show . . . maybe even whispering lyrics and stuff from the wings. You understand? *The song and the people is the same.*

The reaction to any expression moves the deepest part of the psyche and makes its identifications throughout. The middle-class Negro wants a different content (image) from James Brown, because he has come from a different place, and wants a different thing (he thinks). The something you want to hear is the thing you already are or move toward.

We feel, Where is the expression going? What will it lead to? What does it characterize? What does it make us feel like? What is its image? Jazz content, of course, is as pregnant.

The implications of content.

The form content of much of what is called New Thing or Avant-Garde or New Music differs (or seems to differ) from Rhythm and Blues, R&B oriented jazz, or what the cat on the block digs. (And here I'm talking about what is essentially *Black Music.* Although, to be sure, too often the "unswinging ness" of much of the "new" is because of its association, derivation and even straight-out imitation of certain aspects of contemporary European and white Euro-American music . . . whether they are making believe they are Bach or Webern.) Avant-garde, finally, is a bad term because it also means a lot of quacks and quackers, too.

But the significant difference is, again, direction, intent, sense of identification . . . "kind" of consciousness. And that's what its about; consciousness. What are you *with* (the word Con-With/Scio-Know). The "new" musicians are self-conscious. Just as the boppers were. Extremely conscious of self. They are more conscious of a total self (or *want* to be) than the R&B people who, for the most part, are all-expression. Emotional expression. Many times self-consciousness turns out to be just what it is as a common figure of speech. It produces world-weariness, cynicism, corniness. Even in the name of Art. Or what have you . . . social uplift, "Now we can play good as white folks," or "I went to Juilliard, and this piece exhibits a Bach-like contrapuntal line," and so forth right on out to lunch.

But at its best and most expressive, the New Black Music is expression, and expression of reflection as well. What is presented is a consciously proposed learning experience. (See "The New Wave.") It is no wonder that many of the new Black musicians are or say they want to be "Spiritual Men" (Some of the boppers embraced Islam), or else they are interested in the Wisdom Religion itself, i.e., the rise to spirit. It is expanding the consciousness of the given that they are interested in, not merely expressing what is already there, or alluded to. They are interested in the *unknown.* The mystical.

But it is interpretation. The Miracles are spiritual. They sing (and sing about) feeling. Their content is about feeling . . . the form is to make feeling, etc. The self-conscious (reflective, long-form, New Thing, bop, etc.) Art Musicians cultivate consciousness that wants more feeling, to rise . . . up a scale one measures with one's life. It is about thought, but thought can kill it. Life is complex in the same simplicity.

R&B is about emotion, issues purely out of emotion. New Black Music is also about emotion, but from a different place, and, finally, towards a different end. What these musicians feel is a more complete existence. That is, the digging of everything. What the wisdom religion preaches.

(But the actual New Black Music will be a larger expression. It will include the pretension of The New Music, as actuality, as summoner of Black Spirit, the evolved music of the then evolved people.)

The differences between rhythm and blues and the so-called new music or art jazz, the different places, are artificial, or they are merely indicative of the different placements of spirit. (Even "purely" social, like what the musicians want, etc.)

For instance, use of Indian music, old spirituals, even heavily rhythmic blues licks (and soon electronic devices) by new music musicians point toward the final close in the spectrum of the sound that will come. A really new, really all inclusive music. The whole people.

Any analysis of the content of R&B, the lyrics, or the total musical will and direction, will give a placement in contrast to analysis of new jazz content. (Even to the analysis of the implied vocalism of the new music: what are its intent and direction, what place it makes, etc., are concerned.) Again even the purely social, as analyzing reference, will give the sense of difference, what directions, what needs are present in the performers, and then, why the music naturally flows out of this.

The songs of R&B, for instance, what are they about? What are the people, for the most part, singing about? Their lives. That's what the New Musicians are playing about, and the projection of forms for those lives. (And I think any analysis will immediately show, as I pointed out in *Blues People,* that the songs, the music, changed, as the people did.) Mainly, I think the songs are about what is known as "love," requited and un. But the most popular songs are always a little sad, in tune with the temper of the people's lives. The extremes. Wild Joy—Deep Hurt.

The songs about unrequited, incompleted, obstructed, etc., love probably outnumber the others very easily. Thinking very quickly of just the songs that come readily to my mind, generally current, and favorites of mine (and on that other *top ten,* which is, you bet, the indication of where the minds, the people, are). "Walk On By" "Where Did Our Love Go?" "What Becomes of the Broken Hearted?" "The Tracks of My Tears," high poetry in the final character of their delivery . . . but to a very large extent, the songs are about love affairs which do not, did not, come off. For God knows how many reasons. Infidelity, not enough dough, incredibly "secret" reasons where the loved and the lover or the lovers are already separated and longing one for the other, according to who's singing, male or female. And all more precise and specific than the Moynihan Report, e.g., listen to Jr. Walker's "Road Runner." And this missed love that runs through these songs is exactly reflect of what is the term of love and loving in the Black world of America Twentieth Century.

The miss-understanding, nay, gap . . . abyss, that separates Black man and

Black woman is always, over and over, again and again, told about and cried about. And it's old, in this country, to us. "Come back baby, Baby, please don't go . . . Cause the way I love you, Baby, you will never know . . . So come back, Baby, let's talk it over . . . one more time." A blues which bees older than Ray Charles or Lightnin' Hopkins, for that matter. "I got to laugh to keep from cryin'," which The Miracles make, "I got to dance to keep from cryin'," is not only a song but the culture itself. It is finally the same cry, the same people. You really got a hold on me. As old as our breath here.

But there are many songs about love triumphant. "I feel good . . . I got you . . . Hey!" the score, the together self, at one and in love and swinging, flying God-like. But a differently realized life-triumph than in the older more formally religious songs. The Jordans, the Promised Lands, now be cars and women-flesh, and especially dough. (Like *power.*) There are many many songs about Money, e.g., Barrett Deems' "Money," J.B.'s "I Got Money . . . now all I need is love," among so many others. But the songs are dealing with the everyday, and how to get through it and to the other side (or maybe not) which for the most part still bees that world, but on top of it, power full, and beauty full.

The older religiosity falls away from the music, but the deepest feel of spirit worship always remains, as the music's emotional patterns continue to make reference to. The new jazz people are usually much more self-consciously concerned about "God" than the R&B folks. But most of the R&B people were *really* in the church at one time, and sang there first, only to drift or rush away later.

Even the poorest, Blackest, Black people drifted away from the church. Away from a church, usually corrupted, Europeanized, or both, that could no longer provide for their complete vision of what this world ought to be, or the next. The refuge the church had provided during the early days of the Black man's captivity in America, when it was really the one place he could completely unleash his emotions and hear words of encouragement for his life here on earth. Now the world had opened up, and the church had not. But the emotionalism the church contained, and the spirit it signified, would always demand the animating life of the Black man, and as Frazier says, "The masses of Negroes may increasingly criticize their church and their ministers, but they cannot escape from their heritage. They may develop a more secular outlook on life and complain that the church and the ministers are not sufficiently concerned with the problems of the Negro race, yet they find in their religious heritage an opportunity to satisfy their deepest emotional yearnings." *(The Negro Church in America,* E. Franklin Frazier, Shocken, 1963, p. 73.)

It was the more emotional Blacker churches that the blues people were members of, rather than the usually whiter, more middle-class churches the jazz people went to. The church, as I said, carries directly over into the secular music, which is really not secular at all. It's an old cliché that if you just change the lyrics of the spirituals they are R&B songs. That's true by and large, though there are more brazen, even whiter, strings and echo effects the blues people use that most of the spiritual and gospel people don't use. But that's changed and changing, too, and in the straight city jamup gospel, echo chambers, strings, electric guitars, all are in evidence, and Jesus is jamup contemporary, with a process and silk suit too, my man.

But the gospel singers have always had a more direct connection with the blues than the other religious singers. In fact, gospel singing is a city blues phenomenon, and Professor Thomas Dorsey, who is generally credited with popularizing the gospel form back in Chicago in the late twenties and thirties, was once a blues singer-piano player named Georgia Tom, and even worked with Ma Rainey. (He was last known to be arranging for Mahalia Jackson, who with Ray Charles at another much more legitimate and powerful level, were the popularizers of Black church sound in "popular" music during the 50's.) But then so many of them, from G.T., and even before that to J.B., have all come that way.

The meeting of the practical God (i.e., of the existent American idiom) and the mystical (abstract) God is also the meeting of the tones, of the moods, of the knowledge, the different musics and the emergence of the new music, the really new music, the all-inclusive whole. The emergence also of the new people, the Black people conscious of all their strength, in a unified portrait of strength, beauty and contemplation.

The new music began by calling itself "free," and this is social and is in direct commentary on the scene it appears in. Once free, it is spiritual. But it is soulful before, after, any time, anyway. And the spiritual and free and soulful must mingle with the practical, as practical, as existent, anywhere.

The R&B people left the practical God behind to slide into the slicker scene, where the dough was, and the swift folks congregated. The new jazz people never had that practical God, as practical, and seek the mystical God both emotionally and intellectually.

John Coltrane, Albert Ayler, Sun-Ra, Pharoah Sanders, come to mind immediately as God-seekers. In the name of energy sometimes, as with Ayler and drummer Sonny Murray. Since God is, indeed, energy. To play strong forever would be the cry and the worshipful purpose of life.

The titles of Trane's tunes, "A Love Supreme," "Meditations," "Ascension," imply a strong religious will, conscious of the religious evolution the pure mind seeks. The music is a way into God. The absolute open expression of everything.

Albert Ayler uses the older practical religion as key and description of his own quest. *Spirits. Ghosts. Spiritual Unity, Angels,* etc. And his music shows a graphic connection with an older sense of the self. The music sounds like old timey religious tunes and some kind of spiritual march music, or probably the combination as a religious marching song if you can get to that. (New crusades, so to speak. A recent interview article, with Albert Ayler and his brother, trumpet player Donald Ayler, was titled "The Truth Is Marching In," and this is an excellent metaphor of where Albert and his brother Donald want to move.)

Albert's music, which he characterizes as "spiritual," has much in common with older Black-American religious forms. An openness that characterizes the "shouts" and "hollers." But having the instruments shout and holler, say a saxophone, which was made by a German, and played, as white folks call it, "legitimately" sounds like dead Lily Pons at a funeral, is changed by Ayler, or by members of any Sanctified or Holy Roller church (the blacker churches) into howling spirit summoner tied around the "mad" Black man's neck. The Daddy Grace band on 125th Street and 8th Avenue in Harlem, in the Grace Temple, is a brass band, with somewhat the same instrumentation as a European brass choir, but at the lips of Daddy's summoners, the band is "free" and makes sounds to tear down the walls of anywhere. The instruments shout and holler just like the folks. It is their lives being projected then, and they are different from the lives Telemann, or Vivaldi sought to reanimate with their music.

But James Brown still shouts, and he is as secular as the old shouters, and the new ones. With the instruments, however, many people would like them to be more securely European oriented, playing notes of the European tempered scale. While the Eastern Colored peoples' music demands, at least, that many many half, quarter, etc. tones be sounded, implied, hummed, slurred, that the whole sound of a life get in ... no matter the "precision" the Europeans claim with their "reasonable" scale which will get only the sounds of an order and reason that patently deny most colored peoples the right to exist. To play their music is to be them and to act out their lives, as if you were them. There is then, a whole world of most intimacy and most expression, which is yours, colored man, but which you will lose playing melancholy baby in B-flat, or the *Emperor Concerto,* for that matter. Music lessons of a dying people.

Albert Ayler has talked about his music as a contemporary form of collective improvisation (Sun-Ra and John Coltrane are working in this area as well). Which is where our music was when we arrived on these shores, a collective expression. And to my mind, the *solo,* in the sense it came to be represented on these Western shores, and as first exemplified by Louis Armstrong, is very plain indication of the changed sensibility the West enforced.

The return to collective improvisations, which finally, the West-oriented, the whitened, say, is chaos, is the *all-force* put together, and is what is wanted. Rather than accompaniment and a solo voice, the miniature "thing" securing its "greatness." Which is where the West is.

The Ornette Coleman *Double Quartet* which was called *Free Jazz* was one breakthrough to open the 60's. (It seems now to me that some of bassist Charlie Mingus' earlier efforts, e.g., *Pithecanthropus Erectus*, provide a still earlier version of this kind of massive orchestral breakthrough. And called rightly, too, I think. *Pithecanthropus Erectus*, the first man to stand. As what we are, a first people, and the first people, the primitives, now evolving, to recivilize the world. And all these and Sun-Ra who seems to me to have made the most moving orchestral statements with the New Music, all seem not so curiously joined to Duke Ellington. Ellington's "KoKo" and "Diminuendo and Crescendo . . ." can provide some immediate reference to freed orchestral form.)

The secular voice seeking clarity, or seeking religion (a spirit worship) compatible with itself. They are both pushed by an emotionalism that seeks freedom. Its answering category, the definition of the freedom sought, is equally descriptive of who is playing what? If we say we want social freedom, i.e., we do not want to be exploited or have our lives obstructed, there are roots now spreading everywhere. People even carry signs, etc. There is also the "freedom" to be a white man, which, for the most part is denied the majority of people on the earth, which includes jazz players, or for that matter, blues people. The freedom to want your own particular hip self is a freedom of a somewhat different and more difficult nature.

Then, there are all kinds of freedom, and even all kinds of spirits. We can use the past as shrines of our suffering, as a poeticizing beyond what we think the present (the "actual") has to offer. But that *is* true in the sense that any clear present must include as much of the past as it needs to clearly illuminate it.

Archie Shepp is a tenor man of the new jazz, who came out (see *Archie Shepp, New Tenor)* of an American background of Black slums and white palaces. He is a Marxist playwrighting tenor-saxophone player now. His music sounds like a perculiar barrelhouse whore tip. It wavers chunks of vibrato Ben Webster Kansas City style, but turns that character actor wail into a kind of polished cry. Which, finally, if you have ever heard him speak at some public social gathering, is articulate at a very definite place in America.

Archie's is a secular music, that remains, demands secularity, as its insistence. He probably even has theories explaining why there is no God. But he makes obeisances to the spirits of ancient, "traditional," colored people ("Hambone," "The Mac Man," "The Picaninny") and what has happened to them from ancient times, traditionally, here *(Rufus, Swung, his face at last to the wind. Then his neck snapped* or *Malcolm* or *picked clean.).*

Archie is the secular demanding clarity of itself. A reordering according to the known ("The Age of Cities"). Modern in this sense. But of "modern" we must begin to ask, "What does Modern Mean?" and "What is The Future?" or "Where Does One Want To Go?" or "What Does One *Want* to Happen?"

You hear in Archie's music moans that are pleas for understanding.

Cecil Taylor is also secular. He is very much an *artist*. His references determinedly Western and modern, contemporary in the most Western sense. One hears Europe and the influence of French poets on America and the world of "pure art" in Cecil's total approach to his playing. Cecil's is perhaps the most European sounding of the New Music, but his music is moving because he is still Black, still has imposed an emotional sensibility on the music that knows of actual beauty beyond "what is given."

Even though Cecil is close to what's been called Third Stream, an "integrated" Western modernism, he is always *hotter, sassier* and newer than that music. But the Black artist is most often always hip to European art, often at his jeopardy.

The most complete change must be a spiritual change. A change of Essences. The secular is not complete enough. It is not the new music, it is a breaking away from old American forms. Toward new American forms. Ornette Coleman is the elemental land change, the migratory earth man, the country blues person of old come in the city with a funkier wilder blues. Such energy forces all kinds of movement. The freshness of this Americana. A bebopier bebop, a funkier funky. But tuxedoes can be planted among such vegetation, strings and cords tied up to send the life stretched out along a very definite path. Like ivy, finally growed up fastened to an academy. No longer wild, no longer funky, but domesticated like common silence.

Ornette, Archie and Cecil. Three versions of a contemporary Black Secularism. Making it in America, from the country, the ghetto, into the gnashing maw of the Western art world. The freedom they, the music, want is *the freedom to exist in this.* (What of the New? Where?) The freedom of the given. The freedom to exist as artists. Freedom would be the change.

But the device of their asking for this freedom remains a device for asking if the actual is not achieved. Literary Negro-ness, the exotic instance of abstract cultural resource, say in one's head, is not the Black Life Force for long if we are isolated from the real force itself, and, in effect, cooled off. Cool Jazz was the abstraction of these life forces. There can be a cool avant, in fact there is, already. The isolation of the Black artist relating to, performing and accommodating his expression for aliens. Where is the returned energy the artist demands to go on? His battery (guns and engines)?

We want to please the people we see (feel with and/or for) all the time, in the respect of actual living with. Our neighbors? Our people? Who are these? Our definitions change. Our speech and projection. Is that a chick or a broad or a woman or a girl or a bird . . . or what is it? Where are you? What is this place that you describe with all your energies? Is it your own face coloring the walls, echoing in the halls, like hip talk by knowledgeable millionaires. What does a millionaire want as he passes through the eye of the needle? Can he really pass?

The New Music (any Black Music) is cooled off when it begins to reflect blank, any place "universal" humbug. It is this fag or that kook, and not the fire and promise and need for evolution into a higher species. The artist's resources must be of the strongest, purest possible caliber. They must be truest and straightest and deepest. Where is the deepest feeling in our lives? There is the deepest and most meaningful art and life. Beware "the golden touch," it will kill everything you useta (used to) love.

There are other new musicians, new music, that take freedom as already being. Ornette was a cool breath of open space. Space, to move. So freedom already exists. The change is spiritual. The total. The absolutely new. That is the absolute realization. John Coltrane, who has been an innovator of one period in jazz and a master in another period, is an example of the secular yearning for the complete change, for the religious, the spiritual.

Sun-Ra is spiritually oriented. He understands "the future" as an ever widening comprehension of what space is, even to the "physical" travel between the planets as we do anyway in the long human chain of progress. Sun-Ra's Arkestra sings in one of his songs, "We travel the spaceways, from planet to planet." It is science-fact that Sun-Ra is interested in, not science-fiction. It is evolution itself, and its fruits. God as evolution. The flow of *is*.

So the future revealed is man explained to himself. The travel through inner space as well as outer. Sun-Ra's is a new content for jazz, for Black music, but it is merely, again, the spiritual defining itself. ("Love in Outer Space," "Ankh," "Outer Nothingness," "The Heliocentric World," "When Angels Speak of Love," "Other Worlds," "The Infinity of the Universe," "Of Heavenly Things," etc., etc.) And the mortal seeking, the human knowing spiritual, and willing the evolution. Which is the Wisdom Religion.

But the content of The New Music, or The New Black Music, is toward change. It is change. It wants to change forms. From physical to physical (social to social) or from physical to mental, or from physical-mental to spiritual. Soon essences. Albert Ayler no longer wants notes. He says he wants sound. The total articulation. Ra's music changes places, like Duke's "jungle music." Duke took people to a spiritual past, Ra to a spiritual future (which also contains "Little Sally Walker . . . sitting in a saucer . . . what kind'a saucer? . . . a flying saucer").

African sounds, too; the beginnings of our sensibility. The new, the "primitive," meaning *first*, new. Just as Picasso's borrowings were Western avant-garde and "the new" from centuries ago, and Stravinsky's borrowings were new and "savage," centuries old and brand new.

The Black musicians who know about the European tempered scale (Mind) no longer want it, if only just to be contemporary. That changed. The other Black musicians never wanted it, anyway.

Change

Freedom

and finally Spirit. (But spirit makes the first two possible. A cycle, again?)

What are the qualitative meanings and implications of these words?

There is the freedom to exist (and the change to) in the existing, or to reemerge in a new thing.

Essence

How does this content differ from that of R&B.

Love, for R&B, is an absolute good. There is love but there is little of it, and it is a valuable possession. How Sweet It Is To Be Loved By You. But the practical love, like the practical church the R&B people left, a much more emotional church and spirit worship than most jazz people had, is a day-to-day physical, social, sensual love. Its presence making the other categories of human experience mesh favorably with beautiful conclusions. "Since I Lost My Baby" (or older) "When I Lost My Baby . . . I almost lost my mind." There is the object (even, the person). But what is the *object* of John Coltrane's "Love" . . . There is none. It is for the sake of Loving, Trane speaks of. As Ra's "When Angels Speak of Love."

I said before, "the cleansed purpose." The rise, the will *to be* love. The contemplative and the expressive, side by side, feeding each other. Finally, the rhythms carry to the body, the one (R&B) more "quickly," since its form definitely includes the body as a high register of the love one seeks.

The change to Love. The freedom to (of) Love. And in this constant evocation of Love, its need, its demands, its birth, its death, there is a morality that shapes such a sensibility, and a sensibility shaped by such moralizing.

Sometimes through Archie Shepp's wailing comes a dark yowl of desire in the place we are at, and for that place, to love him. And of actual flesh, that also comes through, that it is a man, perhaps crying. But he will reason it (logic as popping fingers, a hip chorus with arcane reference) down to what you hear.

Otis Redding will sing "You Don't Miss Your Water," and it is love asked for. Some warm man begging to be with a woman. Or The Temptations' "If It's Love That You're Running From" . . . there's no hiding place . . . But the cry in Shepp's sound is not for a woman, it is a cry, a wail. But not so freed from the object, the specific, as say Trane's.

Content Analysis, total content. Musical, Poetic, Dramatic, Literary, is the analysis in total, which must come, too. But, briefly, the R&B content is usually about this world in a very practical, where we literally are, approach. Spiritual Concern, in big letters, or "Other World" would be corn or maudlin, would not serve, in most R&B, because to the performers it would mean a formal church thing. But this will change, too. Again, "I got money, now all I need is love," and that insistence will demand a clearer vision of a *new* spiritual life.

The Black Man in R&B is the Black Man you can readily see. Maybe Sadder or Happier or Swifter or Slower than the actual, as with all poetry, but that average is still where the real is to be seen. (Even the "process" on the haid is practical in a turned around way, to say, "I'monna get me some hair like that . . . blow stuff." Badge of power, etc. The more literary or bourgeois Black man would never wear his badge (of oppression) so openly. His is more hidden (he thinks). He will tell you about Mozart and Kafka, or he will tell you about Frank Sinatra and James Michener. It works out the same, to the same obstruction to self. And, finally, the conk is easier to get rid of. If you can dig that.

R&B is straight on and from straight back out of traditional Black spirit feeling. It has the feeling of an actual spontaneity and *happiness,* or at least *mastery,* at the time. Even so, as the arrangements get more complicated in a useless sense, or whitened, this spontaneity and mastery is reduced. The R&B presents expression and spontaneity, but can be taken off by the same subjection to whitening influences. A performer like Dionne Warwick (and The Supremes sometimes as well among others) with something of the light quickness of the "Detroit (Motown) Sound," treads a center line with something like grace. The strings and softness of her arrangements, and of many of her songs, are like white torch singers' delight, but her beat (she used to be a gospel singer in New Jersey) and sound take her most times into a warmth undreamed of by the whites. Though as the $$$ come in, and she leans for a "bigger audience," traveling in them circles, too, etc., then she may get even whiter perhaps. It is a social phenomenon and a spiritual-artistic phenomenon as well.

The New Black Music people, by and large, have been exposed to more white influences than the R&B people. Most of the new musicians have had to break through these whiteners to get at the sound and music they play now. That is, there is more "formal" training among the jazz people. Hence a doctrinaire whitening.

It is easier to whiten a Cecil Taylor form than a James Brown form because the Taylor form proposes to take in more influences in the first place. It sets itself up as more inclusive of what the world is. Many times it is. But this is true with any of the new forms. Finally, it depends on the activating energy and vision, where that is, how it can be got to. The new forms are many times the result of contemplation and reflection. Through these and the natural emotional outline of the performer, the new music hopes to arrive at expression and spontaneity. The R&B begins with expression and spontaneity as its ends. Which are the ends of any Black music. Though this is not to say that this is always the result. Much R&B sounds contrived and simple-minded (much of any form, for sure) because that's what is working with the sounds and forms, but what R&B proposes to be about is more readily available to us from where we are, with just what materials the world immediately has given us. The "widening" and extension, the more intellectual, new music people want many times is just funny-time shit, very very boring. That is, it may *just* be about something intellectual. The R&B might just be about something small and contrived, which is the same thing.

But the new music is consciously said to be about the mind and the spirit, as well as the heart. The beauty of an older hence "simpler" form is that it will be about the mind (and the spirit) if it is *really* about the heart. "Money won't change you . . . but time will take you out." Which can be said some other ways, but then get to them.

And Rhythm and Blues music is "new" as well. It is contemporary and has changed, as jazz has remained the changing same. Fresh Life. R&B has gone through evolution, as its singers have, gotten "modern," taken things from jazz, as jazz has taken things from R&B. New R&B takes things from old blues, gospel, white popular music, instrumentation, harmonies (just as these musics have in turn borrowed) and made these diverse elements its own.

But the Black religious roots are still held on to conspicuously in the most moving of the music. That Black emotionalism which came directly out of, and from as far back as, pre-church religious gatherings, the music of which might just be preacher to congregation, in an antiphonal rhythmic chant-poem-moan which is the form of most of the Black group vocal music that followed: Preacher-Congregation/Leader-Chorus. It is the oldest and still most common jazz form as well.

The old collective improvisation that was supposed to come out of New Orleans, with lead trumpet and clarinet weaving and trombone stunting and signifying and rhythm pounding, this form is as old as Black religious gatherings in the forests of the West . . . and connects straight on into Black free-Africa.

But the two Black musics—religious and secular—have always cross-fertilized each other, because the musicians and singers have drifted back and forth between the two categories, with whatever music they finally came to make being largely the result of both influences. During the Depression, a lot of blues people, probably most of whom had once been in the church, "got religion" and went back (as I've said, the church was always looked upon by Black People as a refuge, from the alien white world . . . the less it got to be a refuge, i.e., the more it got integrated, the less hold it had on colored people). That was a whole church era in jazz and blues.

In the 50's during the funk-groove-soul revival, the church music, more specifically, Gospel music, was the strongest and healthiest influence on jazz, and R&B, too. (Grays even opened a nightclub, The Sweet Chariot with robed hostesses to make them bux off another people's ultimate concern. But nightclub, or not, they still managed to take the music off to their own advantage.)

In fact it was the Gospel and soul-funk influence, especially as sung by Ray Charles and played by people like Horace Silver, that "rescued" the music from the icebox of cool jazz, which finally turned out to be a white music for elevators, college students, and TV backgrounds. (The last mentioned have recently got the rhythm and blues tint via Rock'n'Roll or "Pop," i.e., the soft white "cool" forms, versions, of Gospel-derived rhythm and blues music. Which is the way it goes.)

The cool was a whitened degenerative form of bebop. And when mainline America was vaguely hipped, the TV people (wizards of total communication) began to use it to make people buy cigarettes and deodorants . . . or put life into effeminate dicks (uhh, detectives). Then the white boys slid into all the studio gigs, playing "their" music, for sure.

So-called "pop," which is a citified version of Rock'n'Roll (just as the Detroit-Motown Sound is a slick citified version of older R&B-Gospel influenced forms) also sees to it that those TV jobs, indeed that dollar-popularity, remains white. Not only the Beatles, but any group of Myddle-class white boys who need a haircut and male hormones can be a pop group. That's what pop means. Which is exactly what "cool" was, and even clearer, exactly what Dixieland was, complete with funny hats and funny names . . . white boys, in lieu of the initial passion, will always make it about funny hats . . . which be their constant minstrel need, the derogation of the real, come out again.

Stealing Music . . . stealing energy (lives): with their own concerns and lives finally, making it White Music (like influenzaing a shrill rites group). From anyplace, anytime to "We all live in a yellow submarine," with all their fiends, etc., the exclusive white . . . *exclusive* meaning *isolated* from the rest of humanity . . . in the yellow submarine, which shoots nuclear weapons. (Content analysis . . . lyrics of white music show equally their concerns, lives, places, ways, to death.) In the yellow submarine. Chances are it will never come up.

They steals, minstrelizes (but here a minstrelsy that "hippens" with cats like Stones and Beatles saying, "Yeh, I got everything I know from Chuck Berry," is a scream dropping the final . . . "But I got all the dough . . .") named Animals, Zombies, in imitation (minstrel-hip) of a life style as names which go to show just what they think we are . . . Animals, Zombies, or where they finally be, trying to be that, i.e., Animals, Zombies, Beatles or Stones or Sam the Sham for that matter, and not ever Ravens, Orioles, Swallows, Spaniels or the contemporary desired excellence of Supremes, Miracles, Imperials, Impressions, Temptations, etc., . . . get to them names.

Actually, the more intelligent the white, the more the realization he has to steal from niggers. They take from us all the way up the line. Finally, what is the difference between Beatles, Stones, etc., and Minstrelsy. Minstrels never convinced anybody they were Black either.

The more adventurous bohemian white groups sing songs with lyric content into where white bohemian poets moved long ago, as say the so-called psychedelic tunes, which may talk about drugs (LSD, Psylocibin, etc.) experience, and may be also shaped by so-called RagaRock (Indian-influenced) or Folk-Rock (i.e., Rock songs with more socially conscious content). Bob

Dylan, Fugs, Blues Project, Mothers, etc. But in awe of the poetic-psychedelic and LSD, the chemical saviour of grays. They hope to evolve (as the rest of us) "thru chemistry," which sounds like Dupont. The "widening of the consciousness" type action into a higher sense of existent life, and thereafter, maybe stop stealing and killing, etc., etc., etc.

The Black tip for them is a super-live thing as well. To "Get more than we got" kind of thing. The music . . . lyrics, with instructions to "tune in, turn on, drop out" and sound an Electronic Indian Raga . . . as a meditative eclipse of present reality, a yoga saddhu pop. But in play will still drop out of their society like new Beat thing. Out of it! Yeh. But what to do about what ain't out of it. Like there are people dying, etc. Bullshit.

But the content of some anti-Viet anti-Bad stuff is a generalizing in passionate luxurious ego demonstration to be good anyway though they exists as super-feelers of their evil cement head brothers, and as flexible copout, to be anything, finally, anything but what they patently are. That is, Fugs, Freaks, Mothers, Dylan, etc. Yet it still bees white kids playing around. Dylan's "Blowin in the Wind," which is abstract and luxury playing around stuff with him, is immediately transformed when Stevie Wonder sings it because it becomes about something that is actual in the world and is substantiated by the life of the man singing it. That is, with Dylan it seems just an idea. A sentiment. But with Wonder (dig the name! and his life-style and singing is, of course, more emotional, too) you dig that it is life meant. In life.

The "new content" of white pop was protest, and with that "widening consciousness" as opposed to jes' love. But it is just this love that the white pop cannot sing about because it is not only sweet, stupid, maudlin, but now, frankly cannot be believed. Nobody can be made to believe they could love anybody. So the move.

The superficial advance. The liberal cool protest. Viet. Oh. Viet-Rock. Yeh. LBJ ain't no good. Yeh. But what, what? will happen $$$$$$ . . . stealin' all from the niggers and they bees starvin' all the time. While crooks is good and hates war, for dough. (Wins either way!)

But the "protest" is not new. Black people's songs have carried the fire and struggle of their lives since they first opened their mouths in this part of the world. They have always wanted a better day. During the socially-conscious thirties, after the city and the social sophistication of white protest movements was acquired, so-called Folk Music was the most ubiquitous Black or near-Black music in the American mainstream. This is the reason "Folk" has been associated with protest. White people saddled that horse with trade unionism, IWW, Spanish Civil War, in the same way the folk-rockers, etc. do today.

Black religious music has always had an element of protest in it. In the so-called "invisible institution," or pre-church worship of the Black slaves, the songs were about freedom, though most times couched in the metaphorical language of the Bible, substituting Jews, etc. for themselves, to escape massa's understanding.

But with secular music, integration (meaning the harnessing of Black energy for dollars by white folks, in this case in the music bizness) spilled the content open to a generalizing that took the bite of specific protest out. ("You know you cain't sell that to white folks.")

Early blues is full of talk about Black people and their exact up-hill lives. In fact you can tell an early blues tune if the word "Black" is even mentioned. Or "white" for that matter. The slickening money process shaved a lot of exactness in one area. They talk of love, and that is exact, but as a preacher said, "Today we're gonna talk about Love. I was gonna talk about Truth, but I figured I might offend somebody. So today we're gonna talk about Love." If you can dig that.

But the cycle will turn round. The more bohemian white people's desire to be at least in a recognizable world of war and stuff will be passed around to Black people, as legitimate part of the music bizness. (Just as the quickest way to get Black people to dig Africa, wear African clothes etc., is to let B. Altman's sell it, it would seem to white people, then watch all the hippies show up like they are worshipping some Orisha.)

Stevie Wonder with Dylan's "Blowin in the Wind" is a case in point. Now James Brown with his social consciousness of "Don't Be a Dropout." Specific, but civil-servant stuff, nevertheless. The Impressions' "Keep On Pushin" or Martha and The Vandellas' "Dancing in the Street" (expecially re: summer riots, i.e., "Summer's here . . .") provided a core of legitimate social feeling, though mainly metaphorical and allegorical for Black people. But it is my thought that soon, with the same cycle of the general "integrated" music bizness, the R&B songs will be more socially oriented. *(Black and Beautiful,* Jihad Singers. I'm reminded that a few years ago, Ben E. King and a few others . . . *Spanish Harlem,* etc. . . . had made a special placement of social music, but that was largely picked up by grays.)

Note: *Let the new people take care of some practical bi-ness and the R&B take care of some new bi-ness and the unity musick, the people-leap, can begin in earnest.*

Social consciousness in jazz is something again because it is largely a purely instrumental music . . . though there have always been musicians who had been deeply conscious of their exact placement in the social world, or at least there was a kind of race pride or consciousness that animated the musicians and their music (again, here, Ellington is a giant. "Black Beauty," "Black, Brown and Beige," "For My People" and so many many others).

In recent times musicians like Charles Mingus (dig "Fables of Faubus," etc.), Max Roach and some others have been outspoken artists on and off the stage, using their music as eloquent vehicles for a consciousness of self in America. The new musicians have been outspoken about the world through their music and off the stage as well. Archie Shepp has perhaps been the most publicized of the new socially conscious musicians. And some of his music is self-consciously socially responsive, e.g., "Malcolm," but this so-called consciousness is actually just a reflection of what a particular generation is heir to, and their various responses from wherever they (are) find themselves.

Also, of course, the music is finally most musicians' strongest statement re: any placement of themselves socially. And the new music, as I have stated before about Black music, is "radical" within the context of mainstream America. Just as the new music begins by being free. That is, freed of the popular song. Freed of American white cocktail droop, tinkle, etc. The strait jacket of American expression *sans* blackness . . . it wants to be freed of that temper, that scale. That life. It screams. It yearns. It pleads. It breaks out (the best of it). But its practitioners sometimes do not. But then the vibrations of a feeling, of a particular place, a conjunction of world spirit, some of everybody can pick up on. (Even imitate, which is Charlie McCarthy shouting freedom! or white snick workers going back to Jumpoff Manor after giving a few months to "The Problem.") It is an ominous world all right. You can say *spiritual.* You can say *Freedom.* But you do not necessarily have to be either one. If you can dig it. White, is abstract. A theory. A saying. A being . . . the verb . . . the energy itself, is what is beautiful, is what we want, sometimes, are.

Music as the consciousness, the expression of where we are. But then Otis Redding in interviews in *Muhammad Speaks* has said things (or Shakey Jake, for that matter) more "radical," Blacker, than many of the new musicians. James Brown's screams, etc., are more "radical" than most jazz musicians sound, etc. Certainly his sound is "further out" than Ornette's. And that sound has been a part of Black music, even out in them backwoods churches since the year one. It is just that on the white man's instrument it is "new." So, again, it is just life need and interpretation.

Sun-Ra speaks of evolution of the cosmic consciousness; that is future, or as old as *purusa.* Where man will go. "Oh you mean space ships?" Which is like the Zen monk answering the student's question about whether or not dogs have souls . . . i.e., "Well, yes . . . and no."

And the social consciousness displayed in that music. Pharoah Sanders will say OMMMMMMMMMMMMMMMMMMMMMMMMMMMMMMMMMMM MMMMMMMMMMMMMMMMMMMMMMMMMMMMMMMMMMMM MMMMMMMM. Which is more radical than sit-ins. We get to Feel-Ins, Know-Ins, Be-Ins.

But here is a theory stated just before. That what will come will be a *Unity Music.* The Black Music which is jazz and blues, religious and secular. Which is New Thing and Rhythm and Blues. The consciousness of social reevaluation and rise, a social spiritualism. A mystical walk up the street to a new neighborhood where all the risen live. Indian-African anti-Western-Western (as geography) Nigger-sharp Black and strong.

The separations, artificial oppositions in Black Music resolved, are the ditty strong classic. (Ditty bop.) That is, the New Black Music and R&B are the same family looking at different things. Or looking at things differently. The collection of wills is a simple unity like on the street. A bigger music, and muscle, for the move necessary. The swell of a music, of action and reaction, a seeing, thrown in swift slick tone along the entire muscle of a people. The Rhythm and Blues mind blowing evolution of James-Ra and Sun-Brown. That growth to include all the resources, all the rhythms, all the yells and cries, all that information about the world, the Black ommmmmmmmmmmm-mmmmm, opening and entering.

NEWARK—
BEFORE BLACK MEN
CONQUERED
from *Raise Race Rays Rage*

A. The city of Newark is the sun object projected, magnified, actually blown-up, with hard guns smacking through night. Killing niggers up and down the streets. Breaking pictures of Jesus. Humbling a people to Allah.

The first night rumors. In the heat of the broke down city. Nobody could live in Newark without being stretched out through the final circus colors of America & alienated, No, not even in any America, except the real one!

The common terror of Newark is its spooky absence of any advertised American ideal. Except it is exactly what America is. A sham of ugliness. A sham gesture of humanity, except where strong black life exists and lights up the righteousness and danger to righteousness.

Black People in Newark are strong. They only need to *KNOW IT.* And ACT on it!

Black People in Newark are more than 63 percent of the listed resident population. And probably closer to 75 percent of the people who actually *live* in the city *all the time.* Central Newark is totally black except a light fringe of PR [1] which trails off from High cross South Broad swelling again S.E. down Neck.

Clinton Hill, once Jewish now Black. North of Sussex and down across Clifton to Broad once Wop, now Black with the complement of Latin. North Newark and way across pushing to Weequahic Ave. now Black: pressing the few Jews in pork panic their backs against Hillside and the newly American park. (I remember many years ago Dr. Burch was the first family up the slope of Meeker Ave. "The Good Parts." Quiet Weequahic, once Jewheaven now is Route 66 of Black desire. And down on Bergen & Custer, where used to be gefillte fishes for asswipe, bees now Home of The Brave Willie, harder and newer and aimin' to kick *somebody's* ass.

One of our small capitols is near those streets. One of our centers. Fat Nigger Police hang out in some spots, collars open sweating and being corny bigshots of a dying world.

Swift Hawthorne Ave. & Berrrrr-gin??

(They stoned devils on Bergen like they was goin outta style! Mu-tha-

---

[1] 10% of total population.

fuckin JewAss Peedabed cocksucka!!!! BamBam—they tore up a piece of sidewalk to throw at one dude and a beast lady wheeled her car to get off Springfield or some shit and almost turned the short over wheelin straight into the 12Foot Ants.)

Junk City Moved South too, in the good section, there's trees. A remnant of The Jews. Also in that section, Lee Bernstein, "A councilman for all the people," just as Hugh Addonizio is "A Mayor For All The People." Bernstein and Addonizio have Nigger STOOGES run around and grin at folks and promise anything unemotional!

Bernstein and Addonizio got in because Negroes were divided and sold out. As usual. Black People will not be divided! Bernstein because Bill Payne, who was Kennedy image Negro *(was* because hopefully his tv speech on how bayonets were thrust through his window and his knowing, in her last hours, Mrs. Eloise Spellman, mother of 11 children whom devil soldiers blasted through the windows of the jail they had her living in ... might indicate he's trying to get some soul), and Earl Harris,[2] an Adamish mature slickster; a Black Republican, fought each other for the South Ward and Bernstein,[3] who is not even really jew-slick, eased back on in.

Payne and Harris supposedly had agreed before to accept the findings of other Negroes as to which one was better equipped to run ... so the Councilmanic spot would be Black to represent Black. However they did not hold with such agreement and each ran and each lost. All Black People lost, even those couple who showed up grinning on Bernstein's posters saying "Buy White"!

Addonizio ... because the ugly Toms he marshals, beat or promised or harassed Negroes into division and left the one Black mayor candidate, Ken Gibson,[4] off in a full lurch that neither Dick Gregory nor Martin Luther King could overcome.

The Mayor-Councilmanic election in 1966 was fantasy on the real side. George Richardson's headquarters are broken into and stuff thrown all over. Independent Black Mayoral candidate Kenneth Gibson's posters and flyers were ripped down or painted black. And Italian Rat Drawings of Gibson began to appear up and down the avenues. (After the rebellion Irish Carey, County Chairman ... the unwholesome Spencer Tracy of our lives ... has named Richardson to run on the Reg. Dem Ticket, in a futile coolout motion,

[2] Now Councilman-at-large, 1970.

[3] Recalled in 1969 by Richardson backed Rev. Horace Sharper, who then lost in 1970 to Community Choice candidate for south ward councilman, Sharpe James.

[4] Became mayor, running as "The Community's Choice" in June 16, run-off election, 1970.

not wanting Richardson's [5] Freedom Ticket to remount. And if it doesn't remount it never existed anyway!)

Away from and deep in America, men threaten black candidates and the Italian candidate a Mayor for all the people is making sure that all the people that do not understand that he is for all the people will understand one way or another. (The Italians understand that Addonizio is for all the people. The Jews know that Bernstein is for all the people . . . even in his vicious attacks on the local anti-poverty agency . . . demanding that it be controlled by city officials . . . all of whom have a direct connection with poverty . . . *Enforcing It!*) Only the honest Black candidates are not for all the people . . . they are just for most of the people.

Councilman Frank Addonizio, the Mayor's cousin, is for all the people too. He said in a recent meeting where there were mostly Black People (like the city itself) and Negroes in the audience, that he "could stack the audience too." I guess he meant like he and his brother have stacked most of the city hall jobs with Italians. Tho in a straight out breakdown as to who could stack what, in an open call, it seems mathematically incorrect to figure he could stack such meetings of *Newarkers* with more Italians, since most of them do not live in Newark anymore. Especially the ones with the goodes' jobs! But for sure he could stack it with police and mafiosi.

The Addonizios, along with Police Director, Dominick Spina (and their more soft spoken paisan Malafronte . . . he a weak gesture in the direction of rationalism . . .) run Newark with an iron foot. (Plus the gangsters.) Their Irish step-brothers they have booted upstairs to County bizness. But Nwk stuff is strictly Italian owned and operated.

In the old days hard feelings between Black and Italian could always lead to minor brushfire war. On any corner near the North ward. In 1947 a Black cat named Hailey, in my 8th grade class, was shot down by two Ginnies for winning too many foot races. There was a race riot following that incident that lasted, in a series of violent happenings, more than a week. (One of the first cops to whip my head during '67 rebellion was an Italian I knew from Barringer, where Italian language was part of the curriculum, Detective Jerry Mellillo.)

And the Italians got Newark the way it's shown in the Spencer Tracy picture that the Irish got Boston, by taking it. Newark's owners understand force and power. Any other approach they think of as weakness.

Carrying Addonizio's slop bucket and giving out free samples to Black folks are quite a few handkerchief heads . . . but the undisputed leaders are

[5] Richardson was paid divider in 1970 Community Choice Campaign. He got only 2000 votes in an ignominious defeat.

Councilman Calvin West,[6] who was elected Councilman-at-large, riding in on Addonizio's tail, and his sister, Larrie Stalks, the real nigger-o representative in the Addonizio machine. She is known in some circles as Madame Nhu.

Mrs. Stalks is a belly punchin Tomette Addonizio follower for the last 15 years. She began as his secretary when he was in congress and has risen to undisputed Chief Nigger slop ladeler for the regime. She now carries the title "Director of Health & Welfare." [7] She once used to shine shoes on Broad Street when she was a little boy, and has shined her way clear to the top of the boots!

Mrs. Stalks is the "man" behind Mr. West, and actually makes most of his decisions for him. Mr. West campaigned in Newark also "for all the people," advocating a new sports stadium and public first aid stations. He made no real appeal to the Black community and was the only nigger-o candidate to get any appreciable amount of white votes.

(During the rebellion Mrs. Stalks and Mr. West were out of town at an NAACP convention.)

The other Negro councilman is old line shuffler Irvine Turner.[8] But shuffling Irvine was not always shuffling Irvine. Anyway, not so completely so. The Honorable Irvine Turner, the first Negro Councilman in Newark, back in 1954. Mr. Turner's breakthrough into American politics was made possible by getting into political shape the Black Central Ward and establishing a leadership category for Black People going for the Democratic party tip. Some of Turner's lieutenants and associates like Arthur Love, John Hicks, &c., in the mostly gangster oriented Central Ward, were far more hoodish in their heyday than they are in the now world, but they still like to go for bad! But Italians always maintained control over the pay-offs and the safer higher paying crime. As they do today, on a nationwide level.

Now Irvine, who once seemed outspoken, is screamed on regularly as a Tom. Though he is a sick man in reality, probably from the scummy air in Nwk City Hall, who just barely knows where or who he is from day to day. Where once he offered some actual inspiration to Black People in Newark, now he represents the impotence and incompetence of one traditional area of Negro leadership. An area of Negro leadership that once could boast that it represented Black People.

Now Turner trails in the Addonizio jetstream by default with pictures shaking hands with NoNeck and LBJ. "Re-elect Dedicated Public Servant # 12 Years of Service # First One Of His Race In America To Serve As Secretary To Congressman Addonizio." That sounds like shit now.

[6] Defeated in 1970, and indicted w/ Addonizio and other members of that council for extortion.

[7] Replaced in 1970.

[8] Defeated in 1970 by Community's Choice candidate, Dennis Westbrooks.

The situation in a city of Black majority 1967 without a single Black Captain on the police force. (Whoops! They just made one!) The second largest insurance center in America . . . the bus carries its workers into the city and takes them and the bus back home to the suburbs. The merchandise sold in Newark has grown shoddier and shoddier, as the greys rushed to the suburbs. And the Springfield Ave. that just got busted was only a shadow of its former self. As Addonizio said after the rebellion, "The city is bankrupt." And now it is paying $800,000 to the police for beating and shooting Black heads, overtime. And of course, the majority of Newark's taxpayers (the most heavily taxed city in New Jersey) are Black. So then Black taxpayers are paying to get their homes shot up! Overtime!

Newark is a ghastly looking place all the time. Even before the out and out shooting war. (In fact it has never seemed as beautiful as it did those nights fire was eating up the sky.) It hangs broken in half with a ghost town—downtown in the center—and just above this ghost town the Central Ward: where Southern Black People fall off greyhounds everyday "too scared to go to Harlem."

Parts of the Ward look just like a rural southern town. People sit out in the street and eat and talk and drink and laugh. And everybody knows everybody from block to block.

Downtown is a ghost town after 5 because the Crackers live off somewhere WestOrange-SouthOrange-Teaneck-Montclair-Bloomfield-Maplewood, &c. &c. &c., a hundred suburbs dripping with money taken out of Newark. And the downtown's for white people in daylight, long gone by fingerpoppin night. There's almost nothing downtown for Black People. (But there'll be property and spots for the asking after the next phase of the rebellion.)

There is a clearer feeling in Newark, than any other city I have ever been in, of Colonialism. Newark is *a colony.* A bankrupt ugly colony, in the classic term, where white people make their money to take away with them. The city is kept up only as far as its money-making capacity, say for Prudential Life Insurance, &c.&c.,&c.

The school system is almost non-existent. Schools are horribly over-crowded, and 80-some percent of the school enrollment is black. And the schools are old and falling. They were old and falling 20 years ago when I passed through. (The coming school year even grammar school classes will start to double up in the so-called team system, though no Newark teachers have been instructed in that system. And they are trying to get the kids at Peshine Ave. school to go to school from 2 in the afternoon until 8:00 PM at night. Also, now 92 white teachers are resigning from Newark School system immediately and there's a "threat" that some 400 more are considering it. Boss! I say. Let us get our own! There are no Black principals.[9] There are

[9] Since rebellion some have been named.

only 2 (Whoops! 3) on The Board of Education, out of eleven, including one Italian who wanted teachers going to a Negro History seminar in Washington, D.C., docked.

Italian Barringer has a new building and one night had a 10 person lobby at the Bd of Ed meeting demanding a parking lot and a pool . . . when most schools in Newark dont even have enough classrooms. SouthSide High, whose Black enrollment is conservatively estimated at 99 percent, not only is falling down but there is talk that it is in danger of losing its accreditation. Central High, about 90 percent Black, is in the same state, falling down even worse. The other high schools and grammar schools with high Black enrollment all look like death traps and are as old as the devil. Only Weequahic (which was once as Jewish as any *schul)* and Barringer, to a certain extent, have any learning school atmosphere. And even in those two schools uneasiness circulates the student blood as the Blood population increases. (Weequahic's all American basketball team is All Black.) And there have been fireworks not only between students but between teachers and students as they grapple with the dying culture.

Our children in most of these so-called schools are not being taught anything. And when they are taught something it is usually to hate themselves. (A teacher sends a pupil home to me from Central, "Catholics is the best religion and Stokely Carmichael, Adam Powell, and 'Cassius Clay' ain't no good!") The Jesuitical malice crowding down the larger streets and twisting and turning . . . till wait! Look!

There is St. Benedicts, almost all out-of-town Irish-Italian-Catholic. They have a new theater which plays stuff like *Oklahoma!, Hello, Dolly, Li'l Abner,* at the edge of the ghetto for same Irish-Italian audience. Except they did do *A Raisin in the Sun* after two months of 8 hour daily rehearsals, for an audience of nigger-o's in tuxedos and NoNeck and his boys, for $7.00 a haid. Lovely!

But Our Lady Queen of Angles on the Belmont Hill does a thriving bizness on Black folks with the same energetic inscrutability. They will soon be building, it's sd, a Center for the Performing Arts, with Fed money! And they work hard at what they do in the Black community because most of the big nigger-o churches are personal glory holes with suitable and appropriate psycho-dramas. (Some of the preachers slid around during the war with little "Cool It" signs made up for them personally by "God.")

The nigger-o churches have worked for nothing in the Black community, with a few exceptions,[10] but collections and Cadillacs. One beautiful exception is Rev. Sharper of Abyssinia Church who has always lent himself to the Black spirit of change.

---

[10] *Among the growing list of exceptions are Rev. Cade, Central Presbyterian; Rev. Thomas, New Hope; Rev. Seward, Mt. Zion; Rev. Grant; Rev. Stephens.*

The nigger-o ministers are, as usual, the worst Toms on the planet.[11] Like my man Rev. Benjamin Franklin Johnson (really!) who arose at the first Medical School hearing to say, "I wouldn't want to live in any all-colored city." I guess he couldn't anyway with the grey faggot he got hanging on the wall over he haid! Also he is about to front a Kislak Co-op "for the people" at the Med School site. It's a hundred and something rent . . . as B.F. Johnson said, "I'm not just talking . . . I'm doing something." It is the B.F. Johnsons who will burn with the rest of the dead wood, when this ol' city catchafire again!

NEGRO REMOVAL

Get to the tone of this place, this Black colony. Where liquor stores close at 10, and they cant even sell beer on Sunday. Except the Brothers bootleg, and even on Sunday Official Jew sits open since before I was born selling poison wine to the slaves, with detectives and uniformed cops leaning on the boxes.

You can pay off anything in Newark, so completely rotten and graft-ridden is the place. It is a graft-oriented city. A city of deals and kickbacks, and low low shit.

The Central Ward is old and beat up and junkie-ridden . . . and where they've torn the old buildings down they've erected 13-story jails named after people the residents dont know. Tall dull red cells, really small towns in themselves where the struggle is being plotted in earnest.

Hayes Homes, one of the oldest of these projects, was a central target for the cops during the war. They shot thousands of rounds into those ugly buildings. And at this very moment workmen are scrambling around trying to clean up the evidence of such cold beastthink. People talk about crawling around the floor all night as the brave police and guardsmen shot and shot into the buildings. Many families crawled out into the halls to escape the shattering glass and murderous lead barrage. The woman, Mrs. Spellman, was killed looking out of her window in Hayes Homes. Several days after the rebellion had been declared officially over, they were still finding dead bodies in Hayes, one of which was already starting to stink!

The Central Ward is Project City. At one point as you stand on West Kinney Street all you can see in any direction are those long red jails, on all sides, full of dangerous black people.

First to be herded into these cold tombs and then to be sprayed with the lethality of barbarianism. But why all these tombs, all these memorials to the sterility and failure of the white mind, and the slavery of the Black.

The plan is to get us all together. In one place, where 50 rolls of barbed wire could solve all the social dilemmas these owners think are crucial. Who don't go in the projects must go somewhere. (The hypothesis.) They hope out

[11] Again, since 1967, many exceptions in the growing black consciousness.

of town. But again crazy-ass greys assuming we are they. We will simply turn the South Ward into a Central Ward. The North, East and WestWards too. When the next fire comes we will walk these streets with complete impunity, and move in the empty stores.

But Negro Removal is the name of the game in Newark. *By any means* necessary. They say the death toll, 26, is phony. Where cops hang out the figure is put in the 40's, the upper 40's. Rumors of hidden dead laying now till they can be eased out, in Newark Morgue, and flying around the black city.

Memories (and photographs) of James Rutledge, 19, with 39 bullet holes in his split open corpse is the early sleep image in a lot of Black People's minds. The constant idiot roar of the scared police guns. Popping and popping are still clogging Black People's ears. The pure white terrible evil jesuitical pall of murder is remembered darting above all our heads. And the blood. The shot off faces and breasts. The screams. The beatings. In this blood inquisition, we finally confess to you butcher priests that we are Heretics. Yes, we are Black and We Will be free!

Negro Removal, by any means necessary. First the Medical School is fresh in our minds. The edging in, the final victory of money and malice over people is still on the boards. The Lies. A mouth where his neck wd be, like a pouting weasel, embarrassed by his naked head. Greasy Liar. Says: I am for all the people.

The Medical School "controversy" set bloods boiling. It was the light action preceding the actual knuckle drill.

The Medical School controversy as it's called in white newspapers is just more Negro Removal but on the (quasi) legal side. 155 acres they say they need for the med school. I doubt that there is a Med School on the planet that needs 155 acres! Some 23,000 Black folks wd have to split behind this stuff too. To somewhere! Public Housing Director Danzing insists there are places for all these "Negroes" to move. Even he knows better. There is a waiting list to get into Public Housing. And no matter what they talked about "turnover," there is still a waiting list. Now.

Also many Black People, myself included, see this Med School thing as a practical political move, a political act, aimed at cutting through the potential strength of the Ward, killing off the growing Black Power!

Black Power Black Power Black Power Black Power Black Power! Dig It? It *Will* prevail!

Running the Black People out of town, Plus 3 highways also scheduled to come through. The 16th District has already been leveled and soon on up West Market Street including a hundred year old baptist church, with a framed bronze plaque to my Godfather in the lobby. No Roman Catholic churches will be leveled. That God dont have to leave for the highway, the med school or nothing the fuck else!

But Black People need a Community College, a free Community College so that our children can get into the first part of so-called higher education. Black children by and large will not be in any Med School in Newark, though they will have to move out of the way for those white people that will. And that is pure ugly bullshit, and everybody knows it. (They are building a community college in Bloomfield, a distant extension of Naples.)

There have been meetin's and scream-ins so-called blight hearings all "to determine whether or not the Medical School shd be put in the place designated." Certainly the Greys have already decided where the Med School is to go (they told us!) and that it needs 155 acres (even tho HUD agency says they only asked for 46). And that these Black People have to get out, any way they can. Most of the property is being "roughed off" in condemnation proceedings, which is out and out fraud. The area has not ever been officially designated a "Blighted Area."

A cold subfreezing wind blows between the Black and white. Cave echoes. Arms in stroboscopic detail coming down on heads. All in between. Do you understand what slavery is? What the things that enslave must be?? And we are told to talk to them. (We have.) Rationally. To! God! Love them! This criminal blowing frozen shit blocks any direct connection. We are separate and we have always been/separate. They ask if we are separatists. If we want a separate state. We have always been separate here. And wherever we were. Separate from them. You ever hear of a ghetto? That's separate. A separate state.

But now we understand. A lot of us. That separate is cool, is Right, is NATURAL. What we want is the power to control that separate state. To control its politics and its economics. The absolute power over *OUR* lives. *OUR* lives. Get it? *Our Lives.* Over our children's lives and education. Our employment. All the things that describe and circumscribe men. We want to control. We want to be ourselves . . . and benefit by it. Can you dig that? *And Benefit By It!* All Praises Due To The Black Man!

To control it. To keep the money in our communities to own and operate the businesses. To own and operate the politicians, for our own benefit . . . not the dazzling madness of self hatred double think "Massa, I'se here killin' off my own folks agin" type Calvin West–Larrie Stalks style to Roy Wilkins . . . To Control all Sayers for and of Black.

What the "Med School Controversy" represents (and it is still there, to be talked about already decided decisions) is the attempted political murder of Black Power in Newark. This district they want to raze has a good percentage of the registered Black voters and Black businesses. Nomads cannot register. NoNeck wants in by remote control in '70 through the sambo puppet, West. Addonizio himself has visions of a beatified ascension through garlicky golden clouds to GOVERNOR. (He wont make it He dont have enough style . . . even for devils.)

We say control. And there is another so-called "controversy" giggling up

blood like a gagging cave-ite drenching our Black consciousness. Hate Hate
... hot faced and speechless! The simple striking arm. What can the Black
Man Say? But Fuck You man! Fuck you all! But the strong move will be
when all of us say that together, like all of us say fuck you! Then comes
control. Black control.

The Callahan affair was the other "controversy." A certain Mr. Callahan[12]
was supposed to get a good job as Secretary to The Board Of Education. It
seems that there was also a Negro named Parker who alot of folks thought
should've got the job. A lot of Black folks. NoNeck had a political commit-
ment to give Callahan the job . . . plus an emotional one. Callahan had a high
school education . . . Parker, the spook, degrees' mama-plus 87 percent school
enrollment-Black-minority representation on Bd. of Ed. &c., &c.. Verdict:
Callahan. Addonizio said For all the people I choose Callahan! And the
Black people made polite protest then more fittingly impolite protest, Even
some wd be Toms shouted at NoNeck his thing was so ugly.

Rumors. Each weekend night there's talk of beatings. If you ever been up
against the cops (or even seen them in action) in Newark you know why the
rumors. Cops are very heavy handed South type; the colored ones too like to
swing, but not in killer madness like Sinatra and O'Brien's brothers who will
tell you straight off they'd like to kill you (if you Black). These police are w/o
sophistication and cowardly. Very frightened of Black people . . . their only
impulse is to go for their piece whether traffic violation or loud party. The
picture in *Life* magazine of the calm dispatch w/which the cop put a bullet in
the young man's back, wounding a child, and while both lay bleeding he
began to put some more shells in his pump gun.[13] White Cop Black Death
Syndrome!

The fear again is responsible for most of the killing and beating. Their fear
and their hatred. Because let no one forget that white people hate us much
more than we hate them. And they started the hating business, brother. They
took you from your home to make money off your ass. The hatred of the
Black Man, like Rap sd about violence, is 'Merican as Lady Bird's
hideousness.

The hatred and murder of the Black man is old shit in 'Merica. Do not
forget that. None of this stuff is new. We have been beat and killed before,
but we are still here and stronger than we was.

The cab driver Smith could be a focus. But what spark is needed? Like they
want Rap's ass or Stokely for inciting. But if the sparks from clicking your
teeth together make flame . . . you around some combustible shit.

12 Indicted w/ Addonizio, 1970.

13 A poster of this incident was used for Voter Registration in 1969–70 campaign.
Addonizio screamed!

Did we make this concoction of Hate leaning to explode? If we are men . . .
dog . . . if we are only live even yr physics sez react. ▲ . The Symbol ▲ .
Explode.

You try to talk to a Newark Policeman. He says WHATTA YOU WANT?
SHUT UP?? GET OUTTA HERE! These are the first words in the policeman's handbook: WHAT? WHATTA YOU A WISE GUY? Dumb bastards.
People were lined up on 17th Ave between Hayes Homes and the precinct.
Core's Curvin was out there as pickets marched and policemen made their
cracks. Crowd had walked there from round the Ward; trying to dig what was
happening. The day after stones and cries and bottles and wishes bashed
against the precinct. John Smith, a cab driver, had been beaten. "Man they
beat his ass . . . but he took a couple them crackers out . . . ," the word, out,
traveling. And people showed up that night, to see. To confront the devil in
one lair, the 4th precinct, where they lay in blue scheming broke black ass for
promotions. Spina showed his "restraint," in such an "isolated" issue. Too
many eyes right there nailed to the spot. So the cops just stared. They wdn't
do nothing anyway, not with no bunch of black people pinning them. They
heart and balls are those city issue pieces. No more, no less. Six shotsa "soul,"
an Italian rock group called *Bloody Teeth and The Slobberers.* But now
everybody was trying to dig what was happening, some to make something
happen. The ways and means. All collect to stare into Allah's sun, but not of
the same breed, their separate vision. The eyes. And shit broke out night
flying shit in the air, and the police with their shit. A heavy violence struggled.
So the cops just stand. But get them off by themselves man and these cats will
stretch out on you . . . will stretch you out. "Yeh, they'll kill yo ass dead."
The heat sent along the blood. Bloods sent along the streets all that night.
By morning blood and violence hung in the air walked the air in Newark
thick heavy you thought it was mus-keetas or invisible rain. Crowd was there
in the afternoon, on the spot, where last night rocks and tempers flew, to
begin the long drama. By afternoon the crowd made it hard for three or four
cars to go up Belmont Ave. People moved in South and Central Wards,
shopping out like it was Saturday (this was Thursday afternoon.) Something
was speeding but blocked. A stopped motion!
By time the light began to leave the sky. Something was wiggling loose.
And rumors. Talk. On those porches people were standing not sitting. A soft
summer dancing tension. People a little stiff or moving, now the young boys
walking fast, stopping with little pinched Charlie Chan hats. By early evening
and the sirens had started and words tripped back and forth cross town. *Yeh
they breaking out windows!*
Suddenly in a half hour or so the sirens were at full up screeching pitch.
With a darkness, people were running across Howard Street and Springfield
Ave. From Howard up had turned into circus time.

In another few minutes what was tied was raging in the streets. At the top voice full out! A roadblock at one corner. People turning corners or beginning to pull up on porches or back in the shadowy homes. Something going down.

Fires. At Spruce. It licked moon base dancing a shoe store away. Shoes goin every which way. Black track cross and wild moves. I mean. Shoes. Clothes. It was out now, all. Except the spectre to come. But before the blood, fire and crazy spooks raged and raged. Windows, one bunch just wanted to tear out glass. They'd run at it and smash it out, and keep gettin up. Then the takers wd leap through. And all that stuff they seen on television wd come out too. Hip lamps super trash chairs. Cameras. Scotch was the preference my man scotch . . . the best. Wine is madness survival and it stayed put. Except Harvey by the case. What you see in the movies these cool white folks got.

When the mad red eye turned on near you everybody swept away. Crack crack. Devil waving death. Crack. Bicycles. Weird lamps. Tooth paste. All gettin' up. All the windows in Foodtown tore out. Folks jumping through. Them carts, sometimes, sailing full of stuff. People shopping. All kinds hip bargains. Fire sale! No sale, at all.

If you could feel that. Smoke and flame in the wind. If you could see that, in it, the coming attractions of the actual fall of devildom! Alhomdulillah!

The wounded Blacks . . . from falls or bullets or flying paddy wagons lay on the ground, except when some Black people in cars moved to pick them up . . . but still they had to go to the Devil's hospitals, and gunshot wounded were arrested on the spot. In the hospital by midnight lines and stacks of Black people. Women bayoneted, shot in the breast clothes torn off screaming and crying in the halls. "You a poet?" a small semitic eyeglassed nose, "Itll be along time before you write anymore poetry." A thing like a smile slithered through the vomit wheels and humanoid engines. This was a "doctor" speaking, in The City Hospital.

4 dead that night. 10 killed the next. As the blood, the spectre crouched in even the shiny America, opened the wops' noses and their state police brothers. They began killing, when the word was given. Shotguns spitting like the live dicks of their fantasies. They walked down the center of the streets shooting. For every so-called sniper's bullet, the police issued 1000 rounds. In all directions. Yet where were the snipers?? Have any been captured?? Can anyone prove such a thing as a Black sniper exists?? Most of the sniper stories were started by devils to legitimize their murdering. But it was not snipers who were killed, but any (black) body. Where there was the actual danger of someone having something to shoot back at police, &c. they hit the ground like they wanted to go through it.

Saturday night some Brothers shot into the jail. Shot out the round bulb lights in front of the jail. Crackers thought it came from a factory roof cross from the jail. Suddenly all the devil music playing on the radio (Joni James or one of them no singin' bitches) was turned up full blast on the radio, the lights all over the jail are turned out. The brothers pop pop pop. Dudes hitting the concrete floor, the pavement, and it was a full five minutes before any of the national guard and police and stuff returned the fire. By that time they were shooting at the night. A great swell of happy Black noise rocks the jail and the guards shrink into the shadows quiet and breathing heavy. They ease down the stairs to the center, and huddle down there, getting their pieces checked out.

For this fear, this centuries of fear and hatred, bodies are on roofs, to be gotten down silently at night, in vans, to the morgue, disposed of however, the grim ugly faces of the beasts that must do this, and want this for you, and your children. Shooting small boys carrying garbage, shooting someone 39 times, 5 in the top of the skull. Bayoneting young women, flinging women and babies against walls. (We saw this from the jail, on the Wilsey Street side, a car pulled slowly around Warren Street coming up New Street, very slowly, in the direction of the jail. This was Saturday afternoon. The Guards flopped down on their stomachs immediately there were no words exchanged, in broad daylight, they began shooting raking the car over. The brother inside, stopped and tried to back up to pull back around the corner . . . the guard kept shooting. Inside the car two Black couples and a child. When the car stopped the door pushed open, and one of the women came out clutching her breast crumpling to the ground blood all over the front of her. The other woman with a child, one punk threw against the wall. Later that same goddam night some nigger guard tries to run the tale of a Sniper getting the woman, when half the goddam jail was looking right down at what happened. "We should do that to one of their goddam devil bitches. See how they like that. Shoot one of them pale bitches through her fuckin titty then see how these Crackers could dig that," a brother said, shouting through the bars at everybody.) To say what. Ask for what. From whom. For what. Are you madness trickling out of an ear?

Why Brother Malcolm said we must seek to internationalize our situation. Why we must go to the United Nations and charge genocide and call for intervention by the world body. It is stupid to seek justice from the unjust, from the murderer. As long as we are contained in the lie of a "domestic issue" we will be dealt with by these crackers in ways that they see fit. Tanks rolling up our streets to preserve white rule, white economic exploitation, to keep the money flowing out of our cities, our cities where our children cannot even spell their own names, our cities with torn-down shacks full of vermin and disease, these cities that we now must take control of, in order to live. These tanks rolling, and these mad gunmen from the suburbs here to maintain white rule in yet another of their colonies. And they can sit in those shadowy suburbs and justify the roaches, and rats, the 13-story projects, the unemployment, the huge proportion of Black soldiers in Viet-Nam, Slavery, the misery of the rest of the world's peoples, then send actual murderers to maintain their diseased hold on the world.

There is no connection between us and them. Not in anyone's minds but the paid for and the cruelly misdirected. It was never about law and order in Newark. But about Force. It was never about Right in Newark, but about Power. Power legitimizes anything ... even degenerates and beasts. White people murdered Black People in Newark. They are readying to do it again. They murdered in the name of White Needs. The primal energy drive of their "lives." Just as they have been tearing down our houses and keeping our children in dumps they call schools, because of White Needs. If they did not need these things they would not exist. In those "calm" suburbs no feeling exists for human life, only the artificially inseminated beep of white destiny as it passes out to us with Dick Van Dyke and Andy Williams. Some of our children were killed to make the world safe for the Flintstones and Johnny Carson.

In the nightmare of our lives as slaves for white people, where an evil cracker named Lyndon Johnson is supposed to mean something to us, other than Enemy, and fat Italians who tell us they want to kill us or cut off our joints so they can sleep in peace, are characterized by other enemies as our Guardians and fellow countrymen, it is the part of the nightmare where the exit looms sudden large and necessary. We must get out of this definition the white man has us believing of ourselves as "Americans." We have never been anything but the chattel of so-called free men. As long as we are "Americans" we will be the chattel of free men. As long as we seek domestic solutions to our "problems" with white power we will be dealt with as the chattel of free men. In order to be free we must first be absolutely separate from this society. These cities: Newark, Gary, Washington, Detroit, Richmond, Harlem, Oakland, East St. Louis, Bedford-Stuyvesant, &c. any large concentration of Black People ... these cities are in reality city-states, leaderless most times, almost always disunified, but these are our kingdoms, and this is where we first must rule.

This is the only way we can provide decent education for our children, decent homes for our families, a livelihood for ourselves. We are the promise of humanity here in the Western world. But we cannot live in peace or harmony or with intelligent disposition of our energies while we are slaves. Why should we be a part of a society in which we are slaves? Does it make sense? The cities must be Black ruled or they will not be ruled at all! These colonies spread around the globe are responsible for the luxury of the devils and they are spread around this country for the same reason. The only way we will keep wealth and health in our communities is to build businesses and industries of our own. The white man kills competition. We do not want to be with him. We want to be together. We want to have lives which we can enjoy, in our own Black way. We have our music. We have our art. We have our athletes. We have our religions. We have our Black science, older than any on the planet. We have our beautiful people able to do anything and make anything and bring anything into being. We are happy even while enslaved by vicious animals. *In the fact of feeling is the testing of the soul and the future evolution of men.* We will make cities, even cities like Newark, beautiful thrones of man and testaments to the ecstatic vision of the soulful. The white man is not cultured. He knows neither James Brown nor John Coltrane. In the halls of his government when John Coltrane died there was no memorial. They have never even heard of him. How can they judge us? *They do not even understand HOW we feel!*

The stories the rumors the facts of death and murder are everywhere. We know what happened, just as we have always known. We have told white people before what was happening, i.e., that we were suffering, &c. From the very first fucking second of our "relationship." After 300 years my man you think there's anything happening?? No happenins. What will evolve is the future, as usual. The Black Man will be free. That is written in all the holy books.

In Newark, after the five days. A weak stone against the temple too briefly. Boarded up windows all up Springfield, 14th, 15th avenues. Complete wipe out of the cheap kikey biznesses of Prince and Spruce, &c. Merchants want protection. Addonizio leans against the window looking out at "his city," wondering what it is he can give us to kill us. We will make a sacrifice of his body to Shango.

Core has mounted a recall drive of Addonizio. With 25 percent of the registered voters signing a petition NoNeck could be put out right now way before 1970. If it works it will be the start. Somehow, as if it were Portuguese Guinea, where the brothers are digging out, setting the necessary fires, they are already building schools and homes. (Yes it is all over the planet this move to free ourselves! We Colored People Will Be Free!) This must be our way too. Together. Even while we fight. However we must fight.

Unless we Black People can come into peaceful power, and begin the benevolent rule of the just, the next phase of armed rebellion will burn Newark to the ground. This time City Hall and the rest of the GrecoRoman bullshit goes down too, including the last of these GrecoRomans themselves. Yet even so we will inherit this city and rebuild it, once the Jews and Italians and Irish have fled. We will rebuild and turn the city into a Black heart beat.

The elections would be beginning, but we cannot trust elections. We must trust to the building of strong Black forces. The Italians will have and have always, just as the Irish before them, messed with the election machines (and these chumps got the nerve to send people to Viet Nam to check out those phonyass elections!).

But we must move to take over the cities, elections or not. Since we realize the elections will be just a reflection of who beast is, when beast is running them. Again, we must never be tricked into acting in tune with our slave status as a domestic part of the U.S. We are foreigners, aliens, sons and daughters of slaves, people taken forcibly from other lands. Now we wish to establish our new land just where we are, in these cities or on that southern dirt. Nothing can stop us from doing this. By getting in the way, the Americans will merely hasten the destruction of their own bullshit.

1967

I

from *Six Persons*

I, You, He
They, You, We

Who can speak of their birth? Years later someone can testify as to its alleged meaning, heaping on years of subsequent rhythms, edging it toward whatever ideal has come to please them. I am not who was born, nor even less who was thought up. We are all projections of some one, some great being-ing, some be-ing, a verbal process ongoing even today the window presses its sunny-rainy presence, young bloods laugh fight hug day to them. On-going. Be-ing. So I, is a process, a be-ing. Flash back to the beginning, you are adrift in speed faster than light.

I thought sometimes I was here as Jesus to stunt and be crucified. I thought on Dey Street all these people here know I'm Jesus, and they just makin believe they dont. Blankin on divinity like that. And I'd try to whip around and catch them staring. Almost caught 'em that time. Mattie McClean I definitely suspected of digging the actual and not wanting to give it away. Lorraine, some others. I wasn't sure the Davis family knew it. But some people on that street, and environs, I was sure knew, and were just being creepy about it.

Was this the way it went down. Jesus in Newark on Dey Street trying to figure out why no one wd just come right out with it. But that's absolutely weird now. It aint really, but it is to everybody hearing it I guess. The sickness I was weighted with, if it was, and it was, and is. The Jesus Nigger, I guess because I knew no one else had all the shit that was going thru my head and feelings going thru theirs. But that must be simple abstracting of the world. Simple capitalism. Imperialism. The greed of the "I," so removed, totally, from every other be-ing that its process allegedly goes on singularly, unre-latedly, totally in isolation, great Horse Testicles! Its golden legend reaching, its beam a fold of sun around the devil's haid. He on a calendar, cool, and detached. I dug them flicks of Jesus on the calendar. Like Ron O'Neal in *Superfly*. The hairdo, but he was less hysterical than sfly, never imaged as pushing cocaine, had his own thing he pushed. Marx defined it as dope tho? Why I wanna been J.C.? The schizophrenia of the African slave then a yng colored boy in new-erk, bashed by weird stuff.

I thought later about expiring in the electric chair for some reason. That was *Gangbusters* saturday nights that produced that. Strapped in a chair with hoofbeats mashin up the hall. Somehow that whole projection left me unsettled. I thought it cd get me, even being Jesus. God-Devil that came on sundays, and the Jesus thing too. Warden Swartzkopf, black head, was the keeper of the gangbusters, and he sounded like he could get to me.

I wanted to be everything I ever thought of. At 12 years old, I remember that if I'd been born in 1933 I'd have been 13. That was on Dey Street near Sussex Avenue. Near Joyce's fence, and Mattie's house. But all of this is simply to introduce the I. The basis of struggle and weight of absolute craziness. (Not madness, but craziness. Like it just wasn't anything real to me. Nothing. Everything was a figment of my imagination. I created it. Thought it up. It wasn't real. And since then my straight and difficult task has been to convince myself that I am actually in the world, and not vice versa.)

But if I wanted to make a strict chronicle of I. And not be rent and twisted by the weighted flashes booming in, the cackles and silences. The simple shut doors and screams inside my head. It wd be difficult. To make such a straightforward document of my life. Because in fact sometimes I yet cannot face understanding that my life has been a roll of minutes. A series of absolutely connected images, being born and passing almost at the same time. I think my life an incredible maze and blotch of shadows, circuses, dives, and floats. Much sadness. Much happiness. Mostly expectation and desire. And yet it is all here in me to be rerevealed reunderstood.

1934 OCTOBER KINNEY MEMORIAL HOSPITAL

I dont know what happened. Thats not real, just reported to me. Kindergarten in the wind. Kindergarten at central, a room, with children whispering in their hands, coats on a table.

Later I got sick and went to the hospital and learned to read. While with measles and chicken pox and whooping cough which I went to straighten out first, the others came. Kissing a little girl at night in the next crib, we padded out the crib and exchanged diseases. So Ho hospital. When I got back from kissing Meta in the isolation hospital I knew how to read. It was experience that did it. The diseases, the isolation, the little ol girl and me in the nighttime in the hars-pital. And then Target comics, and the Targeteers. That was easy then, coming beneath such heavy experimentation with life. Yeh. Alone in the hospital, miles and miles away, that void of warmth was filled with words. And Meta(?) at night, the necessary Black adventure. All real and unreal. But existent in me, an everywhere song covering my breath and be-ing. Rising laughter at a tide of happiness, hope, blue feeling. I knew how to read good when I got back, in kindergarten ... kinny garden ... targeteers, in the little chairs. It be cold as what not outside and I was readin, jim. And everybody cd dig it!

I's hung to a ribbon of multidimensional minutes. Amen.

Was it the city that made I so crazy? The total environment, of personal history. The history of ah race. Nothing so grandiose, yet precisely that. I carried and carry in me, always probing the maximum consciousness of existence. I could read. I could walk in the halls. And in me then, and now, to some extent. A knowing urge controlled my daylight giving eyes. In a dark hallway my eyes wd light it up, wheeling around like meat lighthouses. Taking in every inch of every existent. Climbing a fence, a spotlight, twin spotlights wd bathe the yard. Bloods in the house pull the curtain, squinting. Smile or ball up they fist. Some momentarily blinded would listen to Lionel Hampton's "Flying Home," in 1940's spook-america, happy, hapeeeee!

I didn't like to fight. The spooky room I carried with me, on my neck, or sometimes like a vacuum chamber, the world squeezed in. Stared at endlessly. I tasted it, felt it, was beat by it. Sat up at night, hearing weird sounds. I looked at shadows, saw old mysterious men with filled bags of questions. I talked to old drunk wino ladies across the street. (Miss Ator) She was hunched over spitting. Men went in and out. Old dudes with tore down bulky skies. In an old shaky house leaning to one side. Eddie Clark was in there running in an out, grinning. Mysteries mysteries mysteries. Yet somehow interpreted as mysteries and understood simply as that, mysteries. I had the consciousness of myself as anything. Sometimes good looking. I'd keep that one afternoon. I wanted my hair to look a certain way. Like combed kinda round, and wavy. My skin wd be shiny. I'd have on some kind of shirt, or maybe moccasins. And you know be clean. I'd like that, being handsome. Then sometimes, I had a pimple and'd be ugly, and sorry to be ugly. Or my mother (another eye) would have some jive on me. Some short suit, or funny lookin tie or something. I'd be in church, or with her with some people patting my head or hand telling me I looked like my father. Of course I did, and my sun, look like me. Over and over again, tho that wasn't bad, being told that, it was just repetitious. Everybody, said that. Everybody. Oh, he look just like his father. Aint he the spittin image of Roy? Who else I suppose to look like. Thank god I dont look like you.

I had a dog name Paulette and the hurricane came and blew a tree down on the dogs house. I think thats what happened to Paulette. That hurricane came and blew a tree down on our bathroom, busted in the roof. Nature was right on our case over there. Another time, it snowed the day after xmas, 5 feet deep, or something, and we had to go help dig the school out. One time Roosevelt was giving out money for killing Japanese beetles. And they was everywhere. We had bottles full of beetles.

Also we had tomatoes in the back yard and a fig tree. Across the street some white people lived in a red and white house. They had cherries and peaches in their back yard. And we were always over there raiding. They had a brick stoop. There were white people in that block. Angel Cordasco, Angel Domenica Cordasco lived on one side of us. On the other side a vacant lot, and driveway to our back yard. They had a big hill we used to play on. Was a house there once. And next to the hill, Old Man Doyle. My grandfather used to call him Ol Man Doyle. Old red faced white man, and faded wife. The white folks with the cherries directly across the street, and next to them some poorer crackers jammed up in a brown and yellow house. A dude named Dominick, a crazy dude always running around talking some stuff. He was an ice man. A little ice man with a ice pick in his belt. Then next to him the Days. About 11ty 11 niggas in a alley, in the worse looking house on the block. Algernon, Lon-el, Board, Fat, Rookie, Evelyn, Will, Frank ... Mrs. Badass Day, like a lady Joe Louis wearin them niggas out daily. A buncha others. But thats all I remember right now, other names'll come. Then another cleaned up white folks house, little nasty snotty nose italian also named Rookie. With little ugly twin sisters tied together in a harness crying. That was the center of the block, on both sides of the street. The center. And under my house, under the stoop, was where our famous club the secret seven met and ate kits and drank kool-aid and plotted to fly.

Around this center, to one side across the street, a vacant lot next to the cherry and peach yard, with its white fence. An old gravel yard, with something at the back I never understood. Then Miss Ator, with Eddie Clark in there. Lorraine who went for my cousin next to him, Mattie, then Joyce's fence and yard, and around the corner New Hope, where some folks still singing praises to the creator of everything!

Going toward Central Avenue, on that same side after Boards house, then Rookie's house, then cement, for a parking lot for a factory, then Dannie Wilson's house, and his grandmother whippin him. His funny brother, and even funnier cousin Clarence, who switched his whatname from the time he came into the world, sucking his thumb. He immediately got more ambitious. On my side, after Doyle, the playground, then Central Avenue School, and the corner and cold big time Central Avenue. With white folks offices and auto parts and other stuff I cdnt use and so wasnt really inerested in. After Clarence's house on the other side, silent brown houses church folks lived in and a restaurant, white enamel outside where schoolchildren ate lunch and office and factory workers ate. Past Angel's house going that way, nothing but a big factory where they took stuff in and out, off a loading dock, it stretched to the corner.

Sociologists do yr mangy thing! Analyze this neighborhood. Negroes and Italians. And an ol oirishmen! See but there's more jimmy! Around the corner on Nwk St. Jammed up with bloods, po as spit. But that weird neighborhood with even an old tenement in it, among the two story houses, which we really thought was way out, all them ol po niggers stuck up in that building like that. Dam, they all in there? It sprinkled with Italians too, and their house generally better than ours. And at the corner Mary Ann Notare, at Sussex and Nwk Street. But across there, same street going to Orange jim jam and them and a hallway smell like pee. That little cross-eyed girl. Plus "The Frenchman" Lafayette, and his sick brother Sammy. He is the one who set dogs and cats on fire. Plus Lawrence and Vivian, J.D., J.B., Ralph, Pearly Mae, Shirley the present wife of the State Assembly man whose ass we getting ready to kick, Frank Cox, The Boose Brothers, also Augie Delappi, Staring Johnny with the strange disease, Norman. Newark Street that was, just a zoomed up version of Dey Street. Integrated neighborhood. One way, you look up a jail, with big stone walls, a subway. Mhisani, lived up at the corner over the subway with Himaya, Harold and Jackie, then. Plus Bad Edna Fields who won all fights legendary in her time. We went up to Irvington to battle the Italians for her just last year. Go another way through Lock Street where Karolis, a really ugly, snotgreen nose stupid cracker, a Greek, i fictionalized for a play for some reason. That was the goofiest doofiest most backward cracker in school. We used to take tech on him. Even I took tech on him. Or at least messed him over every day I saw him. Hey Karolis you dumb bunny!

Why I later then tried to sanctify him in fiction???? Who knows. Ora used to beat him everytime he laid eyes on him. Maybe I felt sorry for him. Big Shot wd punch him knock him down, kick him. But Karolis he just acted goofy. Lock Street Black Norman who said of the Elks that they were "them lidda mens." Leroy Griffith, Leroy Griffin lived on Nwk Street, and they were related. Lock Street was worse than Nwk Street with even poorer Italians and Greeks. And we ran together and apart. We played and fought. And we always won around there because we dominated. Across Lock was Baxter Terrace which in those days was segregated blacks on one side whites mostly Italians i guess on the other. Anthony Arlotta was one dude I hung with in school at least and a dude named Thomas Ravell who's probably in some advertising agency cutting his competitors throat. But the Days Norman Danny Eddie were my young out in the street running buddies. Were these the very beginnings?? What is that? The very beginnings the very end, of the I. Exactly that, and nothing else, but this material throbbing substance—readily "identified"—I've followed yr work, it is a policeman talking through a bullhorn. "I'VE FOLLOWED YR WORK!" Is it a threat, the demeaning I, so surrounded by exact limitations.

My beginnings in the dust of the thundering herd of Egyptian sky deities. In the sperm riding slippery tracks to fertilize me mutter. I AM. I AM MMMMMMMMMMMMMM one hollow ring, a billion fleshy rings, around the universal egg.

My beginned in Community Hospital, called then Kinney Memorial, after a light-skinned Negro who rose to the top of the bloods. Like they say they named buildings after him, but also a street, W. Kinney Street. From there we lived across the street from the pickle factory in the Prudential Projects. To get hit in the head with a rock, by some dude, for a major trauma. To get hit by a car in front of the house, major trauma (I dont even remember this, its been told to me ... the rock I remember. The throw of it, out there under a hard brick light. A brick side the knot. The why of that is no longer in my mind, tho the seeds of it are what grew up big perhaps the reasons people still do that are probably still existent. I called the rock out?? Awww. As goofy as that sounds, its probably demonstrable.

Same place, this earliest of memories, where I was abandoned by my self on a fire escape. This story has been told often, its probably being told now somewhere. I was on a fire escape by myself. A yng dude out there, just a little ways from the opening to the ground! But I didnt go for it, to write this, I edged back and sat looking at the unconscious streets. Cars & stuff. I think I remember that. Having heard it a number of times. Where a man came to teach us ghetto yoots how to play tennis. Nobody learnd. Maybe they did ... I didnt. But there are dudes from the same neighborhood that did learn, whether they learned it from Bro Francis (the wdbe teachers name) or not, I'm not hip.

Where I saw girls walk and could not claim them. And so made up fantasy lives in which we were together some way. Then and later than then and later than then, and later ...

I had a life in which I wd show up at dances alone, and look at people dance. In which I wd fantasize about being able to dance, but could actually dance. If I wd only dance, I wd put under the fantasy, knowing I cd if I only wd. Have dared to open up the whole self construct to anything that was interested, except on paper years later, knowing everything, being omnipotent. How impotent, actually, when it is the world in which life is and where it must be lived, not on paper, as westernized folk wd have us believe. It is only life which is important or valuable. Only life and its projections are but it displaced or reflected.

But I also had a life, in which I wd later show up with friends, and a sense of community appeared and we circulated to watch the few down dudes among us get down, and wd comment like we do, wishing we was the ones. Eyes still, flashing. Whole nations come into being. Old historian rail on. I was a young black child in a hostile world, yet the hostility of that world only slashed in at moments. For instance when this cracker at the Bronx Zoo, an attendant, answered when I held my nose and asked how he could stand it working in the elephant house, said, he lived in Harlem, he could stand anything. And that was a splinter of hate went completely through me. I did not bleed so complete and swift, underhanded even. The little bigeyed boy, browned skinned, round faced, off checking closer than most, who walked and laughed with the group. Miss Powell, the only black teacher in Central Avenue School, had taken us on a trip to the zoo. She was the only teacher that ever took her classes anywhere. You dig? Like the African Free School being started as the first free education for black or white in America, because of our needs. And the poor whites, the longed for working class they show their revolutionary zeal by hammering at black children with putrid distortions of the world . . . that hurt and shape, but they will get it all back, hard as the hardest known element in creation, revolution.

Eyes, I, bigeyed boy. Popeye, they used to say, trying to put me down. Hey popeye. Hey that dude look like a martian. Hey you little martian. Hey pop. Hey Eyes! (I's, over and over, and over and under, the water and the land, the years and the faces, I sought through the eyes to find yet my self intact, and waiting to begin.) Is it that they called me omnivisioned spectacularly endowed, in the seein dept., or just funny looking . . . maybe schizophrenic. Hey I's! This man can definitely SEE! Which meant I was, on a very low level, a seer.

But with such physical see-ability, how come the world came down in fragments and splinters. In flashes and rhythmic thuds, rather than whole and initialed considered like history, real and usable. We need a whole story to see whole, to be really and truly holy. Meaning in tune with every thing. All the reality, its multiple addresses, and parallel appearances. Awash in a see of others. Yet the others (I will talk about those eyes as I's as others, as theys, after . . .) many times have a thing, a bigger more positive (active in touch with reality) self. An I. A presence, an ego, put together in stone and steel. In charter and theory. In law and society that will inundate yr splinter truthed eye. Will cover over like the famous quivering blob, yr lonely loving I.

I—W. Kinney St.

I—Douglass-Harrison

I—Boston Street

I—Dey St.

I—8th Avenue (after McKinley Jr. High experience, moving from black domination in integrated hoax to white domination and black subjugation. I, I, I, I sd, I did, I went, I thought, I felt, I wanted, I didn't, I wdn't. Yes, it was me. All these parts to the same I.

I—Belmont Ave.

I—Hillside Ave.

I—Eckert Ave.

I—7 Morton St.

I—402 W. 20th St.

I—324 E. 14th St.

I—(Somewhere on 17th Street)

I—27 Cooper Sq.

I—4424 7th Ave. (109 W. 130th St.) (This is questionable, to hold yrself up to ridicule. Its not sympathy I want. To kill this I, but change. Transformation. Not death and transfiguration. But life and transformation.

All all this shd have been the milk I drank, bigeyed in my carriage. Across from Tolchinskies pickle works I'm saying I shdve been told about Tolchinsky and all the Tolchinskies of the world. Maybe I cd've helped the bastid. But then I's can only help I's and then not much. But maybe I cd've helped myself? No chance?? But you shd tell me what the world is. Tell me what it is, and who I am in it. Instruct the I to see. Tell it all the things your eye has seen these twenty million years on earth. As the ships the engines the ideologies are ready for the great I to rise from this planet.

I lived with a brown family named Jones and they were family to I. I slept in the house with them I and my sister Elaine slept there. I slept and went to school. I climbed out of windows and back into them. Shot off guns in the playground, watched dogs set on fire, back and forth up the street to school. Being born, moving every few years, like we do, back and across, the town. I cd say it was unfeeling, yet joy and rapture unforseen, linked our hurts, our black eyes together, and made a strength I knew but didnt realize till much later . . . caught in the death urge of the oppressors.

Trace that growingup, through the streets, and to the gaslight in Boston Street, where a yellow light allowed my grandmother to pick glass from my slashedup knee. Like an operation with the midnight oillamp flickering. Busted my head open befoe, you know. Broke my collar bone falling off the stoop. Broke my hand. Measles, chicken pox, whooping cough, mumps, one summer they thought it was meningitis. Plus I got hoarse every summer. And still growing, growing up, growing to what? In the years of turns and twists, still confused, turned around. Splinters and slivers of everything, flying in, upside which way. Strained through red glass, strained thru silent eyes turned to the ground when they shd have been locked deep in mine. Explain the world. Clear up this twisting darkness not my self. This blank explosion draws my tongue and eye and ear toward simple silence. Nothing. Explain the world. Let this I come into it. Growing, to what. Flash Gordon. Governor Roosevelt of the Uncle Don world. Wash white. Kato. Tonto. Who? Explain the world, singers, preachers, walkers, outrageous loud talking brother who ever, sliding in the dust sidewalks.

Always walking toward my own face. (And who?? Then next category to rise. I'm watching . . . who?? Next bub, bud, bloom, fancy dan, riding o country port wine bottles turned up night cold summer IIIIIIII seeing this. IIIII, in love with it all. It's real. Not even that. It's there. I can see it. I even smell stuff. Yeh. I I I I I I I, explain the world. Please. Never stop however. I see me changing forms. From midget, to midget. Of all I survey. I stand, and let it roll in. I take it all in, drink deep of all around me.

Barclay Street, Boston Street, West Market Street, Rufus Spa near our churcĥ, and a little yard to play in, like Obalaji, I'd run around and play, my man, play for all I was worth. West Market Street in them days was pretty fly, Julius' big grocery store, like what a super market wd mean today, and my grandfather was in tight with Julius, and we got stuff on credit and they delivered, and the place smelled boss . . . right up the street from Bethany.

West Market Street, so much of my life spent near there. The Grand Hotel, Bro Russell, big time no. man clean as daylight. Don Newcombe, Monte Irvin, Leon Harvey, Pat Patterson, Leon Ruffing, Larry Doby, Lennie Pearson, all hang out in there. Tough life. With my father watching the Newark Eagles win the black world series, the Negro World Series, I'm sorry. Very Sorry! A no-hitter opening day, raring back then, and all the bloods' moufs fly open . . . jim. Too much. A no-hitter, opening day. Tell me a cracker did that?? Of course (we) . . . all the I's threw the cushions out on the field. And the cracker never let I^{100} have them again. Who needed them seats?

W/ Rheingold and Vat 69. Schenley's and what not. I was a heavy hot dog man. Get me a hot dog and some root beer, jim, and it was me, in paradise city, digging the purity and body and flavor of the world. With my old man who knew about all that. He told me about that. He filled that I complete. Dudes wd say, Hey, Roy, this must be you. Look just like you man. You mighty mf-in right, my man!

The Negro National League was perfect, and so Jackie Robinson was constructed in a small laboratory in the California Hills. Although they never perfected his speech. The way he talked was a dead giveaway. I knew the minute I heard him he wasnt no authentic blood. You cd hear rubber valves contracting when he said "guys," or "jackie robinson" he really sd, jeckee rawbinsun. I cd spot that right away. A plastic man to break up the negro national leagues for branch rickey and unnamed white millionaires.

But then some I's end up going for the blanks. Negro-Blanco cooperation. Sleek white cadillac, and under the hood 360 niggers in tennis shoes. Yeh. Man. Yeh Boy. 360 niggers, a nigger for each degree. Some o them niggers got degrees, and they under the hood too. In Ko-rea, Vitnam, some bloods spilled they blood in Salerno, Cherbourg, Bougainville, Tarawa, yeh, gotta a good thing goin, a goods thing, still still goin. And I's goin for it. Goin goin for it.

Can you remember the Negro National League? I do. And the world champion Newark Eagles, down 'eck at Ruppert Stadium. All the wild pretty bloods be there sunday afternoon. After church, and that madness dealt with. Goin through the turnstile wit my fadda. It was beautiful, beautiful. Colored society blasting . . . till Effa Manley, the light skinned lady what runned the team told Bizz Mackey about the coming of corporate capitalism. Bizz was the fat manager what had to get another gig after the going of his world champions to the crackers . . . since Doby, Irwin, Harvey, Ruffin, Pearson the heart of the squad split. Into the big time. Just like you bloods fount out about integration down south, since you was screaming for it. Some eyes screamin, marchin in d.c. Wit Rabbi Prinz and Walter Reuther, drum majors for JFK. And then this old blood principal look up in Waltavista, SC and he the janitor in the integration. Groovy groovy. Very groovy. You got a good thing goin for you DuPont-o-Gulf. The straight man for mephisto. I cant believe in no devil no more, he got too much power. Cant even let the cracker be no devil, no supernatural shit. Just natural shit. Natural shit what got to be cleaned up. I got that devil shit from P. John Rome's slow s&m man. Squeeze yo peenie in a minie.

This was a whole thing we went for in the 40's ... artificial light. Nigger turn the corner looking for Jua/Panga, get Westinghouse and G.E. Be Maaaad! We shall overcome, true enough. But what, to do what. And how the I get to be all that heavy?

All this time I had been posing for photographs in various parts of the universe. Turning my self into another me, to yet turn, and be re turned. All the way round. That whole 360 degrees of niglews, be my self whistling hey like with a chain. Most times an invisible chain, singin hey bar ba re bop! But I didnt pose like no Louie Jordan tho I cd dig "Joey, Joey, Joey-Joey-Joey ... Joey, Joey, Joey, Joey-Joey ... Moe and Joe had a candy store, sellin numbers behind the door. Cops come in and Joe run out. Brother Moe begin to shout. Run Joe! Hey the man at the door. Run, Joe, and he wont let me go." I cd dig that. Still do. Cd dig Louie and his tympani five. Caledonia. What make yr big head so hard? He stone cold dead in the market man. I kill nobody but me husbin.

But I never pose like that. I always pose like a little colored boy. Smilin. With bald head and gapped teeth. In funny little suits. Sometimes with my sister, who cdnt smile. Sometimes I posed alone, with a ball, on Belmar Beach lookin like Amiri ... anyway. Or in a tub, looking like Ras Jua. Or in a coat and hat at the World's Fair lookin like Obalaji. I's, and big eyes staring into the future. Hoping somebody wd tell me the truth. Tell me what all this is.

This is my story. I. I tell it like I want to. Follow the eye, and you'll see.

This is my story. The story of I who was born in north east america. An African youth, hid under cotton futures. Hid under slavery, oppression. Hid under my people tryin to make it, tryin to raise me. Tryin to put all slavery oppression behind them, when it was on them, in them, in front of them. And mid 60's bloods still saying we shall over come. And how the I get that heavy.

This is my story. The story of an I. A Black I, growin to pieces puzzlin them pieces together. The slivers and slants. The fake magic, the pure political subjugation of the little boy. The little sweet round faced big I'd boy. In the crib. On the fire escape. In the street hit in the head by a car. In the park hit in the head by a stone. In camp watchin niggers do it to each other. Watchin lil homosexual Max go from tent to tent, tryin to get in the present tense. An I to see the various pieces of life in america. Because that's what this was and is.

This is my story. The story about an I who was raised in urban america, in a middle class laboratory, a middleclass negro laboratory, resting in the blood community. Where you went in off blood street, and entered the magic land of confusion and aspiration. Of grand fathers and small fathers and big uncles and sweet grand mothers and pretty mothers. I swore my mother was the most beautiful woman I'd ever seen.

In those laboratories, connected by tunnels to Bethany Baptist Church, to dance classes, to events at which the negro national anthem was sung, and shivers of unknown delight wd buzz my brain, to wake me up micrometers to say, yeh, yeh, dig it, a negro national anthem.

This is the eye story. The story of a brown I. Growin in spite of all the delusion, and mixmatched values. Struggling with radio, and movies and my mother and fathers hallucinations. I cd lie my can off. Yeh. Lie. Make up stuff. Create. Yeh. Look, POOF, this is a whole nother thing here. Can you dig it??

But an I that lived in a brown house with a porch, and hung out underneath the porch plotting the coming Revolution. I had sent a letter to Roosevelt with a detailed drawing of a moving-fort, on wheels. Roosevelt never answered. I never understood that. Nobody mentioned it being in the papers, or on the radio. Hop Harrigan never mentioned it. Roosevelt simply *never* answered. (Obalaji writes to Nyerere!)

An I so confused. At Robt Treat (now Garvey). Central Ave. McKinley Jr Hi. Barringer Hi (Highwopdistrict), Nwk Rutgers (when the only building they had was down on Rector and near the library. And the only other bloods was a long headed dude with glasses named Conrad). This one cracker, an old snuffy smith dude with tobacco, wd always make cracks about the woogies, and we I guessed just grinned and took it. But never grinned nowhere near a grin under the skin, nor am I sure I grinned on top, just finger the tuba, tryin to be Miles Davis. Did that cracker know about Miles Davis?? Cracker are you alive anywhere, no. You ain alive. Yr dust ain alive, it cnt fertilize a nut. At Howard. Confuse. At FSU. At New School. At Columbia.

Speed of light take the I. From a little boy at Douglass Harrison, to watchin my son run up the street with an orange in his hand.

I lived in various houses. Went to various schools. Played various games. Liked baseball (infield, but poor arm, cd always get on base, and run. Slide head first into home. Later pitched (!!!) thats weird, how cd I pitch with a weak arm, cdnt make the throw from shortstop or 3rd base, I cd play 2nd. Football, swift running back. Scatback. Run back punts, weave along the sidelines, throw them fakes, and tuck it in. Cross the line. Yeh. Cd do that. And catch. Cd go up and catch and play good defense, intercept, tuck it in, and get down, cross the line. Cd even play line. And make the tags. But light in the behind. Played good playground ball, with all the highschool pros.

Loved football. Went also with my ol man to see the NY Giants. But that was big time white stuff, and it sat off away from the heart, but still the roar of that, the bigness of that, the wildness of that, tho impersonal, cd transport the little me. And I had Em Tunnell, the defensive genius, to pick off passes, and do the blood number duck and dodge all the way in. That was real and direct and like the monopolists cd dig, straight for the niggers heart.

I dug football.

Red Rover.

Ringaleerio.

Higoseek.

War.

Running around chasin each other. Climin fences. Explorin. Goin weird places in the neighborhood, like new worlds, up over the used car roof, where there was gravel, and you might cd find stuff.

Everything was more dangerous and less dangerous, at the same time. Getting busted for stealing out of white folks cars on Central Avenue was terrifying, being taken down to the station, to talk to the white man sittin at his desk, with my parents standing behind me, lit me up, in terms of cold fear and trembling. But also it was so way out only the fear not the reality took me. And doing it, trying to get in those cars, taking that paltry rubbish was for us only taking stuff that was static, it wasnt active or being claimed. Sitting there for our adventure.

It seemed I was always at the pit end of some adventure. Faced with lies backfiring or tricks that didnt take. Effects from dubious causes. For instance why take that money from the buffet shelf and go to see *The Fighting Sullivans?* No logic to that, cd I dig I'd get caught. And how up tight my parents must've been, not because of the dough, a few measly quarters, but I stayed to see that flick 4 or 5 times, all day. From early in the morning until late at night, about these 5 Irish brothers that got killed in the War. Wiped out this entire family of Irish character actors. On a ship, a flaming carrier, and drunk Thomas Mitchell weeping. I wept a few times, peed on myself, and my head started hurting I was so hungry. Trying to go home, from the Proctors over to Dey Street, I felt sick, and so rested, laid out flat, on a garbage hamper, hands under my head, and rested, I had to walk that Central Avenue hill from Broad Street all the way. A dude stopped his car, and came over, a white man, and asked me if I was all right. I sd ok, I was waiting for a bus. Then got up and trudged wearily, my wet pants sticking to my leg, back to the house, where blood parents leaped with 44 foots.

What made you do that?

Answer yr mother, McGhee.

What made you do that?

The devil.

What?

The devil.

That must have been a high comic dialogue. I sd the devil I guess believing that. Why not. If its wrong, and that dude is in charge of wrong stuff, then you need to get on him. I got beat with a toaster cord, beat half to death. But not clear to sanity!

I stole from my mother even. Why? I wanted the dust. And I didn't feel it was "stealing," just that was where the dough beed. So I was unbee-in it.

I really dont know. Whats to know. Just I thought I needed the change, and used to take it. One time, in the South, my mother caught me going in her pocket book which was left in the car. Again, some kind of weird strap. Plus fists, smacks, grunts, cries. So infuriated was my mother. I was scared because my mother never hit me with her fists, usually just a strap. Which hurt, and brought fear. But fists, was like some extrafamilial attack. It unnverved me, but only temporarily restored my sanity.

"Yr mother and I have decided to stay behind you," my father sd, when I got thru lookin down at the white man's desk, while he bullshitted me about right and wrong.

But what they taught me, my parents, and the others who created this I so perfectly, in its staggering imperfection. They made me too "polite," in one sense. Too removed from the rush and crush of blood. Realities screams disappear into the tunnel now replaced in my head-heart. My heart pumps words, and concepts. Papers and decisions. Screaming death like a black airplane dived down murdering off a building! Walk the real streets feel the warm blood turn. Say, hey, bro, what's to it. What you into, and what not. They pushed me back of a shadowy stair, and there to wait, breathlessly for my self to return, with all the feeling and soul I lost, looking for what??

I was taught all this madness, or had it placed around me, and me around it. The radio sat in the "front room," much sickness got in there. I looked at the *Daily News* everyday, because my father read the sports. Ol man Krotzer, with his dim witted self sd to me. "Why do you read that horrible paper?" And for the first time I saw a shadow ... why indeed, for the sports, I answered. Those sports that sit at Churchill Downs in silk cravats and wager lives for their pleasure.

I was taught good hair and bad hair. Light skinnd folks in moccasins at picnics was hip. Bethany Baptist was the home of lightskinned folks but I didnt find that out till many years later, although I knew it, or was in it, brown skinnd. I didnt even really understand the "war" between my brown grandmother and the cold white boney Miss Banks of the flower committee till years later, although I knew that too. ((coming of the class struggle peeped in right there, in its bubbling bubbling, in its slow accumulation, of lightskinned negro advantage, brown skin negro frustration ... till 1971 suddenly a qualitative leap, and eureka we has the makin of a fullfledged class, goblin, whass that mystical mumbler, well a class Jethro is some throwed together group a studs with the same interests, who defense them together, in 1971 eureka Kingfish Fatso is de boy, what come to show how its done, and suddenly there they be all them middleclassniggas from so long ago diggin, like the Bamberger Boys, them lightskinndfolks what used to run the Bamberger elevators and dress in tuxedoes, and nonea you brown niggas cd be in that ... but color aint the whole carrot, Oxface, niggas throwd around so tough revolution can be made by some light skinned and for sure some niggas black as god want to be capitalist freaks and suck the life outta babies.)) But eureka from lightskinned Miss Banks of the flower committee hoardin a way to whitey, and the preacher he looked like Cecil B. deMille's version of our father who art in heaven—white hair white skin green eyes—yeh, bubba, singin them ol Mozart tunes with a fag with a croquignole setting up there wavin at them wommens like he was directin something, he was just tryin to point his hiney at some protein projectile. ... But the class struggle yeh, then suddenly in 1971, and 2, and 3, fat gibber lip skunky funky declare the opening of the nigro pseudobourgeois hot foots. And other niggers jaws begin to get tighter and tighter! Yeh its called, a "qualitative leap". In the rhythm of any organisms internal dynamism obapadow—salt peanuts salt peanuts.

Pressed into me, this I, filled with the ignoble sentiments of slave labor. I wore a stocking cap, like my father, and used Nunile. Of course! What you youse, Mulligan?? Tryin a get them waves, honey. A rumple-rumple-rumple—lean and clean and intelligent, but greasy jim, very greasy. That was a serious breach in the bourgeois' cover story. Is white peepas greasy?? (You better believe it Sambo, very greasy veddy veddy greasy, indeed!) Look in them ol yearbooks waves and waves, some sitting up hafways like water leaping at a ship, fish in that mammy jammy too (but thats a different group, but all groups the same group in the world, as they unfurl like flags identifying the level of their development.

Petty bourgeois bloods of america, this is most of our storee. The I is fashioned, by the Charlie McCarthy machine. Tho we aint exactly Charlie because we have the choice that Amilcar Cabral explained. We can commit class suicide, and move at one with the masses of our people, and that will be the warmth to heat up our heads into hearts, and turn the paper language into concrete acts of revolution!

The formation of the I. From the old Nile to Nunile. The creation of plasticnigrew. Who is really made to sip the lesser shit of americus. How we I's grew in school, and on the street. How we I's were not the strict crazy niggers of *Ebony* fantasies, but the niggers the fantasies were supposed to trick into being worshipers and followers of the pseudobooshies. Humbled in the glow of yaller skin or brown dust.

But these I's we is ran too far and too wide. Or the potential is in us other than this personal I, to have made a move, and got the trick exposed. As the negro pulled the rabbit out the hat, "you" (I'll deal with this category later)

dug, it wasink no rabbick but a cracker's nasty foot! I mean I cd not dig bein
The Spiro's bodyguard nor The Agnew's bodyguard (two beasts, Bro, Ish
points out)—which is a big unwashed foot Pseudo pull out the hat drippin in
ol dookie he say is magic. Aint magic, tis tragic. I cdnt be no nigger in charge
a no republican shenanigans on the whole west coast. Republican nigger
shenanigans. What this pseudo say to Reagan. Hellaw Raeg, I checked yr last
40 pitchers, dry as a mertherferker! Cdnt say thet. Aint in em to say it. Cda
been inem. Aint now.

All drained out. By these processes I document. By this tragic path, stares
like an open mouth dripping corny music. And (we) are told to follow beasts
or hallowed savages who stand forever dead on the walls of churches and
colored lodges, amen.

Finally, and despite the gigantic institutionalized lie into which we are
suspended without a history or a personality, there is a realization that this is
not total or final. Unless we can drive white brougham cadillacs into concentration camps. When President Brooke (James Earl Jones)—for real! Signs
the paper saying yall worshipers aint worshiping hard enough, all who aint
get on the train take ya to them camps and what not.

BLACK LIBERATION/SOCIALIST REVOLUTION

The slave trade, which brought the masses of Africans to the New World, marks the expansion of capitalism. It is also the beginning of world trade. The so-called triangular trade that Du Bois spoke of, with slaves coming to the Americas in exchange for cotton and tobacco going to England, and English manufactured items going to Africa, was the beginning of world trade as we know it today. And it was slaves that were the foundation of this world trade, and as Karl Marx pointed out, it was slaves and world trade that made the New World important.

Millions of slaves perished during the slave trade, but this lucrative slavery business was the basis for the so-called primitive accumulation of capital, which makes the later expansion of capitalism, including the industrial revolution, possible. Without the trade in African slaves, there would be no industrial capitalist Europe and no prosperous American colonies.

Throughout U.S. history these slaves and ex-slaves have played an extremely important role in the shaping of society, and especially in the U.S.'s democratic revolutions: the Revolutionary War, which made the U.S. an independent developing capitalist state, and the Civil War, which saw the Northern bankers and industrial capitalists defeat the Southern slavocrats for total domination of the U.S. state; and we can include the civil rights movement and the rebellions of the sixties as still another segment of the U.S.'s democratic revolutions. In the first of these, the American Revolutionary War, the black slaves and Indians at first put in with the British because they were promised freedom. When the thirteen colonies came around to seeing the doom this spelled for them, they then took up the same tack of promising freedom, because at that time it was thought that slavery would just fade away since by that time there was no great profit in slaves. But after the Revolutionary War, with the discovery of the cotton gin, cotton became an international commodity, so that onto the burden of patriarchal or feudalistic type slavery was added the murderous weight of capitalism. It was during this period in the early nineteenth century that slavery in the Black Belt became so notoriously brutal that the average slave had a twenty-five-year death expectancy, which the slaver-capitalists had calculated exactly so as to get the most production for their money.

The Revolutionary War against Great Britain did not solve the slavery question, and the celebrated documents of beginning bourgeois democracy that the Declaration of Independence and the Constitution supposedly constitute do not even address themselves to the issue of slavery. And when cotton became an international commodity, bringing millions of dollars, the slavers introduced even harsher measures, and even took the democratic rights away from some of the freed slaves. But this is also the period of the most intense slave rebellions, beginning with Gabriel Prosser, Denmark Vesey, Nat Turner—Harriet Tubman and the Underground Railroad (1830's) and in 1859, the most advanced abolitionist, John Brown, leading black and white.[1]

The same pattern characterized the Civil War. The North was finally backed into using the slaves to fight, because the South was winning, and using slaves meant the North was able to put 186,000 fighters into the field. The end of the Civil War was the point at which there was again a chance for black people to become integrated into a democratic U.S.A., but that was not the intention of the ruling class. After the Northern monopolists defeated the Southern slavocrats, spearheaded by the masses of working people in the North who saw slavery as a direct threat to their lives, and the black slaves who took up arms to ensure their freedom, Reconstruction governments were set up in the South. These Reconstruction governments, many of them with blacks in governing, key and critical roles, brought a measure of democracy to the South, and esured the enforcing of the Thirteenth, Fourteenth, and Fifteenth Amendments, which actually brought education and the vote to many poor whites as well as blacks. These Reconstruction governments were necessary at first for the big Northern capitalists to thoroughly put down the defeated Southerners. And who was more loyal than the blacks to the federal government, which had just freed them? But once having achieved this stability, the Northern bourgeoisie, in the notorious Hayes-Tilden Compromise of 1876, removed federal troops from the South, delivered the governments of Southern states back to the defeated Southern plantation owners, who were now a comprador[2] for the Northern monopolists, and through armed counterrevolution and terror destroyed the Reconstruction governments and plunged black people back into near slavery, with the black codes, segregation, Jim Crow laws, KKK, guerrilla terror—all bought paid for and directed by the Northern bankers and industrialists on Wall Street. And to this day, the Southern bourgeoisie and managerial class is still tied directly to Wall Street.

With the destruction of the Reconstruction governments, and the imposition of rigid segregation and discrimination, all conditions now had come together

---

[1] *PreCivil War Black Nationalism,* Bill McAdoo, Report, Peoples War, Newark, 1977.

* Compradors are a class serving imperialism—the national sector amasses its capital within the black community.

for the emergence of an AFRO-AMERICAN NATION in the Black Belt South. J. Stalin defines a nation as "a historically constituted stable community of people, based on a common territory, language, economic life, and a common psychological development manifest as a common culture." The Black Belt is an area some 1600 miles long and 300 deep stretching from Delaware to Texas. It could also be called the Cotton Belt. For many years blacks existed as slaves delivering up a cotton crop for international distribution, speaking English or the Afro-American dialect of American English; they had a common economic life expressed by the development of all the classes found in a modern nation, from at first a largely peasant people, with a petty bourgeoisie developing even during slavery among the freed slaves, and the bourgeoisie emerging, after the destruction of the Reconstruction governments, serving a segregated black market, beginning with catering, funeral service, savings and loan and insurance. The existence of an Afro-American culture is by now well known.

It is this Afro-American nation, which still exists in the Black Belt South, that was and is oppressed by U.S. imperialism, in the same fashion imperialism oppresses other nations in the Third World (Asia, Africa and Latin America). But since the Afro-American nation actually exists on the land base of the United States, the approach to its liberation is somewhat more complex than many of the colonial questions whose solution is to be made by revolution, though make no mistake, the only solution to the Afro-American national question is by violent armed revolution, socialist revolution!

The newly emergent black bourgeoisie, for a time, were the leaders of the black liberation movement, what was called the freedom struggle, But the peculiar economic and political flabbiness of the black bourgeoisie made it lose leadership of the freedom movement in the twenties, when, after the sharpest economic crisis in monopoly capitalism, half of all black businesses closed. So that the struggle between the comprador sector of the black bourgeoisie articulated by Booker T. Washington and the national sector articulated by W. E. B. Du Bois, was replaced by the debate between Du Bois and Marcus Garvey, who represented the impoverished sector of the petty bourgeoisie—the lawyers without clients, the doctors without patients, the small-business men—who seized leadership over a great mass of black people, predominantly the newly displaced Southern peasants just arriving in the North. The idealism and utopianism of this petty bourgeoisie with their Pan-Africanism was positive only insofar as it expressed the idea of solidarity between Africans and Afro-Americans, and the need for black sovereignty and pride, but in most other respects it was wanting. But it revealed clearly that the black bourgeoisie had forfeited leadership of the black liberation movement.

By the thirties a working-class leadership had arisen, given impetus by the militant work and correct lines of the Communist Party USA. By 1928 thousands of blacks had been recruited into the party. And the 1928 Comintern and CPUSA position on the Afro-American national question reaffirmed the Leninist position that black people constitute a nation in the Black Belt of the U.S. South with the right of self-determination up to and including secession! The struggles to build the unions, the Scottsboro boys' fight, the founding of the militant sharecroppers' union in the South, were all part of the revolutionary work that the CPUSA performed. It was also the deepest incursion of Marxism-Leninism into the black masses. But by the forties, the opportunist leadership of the CPUSA in the person of Earl Browder and others had used the Second World War and the correct united front tactic put forward by the Comintern to legitimize their desired collaboration with the U.S. bourgeoisie. They put out theories of American Exceptionalism, that somehow U.S. capitalism was different from all the rest of the capitalism, that it did not adhere to universal laws governing the development of capitalism. Browder said that American capitalism was still a young progressive competitive capitalism, that it had not turned into its opposite, imperialism, as Lenin pointed out. Therefore, the traitor Browder "reasoned," since American capitalism was an exception it could be collaborated with: American capitalism would help the U.S. working class. But this was and is pure bullshit. Pure traitorous bullshit! Capitalism is the enemy of working people everywhere, and in its present monopoly stage, called imperialism, it is a menace to the majority of peoples on the planet. Capitalism is an economic system, a mode of production, characterized by private ownership of the means of production, the land, factories, mineral wealth, transportation, communication, waterways. This means of production is owned privately by a single class in capitalist society called the capitalist class or the bourgeoisie. The principal contradiction in this bourgeois society, and the U.S. is the leading bourgeois society in the world, is the contradiction between the private ownership of the means of producing wealth, against the public character of the production process itself. That is, it takes millions of people to produce the wealth by laboring long hours in factories, mines, on docks, in shops, yet the class that makes the gigantic wealth off this labor is the bourgeoisie, who do no work at all. All the wealth that the workers produce that they do not get is called *surplus value,* and this is the secret of capitalism that Karl Marx discovered. One hundred workers in a hour put together 100 automobiles from which a gross profit of $500,000 can be realized. Each worker is paid $10 for that hour; $10 times 100 is $1000. Subtract that from $500,000 and you understand what surplus value is, and you also understand why capitalism must be destroyed, why working people will always be relegated to the bottom of the heap as long as the fruit of their labor is appropriated by the six tenths of 1 percent who constitute the U.S. bourgeoisie! [3]

---

[3] LENNY. Gettin paid? Man, you think somebody's a fool! We gettin seven dollars an hour. In one hour a hundred of us make a hundred goddamn cars for these bloodsuckers. In that same hour that mean management gettin off seven hundred dollars.

Imperialism is capitalism in its monopoly stage, where it has left the boundaries of one country, having used up and controlled the raw materials and capital inside its own boundaries. It then begins to look for new sources of raw materials, new markets for its goods, new places to export capital (capital is wealth used to exploit labor). And to do this it must scramble around the world, overturning governments, setting up colonies and neo-colonies, supporting tyrants.

When the leadership of the CPUSA came out lying that U.S. imperialism

---

FOREMAN. You get five or six dollars benefits every hour too, loudmouth.

LENNY. OK, say we made ten dollars an hour then or even fifteen dollars an hour. That would still be only fifteen hundred dollars management would have to pay us in an hour. But those hundred cars we put together each sell for nearly five thousand dollars apiece. That's five hundred thousand dollars in one hour minus our fifteen hundred dollars. They making four hundred eighty-five thousand an hour off our work, and you talking about speed up. Your ass is loose.

FOREMAN. Hey, the company's profit is not the dealer's selling price minus the workers' wages—that's simpleminded. A dealer buys a car from a company at a fifteen to twenty-five percent discount—and the car wasn't manufactured out of air—you think the steel, glass, plastic cloth, paint, cost nothing? The company's got to pay for these.

LENNY. Hah, but all you doin' now is calling for more explanation—which is good. First, what we saying, and what these workers here need to understand, is that if it wasn't for their work there wouldn't even be a car in the first place. And if it wasn't for the work of workers other places wouldn't be no steel, glass, plastic, cloth, paint and stuff. The workers' work creates it, not the owners' bullshit. The workers create, the owners rip off and do no work. And their companies make so much profit at the end of the operation that the little discount so-called they give the dealer is nothing. And the dealer is just a small owner, a petty capitalist functionary of the big owners anyway. And as for the sources of these materials, now you just talking about something called imperialism. Which is when these factory owners, and banks, these capitalists get so swoll up they had to spread past the boundaries of "their own" countries and spread around the world. Looking for new sources of raw material, new markets, new spheres of influence, and new places to export capital. And the essence of imperialism is that these big corporations *don't* pay for the raw materials they make these car parts from, that's why their profits are so huge. The rubber, glass, paint—they rip them out of these Third World countries, Asia, Afrika, Latin America, and make super profits! Super profits. So much that they can spend a few pennies of those enormous profits to delude some of us workers in the USA, bribe a few of us
(Nods toward Foreman)
and get us to support this bullshit rather than whip it to death! Naw, man, all the wealth workers create which they don't get, it's called *surplus value,* is so large that the so-called expenses of the big capitalists are nothing! And what are those expenses?? Keepin us livin in shacks, which we pay rent for—right back to them—givin us just enough pennies to barely feed our families and buy a few clothes. And all that dough goes right back to them, cause they own the big farms *and* the supermarkets. The department stores to boot. If we don't like it, and try to do something about it, they got a private army called the police to cool us right out—pay 'em with our money too, not their profits. 'Scalled taxes!

From *The Motion of History,* Amiri Baraka, pp. 114-15 (New York: Morrow, 1977).

was an exception, they were merely laying the stage for their own liquidation, and their following of the bankrupt Communist Party of the Soviet Union onto the tragic traitor path of revisionism. The once proud party of the Soviet Union turned revisionist after the death of Stalin, as the result of a political coup led by Nikita Khrushchev, who was an agent of the old and new bourgeoisie within the Communist Party of the Soviet Union. The CPUSA, with its own opportunist leadership, and history of critical struggle against opportunism and chauvinism, now degenerated completely into revisionism. Revisionism is the using of M-L phrases and terminology to cover reformism and collaboration with the bourgeoisie. The CPUSA abandoned the militant sharecroppers union in the Black Belt, and then reversed itself on the Afro-American National Question eliminating the call for self-determination for the Afro-American nation in the Black Belt South. By 1957, the CPUSA was a completely consolidated revisionist clique, a pack of new liberals (who one day will probably run their lies from the official buildings in Washington, D.C.) babbling about the "peaceful transition to socialism," completely liquidating revolution.

The effect on the black liberation movement, and on the working-class struggles and struggles of other oppressed nationalities, was grave. Without a revolutionary Marxist-Leninist party to give leadership to the various mass struggles, they remain spontaneous, rising and falling in waves. The black liberation movement (BLM) is a particular classic example of this. First the CPUSA began to support the comprador sector of the black bourgeoisie as the leadership of the black liberation movement, the Wilkinses, Whitney Youngs and the like. Martin Luther King emerged as spokesman for the black bourgeoisie, its national sector, the sector that still has some militance in that objectively it is in contradiction with the big bourgeoisie over its market, black people. The national sector of the black bourgeoisie wants control over its market, but this is impossible because the Afro-American nation is oppressed by imperialism, and to gain control over that black market, the black bourgeoisie would have to fight an anti-imperialist war of liberation against foreign domination. The bitter irony of this for them, however, is that any such war would invariably be led by the black working class, which might include them as part of a united front, but would never let them lead. And the goal of such a liberation struggle would be new democracy or people's democracy, and then upward to socialism.[4] It certainly would not have as its aim the delivering of the black masses into the hands of a black bourgeoisie in place of the white imperialists. But because of the traitorous actions of the CPUSA the leadership of the BLM was delivered

[4] But because the U.S. is a highly developed capitalist/imperialist state and the Afro-American nation exists within it, revolution in the U.S. will be a one-stage revolution, directly to socialism.

back into the hands of the black bourgeoisie. This was the era of the civil rights movement, a mass movement for democratic rights led by the national sector of the black bourgeoisie and petty bourgeoisie. The contrast between the black bourgeois position and the position of the actual masses of working people is the contrast between Dr. King's political lines and the line articulated by Malcolm X, who was a spokesman for the black sector of the working class. Without a doubt Malcolm X was the most influential black leader of his time, and historically will be summed up to be the most significant leader of the entire period (fifties and sixties).

It was Malcolm who in the face of the line of "we shall overcome" and "turn the other cheek," which were the metaphysical watchwords of the black bourgeois leadership, put forward the line that black people had the right to *Self-Determination, Self-Respect, and Self-Defense.* He sd that if we had to struggle for civil rights, which are merely the democratic rights of any citizen of a society, then we must not be citizens in the first place. Malcolm made us aware of our connection with Africa, both historically and politically. It was also Malcolm X who declared the March on Washington a black bourgeois status symbol which would solve nothing!

Malcolm X influenced a whole generation of black people and people of other nationalities as well. And his expulsion by the Nation of Islam for remarks he made about the Kennedy Assassination was merely *one splitting into two,* showing that the revolutionary nationalism of Malcolm X could not exist within the cultural and religious nationalist and black capitalist framework of Elijah Muhammad's Nation of Islam.

The line of self-defense was picked up by people like Robert Williams, who comprador Wilkins also fired for firing up some Klansmen in Monroe, North Carolina. Also the Deacons for Self-Defense in Bogaloosa, and the Black Panther Party in California were deeply influenced by Malcolm as well as Stokely Carmichael and Rap Brown of SNCC. Carmichael's cry of "black power" was merely putting forward Malcolm's line on black nationalism, and Huey Newton and Bobby Seale, marching into the California legislature with arms, were simply carrying into practice Malcolm's message to the grass roots of armed self-defense.

As a result of Malcolm's great leadership the BLM moved very quickly from an idealist-led mass movement with metaphysical goals to a revolutionary mass movement culminated by the mass rebellions in the late sixties carried out predominantly by black working-class people. The motion from Dr. King's "we shall overcome" to Rap Brown's revolutionary cry, "If America don't come round America need to be burnt to the ground," is not possible without Malcolm X's revolutionary leadership and example!

But the lack of a revolutionary Marxist-Leninist party remained a tragic vacuum, dooming the black liberation movement and the other workers' movements to spontaneity. It shd be clear that the reason the black rebellions of the sixties could not become revolution is that there was no Marxist-Leninist leadership. And renegades like the CPUSA played the bourgeoisie's game by constantly denouncing leaders like Malcolm, calling him a police agent, and the same as the Ku Klux Klan. If they were examples of Marxists, of communists, then we wanted nothing to do with them. But they weren't. It was obvious they were simply misguided petty bourgeois reformists and white chauvinists to boot.

Malcolm X's assassination left a vacuum in the black liberation movement, one made even more glaring and tragic by the principal vacuum left by the absence of a genuine Communist Party in the U.S.A. For one thing, petty bourgeois leadership moved into this vacuum, and leading forces in the black liberation movement made tragic errors. On one hand, the cultural nationalism that ascribed black oppression simply to all white people was finally simply the ideology of the small merchants protecting their tiny market, bourgeois philosophy that objectively served the bourgeois ruling class by dividing the working class. Chauvinism has the same political base as opportunism: collaboration with the bourgeoisie, even as far as to work with the bourgeoisie against the workers of other nations. The economic base of opportunism is the superprofits ripped out of the Third World by imperialism that allows it to bribe a small sector of the working class and the petty bourgeoisie, the so-called labor aristocrats.

The absence of a vanguard party, and the practice of the revisionists and chauvinists who masqueraded as communists, such as the CPUSA, was also another catalyst for the bourgeois cultural nationalism that developed in a large sector of the black liberation movement. The organization I was a member of at that time, the Congress of Afrikan People, has made self-criticism for being involved with this bourgeois ideology, and some time ago removed itself from the ranks of cultural nationalists to embrace M-L-M.

The other major trend of the BLM during the sixties was represented by the Black Panther Party, who initially forcefully carried out Malcolm's correct line of armed self-defense, the right to bear arms in the defense of our lives, in contrast to turn the other cheek—and let it get blown away too! But without Marxist-Leninist guidance this line was perverted into a kind of gun cult, which quickly brought the brutal forces of the bourgeois state down on the Panthers in bloody repression. Also, under the sinister influence of the Bakuninist-Anarchist ideology spread by Elder Cleaver, which masqueraded as Marxism, the Panthers pushed the incorrect line that the revolutionary class that wd lead socialist revolution was the lumpen, i.e., the pimps, hustlers, dope pushers and prostitutes, romanticizing an inconsistent, sometimes dangerous class, already destroyed by capitalism. But the revolutionary social force of proletarian revolution is the working class, the masses of workers, who, armed with the science of revolution, Marxism-Leninism-Mao Tse-tung Thought, by means of a revolutionary vanguard party, will smash capitalism and establish the dictatorship of the proletariat and build socialism.

The black liberation movement includes a number of tendencies and organizations and classes all struggling in some way to some degree against national oppression and for democracy. There are black capitalists such as the Nation of Islam who consider themselves part of it, right-wing nationalists such as CORE, who recently advocated sending black Vietnam veterans to Angola in a scheme that seemed to have leaped directly from the State Department's feverish brow. There are cultural nationalists, who are also part of the broad and contradictory black liberation movement, some of whom are still including health tips for chewing yr grains 1000 times as methods of liberation; there are Pan-Africanists and Black Zionists who still think we must return to Africa to find our home. And while we must realize the historical and political significance of our relationship to Africa, we must abandon the idealism and confusion that does not allow us to see that our principal struggle is for the land we have lived on for almost four centuries, including the liberation of the black nation in the Black Belt South, and equal rights for the black oppressed nationality throughout the rest of this country. The broad masses of black people who are struggling day after day against the robbery and exploitation and limitation of democratic rights that characterizes national oppression, realize it and are struggling day after day against this national oppression which has the added horrors of racism, the monster created by capitalism and its slave ships.

But we must understand that there will be no black liberation until the system of monopoly capitalism is destroyed, that this is the economic base and root of our oppression. And finally only those aspects of the black liberation movement which oppose imperialism and fight for consistent democracy can really be considered revolutionary; the rest must be exposed as reactionary and as aides to our oppressors.

We must also be very clear by now that skin color is no indicator of one's political line, and that black liberation, the self-determination of the Afro-American nation and the liberation of the black oppressed nationality will only come through armed violent socialist revolution, a revolution made in concert with the entire multinational working class. But in order for such a revolution to become a reality, the masses of working people must be led by a Marxist-Leninist Communist Party, the party Lenin described as the party of a new type, a party of the working class, a party composed of the advanced sector of the working class, advanced because they are armed with the science of revolution. This is why the central task of all revolutionaries in the U.S.A. today must be the building of such a Marxist-Leninist party, because without such a party we are at the mercy of monopoly capitalism and its bloody bourgeois rulers.

In the U.S. today there is a severe economic crisis, no matter the constant yatter of the bourgeoisie's paid liars who tell us different, who try to conjure up once a week a new "upturn." Depressions are a cyclical occurrence in capitalism due to the anarchistic production of commodities for profit rather than for people's needs. Periodically the markets are flooded because the impoverished masses simply cannot absorb the torrent of unnecessary commodities. Workers are then laid off, but sometimes prices rise at the same time, because the capitalists try to make the same profit off a lower volume of sales; also the largely paper money of the decadent society no longer represents actual labor, merely printer's ink and bourgeois desperation, and so we have inflation.

In the wave of this economic crisis which grips the entire capitalist world, is added the searing force of the peoples and nations of the Third World—Africa, Asia, and Latin America and other regions—who are the main fighters against imperialism, colonialism, neocolonialism, Zionism and superpower bullying and control called hegemonism. As the revolutionary forces drive U.S. imperialism out of Asia and Africa and Latin America, the economic crisis grows even more intense, because the captive markets and sources of cheap raw materials and labor that the imperialists counted on to make superprofits are forcibly ripped away from them. And the exploitation of workers inside the U.S. must also intensify as the bourgeoisie cuts back and lays off. It is these struggles that make revolution the main trend in the world today. Countries want independence, Nations want liberation, and the People want revolution, was how Chairman Mao termed it! There are four fundamental contradictions in the world today: labor vs. capital in the advanced capitalist countries; imperialism vs. imperialism, with the sharpest struggle between the two superpowers (the U.S.S.R., socialism in words and imperialism in deeds, and the U.S.A.); imperialism vs. the Third World; and imperialism vs. the socialist countries, a contradiction between what is dying and what is invincible. The sharpest of these contradictions is the one between imperialism and the Third World, which we described, which is the motor driving revolution around the world; and the other sharp contradiction between the two superpower imperialisms for redivision of the world, just as the big imperialist powers contended and struggled and finally declared world wars to redivide the world between them which was World War I and World War II. Even tho revolution is the main trend in the world today, the factors for both war and revolution are rising. And the people must prepare for this imperialist war no matter the fraudulent line of détente which one superpower throws around and the other conjures with. The politics of imperialism is war, and the people must prepare for such a war, or suffer. The main preparation for such a war, just like the main preparation for revolution, is the building of a vanguard M-L Communist Party, to smash capitalism and transform the privately owned means of production—the land, factories, mineral wealth, mines, transportation—into publicly owned state property under the revolutionary dictatorship of the proletariat.

Black liberation will come only through socialist revolution, and it is part and parcel of proletarian revolution, and socialist revolution can only come led by a party which combines the entire multinational working class guided by Marxism-Leninism-Mao Tse-tung Thought. Jimmy Carter's 88 teeth, his colored stooges, his women stooges and his trade union bureaucrat stooges will change nothing in this society but the accent in which the lies will be told. There will never be the change we seek under capitalism; only revolution and socialism can bring a truly just & equitable society.

MARXIST-LENINISTS UNITE—WIN THE ADVANCED TO COMMUNISM!!
BUILD A REVOLUTIONARY MARXIST-LENINIST PARTY IN THE USA!!
BLACK LIBERATION—SOCIALIST REVOLUTION!!

NATIONAL LIBERATION
MOVEMENTS

There are four fundamental contradictions in the world today, contradictions of capitalism turned to imperialism! These were first clearly pointed out by Lenin in *Imperialism: The Highest Stage of Capitalism.* Stalin reiterates these in his seminal work *The Foundations of Leninism.* Lenin pointed out that imperialism, which is moribund or dying capitalism, "carries the contradictions of capitalism to their last bounds, to the extreme limit beyond which revolution begins." The first contradiction, in the Western industrial countries, is that of labor vs. capital. "Imperialism brings the workers to revolution" because under imperialism, trade unions, cooperatives, parliamentary parties and parliamentary methods have all been proven totally inadequate.

The second of these contradictions is between the financial groups and imperialist powers themselves. Imperialism vs. Imperialism. It is these intraimperialist struggles that invariably lead to imperialist war, such as World War I and World War II. The imperialists contend for new sources of raw materials, new markets. new spheres of influence, new places to export capital, they struggle to redivide the world, and this struggle leads to war. In the present era, the sharpest of these struggles is the constant contention between the two superpowers, the U.S.A. and U.S.S.R, i.e., between U.S. imperialism and Soviet Social Imperialism, which is socialism in words, imperialism in deeds.

The third contradiction is the sharpest one in the world today, imperialism vs. the peoples and nations of the Third World (i.e., the colonies and semicolonies)—Asia, Africa, Latin America and other regions. It is these struggles that drive the flame of revolution around the world, they are the motive force of revolution, and the people and nations of the Third World are the main strugglers against imperialism, colonialism, racism, Zionism, neocolonialism and the superpower domination called hegemonism.

The fourth contradiction is between imperialism and the socialist countries, and as such it is the confrontation between that which is dying and going out of existence—imperialism and monopoly capitalism—and that which is coming into being and therefore invincible, socialism.

These contradictions produce two sharp trends in the world today. The contradiction between the imperialists themselves produces the trend toward imperialist war. And it is sharpening daily, hourly, as the two superpowers contend all over the world for domination of the world, which neither will get. No matter the hollow cries of détente, which the one superpower uses, or human rights, which the other uses to lull people into a false sense of security while both of these international bandits go thru the charade of attending yet another security conference or peace conference, meanwhile arming to the teeth and preparing for a new world war. A new world war is already visible on the horizon, and people of the world must prepare or suffer. The superpowers contend in Southeast Asia, the Middle East, Latin America, and now with deepening and clearly warlike intensity in Africa, although the focus of their contention remains Europe, which they both deem a political and economic prize.

But even tho the danger of war is increasing visibly, revolution is still the main trend in the world today. The contradiction between imperialism and the peoples and nations of the Third World is the sharpest of the four fundamental contradictions of imperialism. "The days are gone when imperialism and social imperialism could do as they wished. Countries want independence, nations want liberation, and the people want revolution—this has become the irresistible tide of history." It is out of the struggles of the people of the Third World vs. imperialism that the national liberation movements arose and why they continue and grow in effectiveness and world recognition. The expansion of capitalism worldwide as imperialism is in the main to seek out superprofits. To do this the imperialists must superexploit the peoples and nations of the Third World, and because wherever there is oppression there is resistance, Third World reaction is doubly intense. ". . . In exploiting these countries imperialism is compelled to build there railways, factories and mills, industrial and commerical centers. The appearance of a class of proletarians, the emergence of a native intelligentsia, the awakening of national consciousness, the growth of the liberation movement—such are the inevitable results" of imperialism. "The growth of the revolutionary movement in all colonies and dependent countries without exception clearly testifies to this fact. This circumstance is of importance for the proletariat inasmuch as it saps radically the position of capitalism by converting the colonies and dependent countries from reserves of imperialism into reserves of the proletarian revolution." This is how Stalin put it in *Foundations of Leninism.*

But Lenin goes on to point out "that under imperialism wars cannot be averted, and that a coalition between the proletarian revolution in Europe and the colonial revolution in the East in a united world front of revolution against the world front of imperialism is inevitable." Imperialism is a world system, and it brings about conditions for revolution on a worldwide basis, but most intensely in the colonies and semicolonies. Imperialist war can be stopped only by revolution, and even when the imperialists mount their world war, revolutionaries will turn such a war into revolution. But comrades who belittle the national liberation struggles, the national revolutions in the Third World, saying that world war can be stopped only by revolutions in the two superpower states, U.S.A. & U.S.S.R., miss the points made by Lenin in his great works on imperialism. Stalin says, in *Foundations of Leninism,* "Formerly it was the accepted thing to speak of the proletarian revolution in one or another developed country as of a separate and self-sufficient entity opposing a separate national front of capital as its antipode. Now, this point of view is no longer adequate. Now we must speak of the world proletarian revolution; for the separate national fronts of capital have become links in a single chain called the world front of imperialism, which must be opposed by a common front of the revolutionary movement in all countries. ... Formerly the proletarian revolution was regarded exclusively as the result of the internal development of a given country. Now this point of view is no longer adequate. Now the proletarian revolution must be regarded primarily as the result of the development of the contradictions within the world system of imperialism, as the result of the breaking of the chain of the world imperialist front in one country or another." *(FofL,* p. 29.)

There are liberation struggles against imperialism all over the globe. And their overwhelming success year after year steadily weakens and debilitates imperialism. The liberation movements in Southeast Asia, principally in Vietnam, Cambodia and Laos, drove the United States imperialists into open decline. The billions of dollars and hundreds of thousands of troops the U.S. sank into the S.E. Asian debacle and defeat was much like the fox and the tarbaby: the harder the fox punched, the more pitifully mired in the tar he became, and finally died there trying to punch. The Southeast Asian struggle also raised the level of revolutionary consciousness of the people of the United States as well, causing a series of domestic crises for the U.S. bourgeoisie which ended with the Watergate sacrifice to imply that the Vietnam policy was the concoction of Richard Nixon's sick mind alone, when it was the general policy of the U.S. bourgeoisie, from the "liberal" Kennedy to the repressive Nixon.

The Korean War started the U.S. long decline, and the only answer they have to the massive liberation movements worldwide against imperialism is to fight them in the open as in Southeast Asia, which has proved totally bankrupt, or to prop up fascist gangsters such as Pak Jung Hee in South Korea, where U.S. imperialism opposes democracy and unity for the Korean peninsula, or in cases like Thailand, as the government moved further away from the U.S. orbit, stage coups, murder communists, national revolutionaries and even petty bourgeois democrats. In Africa the U.S. policy of backing repressive colonial governments was clearly exposed with its backing of the Portuguese fascists in Guinea Bissau, Mozambique and Angola, who were defeated utterly by the African masses. U.S. imperialists continue to support racist illegal regimes such as those in Zimbabwe (Rhodesia), Namibia (South-West Africa) and Azania (South Africa), though with the coming of the Jimmy Carter Snake Oil and Holiness Show, the U.S. bourgeoisie is trying to change their image in the Third World by bringing on one of the black bourgeoisie's political cadres, Andy Young, to go around the Third World,

Africa principally, throwing the soul handshake on the Africans pretending the U.S. no longer is the chief supporter of Rhodesia, South Africa, and South-West Africa's fascist racist regimes.

U.S. imperialism has been exposed worldwide as a bloody beast imperialist, and the national liberation movements have caused it to back up around the world. And that is the reason why Soviet Social Imperialism is so dangerous, because it is still somewhat disguised, covering its naked expansionist moves in Africa by calling itself "socialist" and "natural ally of the liberation movements." As the people of the Third World thru their liberation movements kick U.S. imperialism out the front door, Soviet Social Imperialism tries to creep in the back door and set up the same imperialist shop, under a new-style neocolonialism. The S.S.I. actions in Angola last year, where it sent its Cuban mercenaries in to singlehandedly start a civil war between the three Liberation movements in Angola, all of whom had contributed to the defeat of Portuguese colonialism. These three liberation organizations, FNLA, MPLA and UNITA, had already signed two agreements, one in Alvor, Portugal, the other in Nakuru, Kenya, that they would set up a government of national unity combining all three organizations, now that the Portuguese were defeated. But the Soviet Union capitalized on the weakness of the other superpower and the existence of old feuds between the three movements to back one of the movements, term the others reactionary, and using the South Africans as the suface cover story, send thousands of Cuban mercenaries into Angola, plus modern weapons and heavy armaments never sent during the struggle against Portuguese colonialism. In the year or so that the SSI and its mercenaries have been in Angola they have killed over 150,000 Africans, Angolans—more than the Portuguese in seventeen years of national war. And the Cubans continue in Angola as an occupying force of mercenaries in the pay of SSI.

In Zaire the Soviets used the Katanganese gendarmes, Moise Tshombe's old enforcers, to invade Zaire in shameless fashion in a further attempt at expanding SSI control in Africa. These were the same Katanganese mercenaries who helped kill Patrice Lumumba, and they are now being used by the SSI for the same purpose, the attack by imperialism.

SSI has gotten so funky in Africa that both the Egyptians and recently the Sudanese have had to send them packing, denouncing them for interfering in their countries and trying to practice their domination and hegemony. And in countries where national liberation struggles are raging, such as Zimbabwe and Azania, advanced forces are very hip to the bloody expansionism and hegemonistic practice of the SSI, even as they wage war on tottering racist regimes bound to U.S. imperialism hand and foot. In Azania, for instance, where rebellions and armed offensives against the racists are growing in their consistency and intensity, such as in Soweto and Capetown, leading national liberation organizations such as PAC (Pan-African Congress) have openly denounced the machinations of SSI's behind the scenes actual collaboration with the Vorster regime through its puppets such as the so-called Communist Party of South Africa, who until a minute ago were actually preaching *peaceful transition* in South Africa! Meanwhile Moscow ceaselessly makes a big noise about "supporting" Zimbabwe's armed struggle and opposing the Smith racist regime. But the African countries and people know well enough that this so-called support simply means using military aid as its lever to project its influence into the future liberated and independent Zimbabwe. Its opposition simply means replacing the racism there with its own neocolonialism. In Zimbabwe the liberation movements practicing a higher level of unity, and persisting in armed struggle, have caused the racist Smith regime to visibly shake, and their U.S. & British backers to call for Smith to effect some settlement immediately. They try to lull the movement to sleep by babbling about the need for negotiations, but negotations, as the advanced forces understand, must be based on armed struggle. The liberation movement there is now using dual revolutionary tactics, talking negotiation but continuing to fight against the racists' use of counterrevolutionary dual tactics, talk of negotiations but continuing to attack, even carrying their criminal assaults into Mozambique and Zambia. The imperialists meanwhile tried to raise up the reactionary Idi Amin to prominence with daily reports of his lunacy, to make it seem that the problem with Africa is Amin and clownish Africans rather than imperialism. They expose Amin, who they put in in the first place, why not expose Vorster and Smith? But this diversion like the Andy Young trick is a trick the people see through readily, because it does not stop the armed struggle, which is the only method of liberation.

Many liberation movements who wanted to take a noncommittal or even soft position on SSI last year have had to learn the hard way that the Third World's most dangerous enemy is SSI, because it is hidden but no less an imperialist than the U.S. In Ethiopia, for instance, where the U.S. was openly backing the feudal bourgeois military junta, this bloody pack of oppressors have the nerve to call themselves socialists and pretend to kick out imperialism and thus legitimize their claim to be called socialists by closing up U.S. agencies, while simultaneously embracing the infamous imperialists from the Soviet Union. This is a wedding made in blood, both having the same relationship to socialism—social fascists domestically.

This means the social imperialists will also be helping the Ethiopian junta attack the Eritrean national liberation movement, which is struggling for Eritrean self-determination in Ethiopia. It shows clearly that only a high level of unity, self-reliance and armed struggle can resolve the national liberation struggles, not dependence on any so-called natural allies, who want to practice an "avant-garde" imperialism.

In the Palestinian struggle, the liberation movement, though making steady progress against the illegal Zionist racist regime calling itself Israel, nevertheless is being constantly obstructed from pursuing the most direct cause of struggle against the Zionists because of U.S.-Soviet collusion. Israel has become one of South Africa's staunchest allies and is another of the U.S. imperialists' antifreedom projects. But the Soviet Union, again under the guise of aid, has consistently kept the Palestinians in a no-war, no-peace condition, and as the Egyptians exposed so clearly when they terminated their friendship pact with the Soviets, the U.S.S.R. will not give the Arabs the weapons they need, as the U.S. does for Israel, and the U.S.S.R. will not even show the Arabs how to operate the more advanced weapons, an old colonialist trick. And the Soviets are even going along with the imperialist game of offering the Palestinians a little strip of land on the West Bank of the Jordan River to pretend they are getting their land—"a national home," they call it—and the SSI imperialists are urging the PLO to settle for this.

It is the superpowers' contention which is at the base of the disorder and intranquillity in the world today. But as our Chinese comrades say, "No matter how desperately they may struggle, they will not escape their ultimate doom. The people are the masters of history. The future of the world belongs to them, and it is very bright." *(Peking Review* #20, 5/14/76, p. 7) Mao sd, "The world is changing in a direction increasingly favorable to the people of all countries. This is one aspect, a principal aspect. But we must also see the other aspect—the aggressive nature of imperialism will not change. . . . Modern war is born of imperialism, Lenin said. As long as imperialism exists, there will be no tranquillity in the world. The danger of a new world war still exists. This is another trend in the development of today's world." We must be very careful to see both trends in the world, and our tactics must change if the trends themselves change. The superpowers are opposing and interfering with the national liberation movements as they must, one openly siding with colonialism and racism, though trying to hide it more and more, the other superpower calling itself socialist, undermining revolution wherever and whenever it can. Its open line of peaceful transition to socialism is public knowledge; how then can it support armed revolution in peoples' democratic struggles? In the countries fighting by means of liberation movements against imperialism, there are two stages of their revolutions. First is the stage of democratic revolution, against absolutism, colonialism, foreign domination, feudalism, and in such struggles a broad liberation front of all the classes opposed to imperialism can be united to make democratic revolution. But as Lenin pointed out in his great work *Two Tactics of Social Democracy in the Democratic Revolution,* and later Mao Tse-Tung in his works on *New Democracy* at the stage of democratic revolution, it is no longer necessary to stop at that stage as did the countries of Western Europe and the United States, which became bourgeois dictatorships. Lenin pointed out, and the Russian Revolution and the Chinese Revolution and democratic revolutions in the Third World in the main have confirmed it, that if the democratic revolution is led by the proletariat, then at the stage of democratic revolution there is no bourgeois dictatorship, because the proletariat will lead uninterruptedly to the next stage of revolution, socialist revolution. And this process is going on all over the Third World. On the doorstep of the U.S.A., the liberation movement in Puerto Rico against U.S. imperialism is heightening, and the bourgeoisie's talk of statehood is a last-ditch diversion trying to stave off the inevitable, the liberation of the Puerto Rican people from U.S. colonial rule. To exploit this state of affairs, in which the people are driving U.S. imperialism into the sea, SSI is sneaking around trying to penetrate the national liberation movement through the revisionist PSP (Puerto Rican Socialist Party) who have become the open puppets of bankrupt CPUSA. We must support the Puerto Rican liberation movement against both superpowers, and while struggling against U.S. imperialism, don't close our eyes to the dangers of SSI.

But the Puerto Rican people in the U.S. are an oppressed national minority, part of the multinational U.S. proletariat.

In the U.S.A, however, an advanced imperialist country, there is a need for only one stage revolution. And even in the Black Belt South, the land base of the Afro-American nation, the united front against imperialism must be joined together with the multinational proletariat to fight for socialist revolution. However, in the U.S.A. we lack a genuine communist party, to lead the masses of us in revolutionary struggle; a Revolutionary Marxist-Leninist Communist Party, based on Marxism-Leninism-Mao Tse-tung thought. We have had no such party in the U.S.A. since the tragic degeneration in the late fifties and fall into revisionism of the CPUSA, which is now the left wing of the Democratic Party. Because of this, *party building* is the central task of all revolutionaries in the U.S. Party building is part of the revolutionary main trend of revolution which is coursing through the world today. Such a party must be built if we are to make socialist revolution in this country, smashing capitalism and building socialism under the dictatorship of the proletariat. Such a party is also the people's main defense against imperialist war.

As the liberation movements of the Third World drive imperialism out the front door, the normal internal economic crisis of monopoly capitalism intensifies, since now the superprofits gouged out of the Third World are cut back by revolution, and there is less booty to use to spread opportunism inside the fortress of imperialism itself. The bourgeoisie must shift its economic crisis onto the backs of the people. Budget cuts, layoffs, phasing out of social welfare programs and ghetto coolout programs all contribute to the steadily rising tide of revolutionary consciousness inside the U.S. The struggle to build a new communist party in the U.S.A. is part of the world front of revolution aimed at smashing the world front of imperialism. But in the U.S. today there are many sham party-building travesties going on that serve only to confuse the masses, though advanced forces learn even from these petty bourgeois fantasies what the party of the proletariat must not be, as well as what it must be. The so-called Communist Labor Party, the so-called Revolutionary Communist Party, and just recently October League's newly formed Communist Party (Marxist-Leninist) are all examples of petty bourgeois frenzy and impatience but not examples of the party of a new type that Lenin spoke of. These sectarian little groups have neither unified Marxist-Leninists nor won the advanced to Communism so that Advanced Workers form the greatest part of their parties in key industries all over this country. And their programs have more to do with reform than revolution. And in the wings others, such as the bankrupt so-called Revolutionary Wing of PRRWO (Puerto Rican Revolutionary Workers Organization) and RWL (Revolutionary Workers Organization) wait to stumble into the public eye with their latest mistake, which they will call the U.S. Bolshevik Party, which will also not be the party, and now WVO (Workers Viewpoint Organization) threatens to make the same mistake—tho we hope not.

But whatever these groups do, they cannot stop the ultimate formation of The Revolutionary ML Communist Party, based on MLM, which will destroy declining U.S. capitalism from within, just as the liberation movements all over the world are smashing it harder against the wall every day and bringing revolution in the U.S. closer by the minute. Unlike bourgeois nationalist elements like Stokely Carmichael, who thinks that revolution can only be made in Africa, thereby protecting the U.S. bourgeoisie as cleverly as Andy Young, we know that revolution can and will be made in the U.S., and by the multinational proletariat. Our cry:

PEOPLE OF THE WORLD UNITE TO CRUSH THE SUPERPOWERS!
U.S. AND SOVIET SOCIAL IMPERIALISM!
VICTORY FOR THE NATIONAL LIBERATION MOVEMENTS
AGAINST IMPERIALISM
IS A VICTORY FOR THE U.S. PROLETARIAT AND OPPRESSED
NATIONALITIES!
ML UNITE—WIN THE ADVANCED TO COMMUNISM
IN THE USA BUILD A REVOLUTIONARY ML COMMUNIST PARTY
BASED ON MLM

WAR/PHILLY BLUES/
DEEPER BOP
from *John Coltrane:*
Where Does Art Come From?

Around the time the Nazis were beginning to pay for the mistake of invading the Soviet Union, John Coltrane was coming out of high school. This was 1943, the Battle of Stalingrad, and the turning point of the antifascist war. Hitler did not learn from either Napoleon or the fox who f-ed with the tarbaby, i.e., you can get in but getting out's a real problem! By the end of the year, the entire war had been turned around and the back of the German offensive thrust twisted and gnarled. For example, one third of the 300,000 Nazi soldiers were encircled and captured—that is, 100,000 troops—and 147,200 Nazis died. As Stalin said, "Stalingrad signified the decline of the German fascist army. As is well known, the Germans were unable to recover after the Stalingrad slaughter." ("The Twenty-sixth Anniversary of the October Revolution," *The Essential Stalin,* Anchor.)

I point this out in detail because most of us in the U.S. thought it was solely the efforts of the U.S.A., notably Van Johnson, &c, who had beat the Nazis, when in fact the second front that the Allies promised to the Soviet Union, i.e., the invasion of Europe, D-Day so called, did not take place until the next year, 1944, after the Germans had got their behinds kicked hard and regular by the Russians!

John Coltrane had now finished high school and split for Philly with some friends, making the classic journey from the Afro-American homeland to the "promising" North. If you consider it, it is really a journey into the United States from the land of one of the nations the U.S. oppresses. More immigrants into the "melting pot" looking for the streets lined with Gold. Hey. And what you find? For the blacks, the war years offered a further way into industry, toward a further proletarianizing of the masses of Afro-Americans, a further transformation from the largely peasant people black people were at the end of the Civil War (and the later destruction of the Reconstruction governments that completed their consolidation into an oppressed nation in the Black Belt South) into a largely proletarian, i.e., industrial working-class-centered mass, both as an oppressed nation in the South and as an oppressed national minority-oppressed nationality in the rest of the U.S.

Coming into the Phillys and Newarks and Harlems and Chicagos really meant and means coming into miniature versions of the Black Belt homeland itself. The immigrants find out that *they* are the gold that the streets are lined with, and the bosses drop them into their pockets. There *is* more money, it is more regular than the inconsistencies of the farm or small mill in the Black Belt. The exploitation and oppression may take on a slightly different form, but the content is the same. It is a national oppression. The blacks are doubly oppressed, as a working class in relationship to capitalism, and also because of their nationality, Afro-Americans, and the forcible occupation of their land, the Black Belt South, by U.S. imperialism. And this national oppression is made even more hideous by racism, the oppressed being easily identified and the paths and methods of "escape" from the new ghetto trap being all the more easily obstructed.

They did not come to Philly, they came to South or North Philly, or not to Newark but to "The Hill." They didn't check Manhattan so much as Harlem, and South Chi was where you could be you went up that way. They came to secondhand neighborhoods, with secondhand houses, and secondhand schools and sometimes even secondhand factories. But all the time secondhand jobs no matter if the factory was brand-new. But in comparison to before the war, the factories offered "good money"—if you could find somewhere to live, and get your children in school all right. But they lived in reproductions of the Black Belt; as Harry Haywood says, "the shadow of the plantation" extended itself right up into the U.S.A. proper, as it had since the first huge migrations at the turn of the century into the twenties. Even though there was not the same proliferation of "White Only" signs one still saw in the South, in the exact same fashion as in South Africa, the national oppression and racism, and its concomitant outrages, segregation and discrimination, slums, shack houses, shabby health care, unemployment or underemployment. Even during high-employment periods, poor education from low-level schools, police repression and brutality—these were constants that made the Northern cities just like home. For it was to the cities, the urban centers, brought into existence by the great concentrations of industry and commerce, that the Afro-American immigrants came. And to this day, the greatest part of the migrating Afro-American nationality is housed in about twenty-six cities in the U.S.

Factory wages were "good money" only in comparison to the no money of slavery, or the next to no money of sharecropping or small farming. If one considered, however, that working on an assembly line, say, with thousands of other workers, one did not see Henry Ford or his latest mistress on the line with one, and yet for every employee on that line—Ford had 200,000 such employees by 1974—Ford made *himself* a clear two-dollar[1] profit per hour, which is $400,000 an hour profit for *him,* then one might not think that money so good. In fact, one would then be waking up to the principle called *surplus value* that Karl Marx hipped the world to, which is the secret of capitalist accumulation and exploitation.

[1] "The Gap Between The Rich and the Poor Is Becoming Ever Wider," *Albania Today,* reprint #1.)

John Coltrane, like the other immigrants, got a job in a mill. Later on he worked across the river in the Campbell's Soup factory. But John's real focus and interest in Philadelphia was still what had grown up inside him these last few years, music. He started going to music school—first to the Orenstein School, and then for a longer period to the Granoff Studios, where he began to stretch out much more.

In the Northern cities there was more mobility and anonymity for a young man like Trane. The old mores of the Black Belt were changed by the industrial North in all areas. The death of both of the male breadwinners in the Coltrane family had also shifted the family more directely into the proletariat, as is always the case with the lower petty bourgeoisie: they are the first ruined by any negative change in the capitalist economy and are easily broken and pauperized by any rapid shift of fortune. Throughout the whole period of Philadelphia residence Trane mostly went to music school and worked in a factory. In Philadelphia also was a close-up relationship to the slick harsh big-city blues. It is in the cities that the basic twelve bar AAB form is taken to its heights (its depths). What is heaped on it is experience of life, and absorption, understanding, of its forms and processes. Also there is a more thoroughly sophisticated "urbane" use of musical resources. To the four-, eight-, ten-, twelve-stringed guitars with the bottlenecks slid up and down the frets, there are added electricity, wailing horns, and groups on every corner or in every other hallway, cut further away from the church, and the religious framework, though in some ways indelibly linked to it.

From the early city blues, with guitar or boogie piano accompaniment, the changes of the classical singers like Ma Rainey and Bessie Smith, who sang with larger groups or even big "show" bands, were absorbed, and during the late thirties and the war years still further changes developed in the blues form. The cities could contain at the same time (now especially because of phonograph records and the radio, plus the constant migration of people from the Black Belt) all the blues styles and jazz styles, interrelating and influencing each other. (See "The Blues Continuum" in *Blues People*, p. 166.) No matter the various forms and styles Afro-American music took on, the blues, as the blues, still developed directly, i.e., no matter what it was shaped like in other, related expressions, such as jazz. There was still a straight-out blues, going through changes, but still a blues, and still straight out. The great jazz players, the great Afro-American musicians and composers, have always understood this and used the blues one way or another. Pres and Bird could play blues make you weep, and so too would John Coltrane.

Around the early forties in the big cities, rhythm and blues was the straight-out blues style most popular. It especially carried the blues fire of the Kansas City-Southwest area, where a good many big blues bands, including Bill Basie's, came from. There were other bands like Bennie Moten (K.C.), Walter Page and the Blue Devils (Oklahoma City), Charlie Creath (St. Louis), and

Troy Floyd (Texas) were all big blues bands rumbling their most expressive during the thirties. These bands, even during the effetery that commercial swing was spreading around, maintained their big brash dramatic blues sound. The big-band blues "shouters" came out of this tradition. Although the blues shout is as old as the *griots* (singing history tellers) of the African continent, the emergence of the big blues bands, and with them the electrified guitars and smashing driving rhythm sections with many horns, meant that the singers literally had to shout to be heard. The R&B shouters were also hooked up directly to the field hollers and coon yells and blues shouts of the earlier country blues and work song era, i.e. when they predominated, because you can hear both country blues and yells right today.

"The constant use of the riff, heavy drumming, and unison screaming saxophones behind the singers was all a legacy of the blues-oriented Southwestern bands," with singers like Joe Turner and Jimmy Rushing. Men like "Wynonie Harris, Jimmy Witherspoon, Bull Moose Jackson and B. B. King were among the best and the most sophisticated of the shouters; the more 'primitive' school of shouters like Muddy Waters, T-Bone Walker, Bo Diddley, Smokey Hogg seemed to bring a deeper knowledge of older blues forms into the music." (Op cit., p. 170.) During the war years R&B developed to the height of its popularity. It seemed, and was, louder and wilder than the older blues forms. Added to the plaintiveness and wail of blues was a power and dynamism, an aggressiveness. R&B emerged as the basic contemprorary black blues style of the forties. The whole style embraced both show business and performance, but also centered on the deep concerns of black life.

There also developed an instrumental style that went further and further out, in the direction of the ever wilder shouted R&B style. Eddie "Lockjaw" Davis, Illinois Jacquet, Willis "Gatortail" Jackson, Big Jay McNeely, and Lynn Hope were known as "the honkers." During this period there was a reaction among those closest to the blues to the commercialism and vapidity of monopoly music. The R&B shouts, honks and screeches took them outside all that, though to be sure, and this is a constant of capitalist society, soon there were also imitations and imitations of imitations, and indeed a full-blown commercial style of R&B emerged which was as monopoly-controlled and vapid as commercial swing. As long as the motive of making money is an end in itself, to the majority of the people's detriment, commercial watered-down versions of anything will be manufactured and commercialized for just that reason, making money, and nothing else. For someone not to understand this, or to expect something else of this society, is naive and idealistic. The purpose of capitalist society is not the well-being and development of humanity; love, truth, profundity, art or any of that; it is to make money, and it does this by exploiting the majority of the people in the world.

So that Trane entering into Philly entered into two developing streams of black music. The basic blues thrust was rhythm and blues—the most modern blues form, the standard speech of the ghetto. And now, more than in High Point, North Carolina (where Trane spent his early years), this basic modern city blues form became the fundamental environment for Coltrane. With the radio, phonographs and traveling blues bands, there is little doubt that R&B had some entrance into the small towns of the South as well as, naturally, the Black Belt cities. But the earlier, rawer blues styles always were more in evidence in the Belt as the predominant expression than in the North. The screaming style coming out of the Southwest followed the big-band circuits, and the smaller nightclubs that featured full-out blues expression—although some of the bigger bands tried, if they could afford it, to stay out of the deeper South, where they would run into the straight-out presence of U.S. imperialism, and its running dogs racism and repression.

The fact that Coltrane had come from the kind of background he had, and had learned music the way he had and where he had—in the Black Belt—did not mean that he "never heard much black music until he moved to Philadelphia," as some simple souls would have it. Black music is a broad experience and expression. There is a blues continuum wherever a sizable number of black people live and work and have some history of residence. It means almost all the forms of blues expression have got some fluency there. The black spiritual and the dance band both have some connection with the overall expression and life of black music. What Coltrane was exposed to in Philadelphia was the most contemporary urban blues style. But in the national oppression of a people, there is a leveling and gathering of all the elements in that nation, not to the exclusion of class distinctions but in spite of them. And this leveling and gathering makes the resources of the Afro-American folk and contemporary tradition, in whatever area, much more common—and much more accessible—to a wider number of the oppressed. R&B could not have suprised Coltrane; it is much more likely that it simply confirmed and extended what the blues tradition had already taught him. It was the basic contemporary blues expression of the Afro-American urban masses.

The first paying jobs Trane had in music were with R&B groups, and the necessary credentials for the R&B saxist was a big big sound, and blue funky intonation. The rooting in the bad blues, the old blues, was fundamental. To my own view, the Afro-American musical tradition is rooted in blues—i.e., rhythm and blues, in all its basic forms. And without anchoring oneself in those basic traditions, absorbing them and being absorbed by them, the nature of one's approach to black music can only be shallow.

No matter what kind of innovations are made within the overall tradition of Afro-American music, the most impressive of these innovations have reinforced, and raised to a higher level, the Afro-American folk tradition, i.e., those materials and experiences drawn from out of the lives of the masses of workers and farmers who constitute the majority of the Afro-American people. It is critical to understand this because it is the nature of this relationship as it exists in various musicians' musical contributions that has determined the essential character and validity of those contributions. These times Trane finished high school and came to Philadelphia in were hectic times. Times of great transition and rapid-fire change. *The whole world was in turmoil,* as war raged across Europe and Asia. And people all over the world were drawn in some way, whether great or small, into the current of change created by that turmoil.

The same year the U.S. joined the war (1941) was the year that Charlie Parker, born six years before Trane and the greatest of the bebop innovators, the new Afro-American musical expression that erupted at the beginning of the forties, finally reached the Big Apple, New York City. It was only two years later that Trane came to PhillyDilly! The difference in age and experience accounted for the disparity of their accomplishment at this time. But it should be established how much of a *continuer* of a tradition was Coltrane.

The early war years saw Bird (along with Dizzy Gillespie, Thelonius Monk and Kenny Clarke) experimenting in places like Monroe's and Minton's in Harlem, developing the musical explosion of bop. By the time Bird finally stood the world on its ear on "the street" (Fifty-second Street, which was the downtown mecca of the beboppers at full exposure—just as New Orleans had been for early jazz, Chicago in the early twenties, Kansas City in the thirties, and the Village in the sixties), Coltrane had been drafted into the U.S. Navy, where he played clarinet in the band.

From 1942 to 1944 there was a recording ban imposed by the American Federation of Musicians due to disagreements with the major record companies, but also there was a shortage of basic recording materials because of the war. This was the richest period of the developing new music, including the short-lived existence of two of the best of the few big bop bands. The first was the Earl Hines band (in 1942), which included Dizzy Gillespie and Benny Harris in the trumpet section; Benny Green, trombonist; Shadow Wilson, drums; and Bird and Scoops Cary in the reeds. Later on, in 1943, a young female singer joined the band: Sarah Vaughan from Newark, New Jersey. Bird played tenor in this group.

The other was Billy Eckstine's "dream" band, the bebop ultra ultra. B was a middle-class, Howard University ex who fronted the band as, of course, the male vocalist. He later went on to become the most influential male vocalist of his time, before racists whitelisted him for refusing to play porters in movie musicals. B was never a great valve trombonist, but he put together a dynamite band, which was mainly unrecorded. In fact, the chief recordings of the heavy bop years were made by amateur recording nonexperts who were getting it down for their own pleasure. Some of them cut out Bird because they didn't dig him, others cut out everybody else but Bird, because all they wanted to do was dig Bird's solos. (See Ross Russell, *Bird Lives!* Charterhouse.) B's unbelievable band consisted of nine carryovers from the ill-fated Hines band, Dizzy, Bird, Gene Ammons, Leo Parker, Benny Green, John Malachi, Tommy Potter, Shadow Wilson, Sarah Vaughan was the female vocalist, plus Art Blakey, Tadd Dameron, arranger, among others. Miles Davis, another product of the petty bourgeoisie, the son of an East St. Louis dentist, showed up as a temporary substitute for the one of band's trumpet players, Buddy Anderson.

What the recording ban did also was keep the music to more or less a small circle until well into 1945. To a certain extent bebop represented a revolt against the monopoly music of commercial swing and against the big-band "jails," as Bird called them, where this nonmusic was made. Bebop arose out of the small bands which were the experimental laboratories for the development of new ideas, which could never see the light of day in the big nonswing swing bands. The small groups, working out their ideas in small clubs to small audiences, tended to enforce a kind of isolation, some of which could not be avoided. The recording ban saw to that. But some of the musicians held up the isolation as a positive thing in itself, rather than seeing that it was isolation from the commercial garbage of monopoly-controlled music that was positive, but certainly isolation from the people could never be positive.

The recording ban set up a kind of exaggerated "cultural lag" between what the most creative musicians in the Afro-American musical tradition were doing and their widest audience. So by 1945, since the music had not been chronicled step by step through its early growing stages because of the recording ban, when bop was first heard widely it caused quite a few people to misunderstand it and dismiss it foolishly. Though it should be clear that it was taken up by many youth, and other sectors of the people, as the pure breath of change itself!

Trane first heard Bird and Diz in the Navy, as the first records were beginning to get released. "Groovin' High," "A Dizzy Atmosphere," "All the Things You Are," "Salt Peanuts," "Shaw Nuff," "Hot House," "Lover Man" (featuring Sassy Vaughan) are some of the first releases and some of the best, all put out by a small independent label that shot off into the field while the monopolists were still hassling with the musicians' union.

Trane was not a child with heavy influences passing around him invisible to his conscious self. He was already a somewhat acomplished musician. To get in the military bands you have to be able to get around a little on the instrument and read fairly well, because there is a high degree of competition based on all the dudes in the service, especially during the time of the draft, who found themselves in with "them war cats" but who were "not interested in no war shit."

The Bird-Diz-bop influence was a shaping force, a critical element in John Coltrane's musical and intellectual life. And all the things that bop was, as music, as social commentary, as life doctrine, as class expression, had to be, to some extent, absorbed by the youthful but rapidly maturing Trane.

If R&B was the basic contemporary Afro-American urban blues, what was bebop? And what were its roots? Various kinds of bourgeois-oriented, chauvinist and otherwise flawed music and art and social critics had unkind words to say about bop, and by now these are well documented. (See *Blues People* or *Bird Lives!* or *Jazz: A People's Music).* The unhep, then unhip, then corny, music magazine *DownBeat* actually had to *rereview* the bop classics because they had torn their ass so bad when they reviewed the records when they first came out—demanding, as the bourgeoisie always does, that any expression in this society be accountable to and controllable by it. Why Did The Music Have To Sound Like That? was the question. Why didn't it sound like something quiet and invisible and nice or dead and respectable or at least European? (And this is not to make the case that jazz is something that is exclusively black, that there are no white or Asian &c players. That is nonsense. A nationalist friend of mine was genuinely embarrassed but enlightened when he found out from me that a record that he admired, "I Can't Get Started," and the dude who composed and played and sung it, Bunny Berigan, was a tragic Irishman with a derby.) But the heaviest sources of jazz and blues are Afro-American folk sources, and it has been Afro-American people who have been the principal innovators. And this has shaped the peculiar strengths and weaknesses of the music.

Just as the monopoly music manipulators had succeeded in flooding the country with inferior imitations of real big-band swing, the most creative musicians broke away from this sterile form in rebellion, and using small groups as laboratories produced a new music that raised the level of jazz, of Afro-American music, of American music, of "popular" music and of world music in general. Sidney Finkelstein in his important book tells us how the immigrants, "Jewish, Italian, Irish, ... who came to these shores with a cultural heritage that could have added much to American life, were discouraged from using this heritage and instead given not a better culture, but the phony contrived and synthetic 'popular' culture that is good business but bad art. They have nevertheless made a contribution." *(Jazz: A People's Music,* pp. 270-1.) For the Afro-American people, however, the basic foundation of the expoitative capitalist society is built on the fundamental and historical exploitation and oppression of black people, based initially on slavery, and then and now on imperialist control of the Afro-American nation in the Black Belt South.

The added element of racism (i.e., national oppression is basic, the racial aspect of it making it even more hideously effective) has served to isolate and separate the Afro-American people from the American mainstream. The bourgeoisie has desired this, so as to superexploit them, as well as divide the white and black working class to obstruct the development of the multinational rebellion against this bankrupt system of monopoly capitalism. But at the same time the bourgeoisie has tried to impose the same mainstream bourgeois ideas on the Afro-American people so as to tie them to the same system. Of course, there is a contradiction in this: it means that neither the isolation nor the absorption can be completely effective.

Part of the resiliency of the Afro-American culture in the face of the attempt to subjugate and absorb it by the bourgeoisie is its separation. The Afro-American nation in the Black Belt South has not been "assimilated" into the U.S. nation via "the productive forces of imperialism" as the backward social democrats and the bourgeoisie wished. The segregation and discrimination heaped on the black people all over the United States, in the replicas of the Black Belt they are made to live in, serves to keep blacks on the margins of American life, despite the petty bourgeois symbols, i.e., tokens, the bourgeoisie lift up to pretend that there is some "equality" for the Afro-American people in the U.S., or democracy for the masses rather than bourgeois democracy, which is in reality a bourgeois dictatorship. So that even the majority of the petty bourgeois blacks understand the hypocrisy of the capitalist white supremacy system.The black working masses inhabit a marginal stratum in, and have a marginal relationship to, the U.S. economic system, in the sense that they have the worst jobs with the lowest pay, and the highest unemployment. One third of the black population today are in the poverty stratum as defined by the U.S. Department of Commerce.

In the music business, for example, the same frustration and racism was discovered as any other facet of U.S. life. The blacks who had to develop a complete form of more or less self-satisfying self-oriented musical expression because of their national oppression found that even in that area they had been forced to develop staggering competence and creativity but they were still the last and the lowest! So even the black college types who fronted some of the successful big bands in the thirties found that "success" was more artistic than financial, and that it did next to nothing to break down the real exploitation and oppression they and the masses suffered, no matter who said what.

The exploitation of working people in general in the United States must be understood as a fundamental platform for all this national oppression of blacks we are pointing out. But what is key is that the Afro-American people, like the other oppressed nationalities in this capitalist society, are doubly oppressed, by class and by nationality. And it is this *double* oppression, and the attendant isolation, that gives the folk culture, and its modern expression, its strength and resiliency in the face of bourgeois assaults.

Bebop rebelled against the absorption into garbage, monopoly music; it also signified a rebellion by the people who played the music, because it was not just the music that rebelled, as if the music had fallen out the sky! But even more, dig it, it signified a rebellion rising out of the masses themselves, since that is the source of social movement—the people themselves!

The urban blood circa the early forties reacted to life in the U.S., and its constant oppression and exploitation unlike the bloods before them. This is true *only* in terms of the intensity and the level of consciousness, but these are only possible because of what had gone on before. There have been slave rebellions since the slavers grabbed the Africans in Africa and dragged them back to the thirteen colonies to build up the early accumulation of capital of developing capitalism. But the people in the forties had all the past to stand on, as the people in the fifties had the forties and the rest of it. As we in the last part of the seventies have all of what went before to stand on and relate to, or measure our efforts at whatever by. In the music, bebop raised up that the mainstream music was dull sterile garbage, and what they, the serious musicians were doing, was more expressive, vital, beautiful, energetic, esthetic, morally sound, representative, descriptive. Bebop was a much more open rebellion in the sense that the musicians openly talked of the square, hopeless, corny rubbish put forth by the bourgeoisie. They made fun of it, refused to play it except in a mocking fashion, making it even more ridiculous. They took "popular" music (not really popular, but imposed by the music bosses through their absolute control of the media), turned the "heads" or melodies into "bottoms," just their essential chords, and blew what they wanted to, changing the names of the tunes and even getting the new tunes copyrighted.

The whole fabric of Afro-American life raised rebellion to a higher level by the forties. The thirties was a time of struggle. The struggle against the national oppression represented by the Scottsboro Boys frame-up was typical. The struggle then was to try to enact an *anti-lynch* law; the struggle for the vote and education &c would not reach its peak for another decade, after the war. Discrimination and segregation were ways of life even in the North, and this coupled with the basic struggle of working people against the ravages of capitalism had made the thirties generally hot. The fight by working people to build the unions, particularly the CIO, came to a head by the late thirties and the black struggle was one spearhead of this fight.

One important aspect of the militancy that had intensified in the workers' and black national struggle by the end of the thirties was the correct line and revolutionary work of the Communist Party U.S.A. in leading some of those key struggles. For instance, the communist International Labor Committee took the heaviest part of the work to fight against the legal lynching and government frame-up of the Scottsboros. It was the CPUSA, again, that led the struggles to build the unions, and in so doing brought a higher unity between black and white workers. In the Black Belt, the pit of black oppression because it is an oppressed nation subjugated by imperialism, the Communist Party led the largely black Sharecroppers Union in its battles against the big landowners.

As the war came, even though blacks were asked to cool out their protests in the interest of national defense (a tactic that even the CPUSA went along with), the causes of those protests did not cease but intensified. For one thing, as the masses of blacks swept up from the South, just as they had done around the time of World War I, conflicts between blacks and whites intensified, fed by the racist American system. Between 1940 and 1943 at least seventeen blacks are known to have been lynched! (Twombly, *Blacks in White America Since 1865*, McKay.) The service tended to show blacks other ways of life and to break down many inhibitions that were fostered by national oppression. Clashes between black soldiers and white civilian police and military police escalated to almost a commonplace during these years. Sectors of the bourgeoisie resisted the utilization of Afro-Americans in the factories despite the war need. And though the social democrat A. Philip Randolph "threatened" a March on Washington to bring about "fair employment," on June 1, 1941, Roosevelt called an executive conference of these Negro leaders, the day they were to lead the March. Then on June 25, 1941, Roosevelt issued his executive order setting up the FEPC, the Fair Employment Practices Committee. This meant, on the real side, that the sector of the bourgeoisie in control wanted to make sure it could get all the cheap labor necessary for the war effort.

By 1943 the so-called race riots broke out in large Northern cities, exactly as they had in 1919 during the First World War, and exactly as more intense rebellions were to break out in the late sixties around the period of the Vietnam War. Detroit, as it was in the sixties, was the site of intense rebellions and black-white clashes, as was New York City. Detroit is an area with a high concentration of the industrial proletariat, and waves of Southern Black Belt immigrants enlarge that black sector of the working class hourly.

In 1941 Richard Wright's *Native Son* reached Broadway, and was the most talked about work by a black author. The work not only questioned black national oppression but showed the rebellion and illness it caused, and indeed the illness of the entire society. Wright's works all raised up the deepgoing sickness of U.S. society especially in its relationship to black people. Paul Robeson was also on the scene, onstage, in the concert hall and even making films. Both Robeson and Wright were left-oriented: Wright had even been a member of the Communist Party, while Robeson was always close to the party. Paul Robeson's version of Othello was the longest running production of a Shakespeare play on Broadway.

In both of these men's work, attacks on black national oppression and particularly on discrimination and segregation were pronounced. By the midforties, when the war was finally over, black troops came back having bled for this country and not wanting to hear any shit about being segregated, discriminated against, &c. But this happened, on another level, during the Korean War which followed and the Vietnam War which followed that.

In the stream of protest is the stream of development as well. It is the new coming into existence, confronting and destroying what does not serve it. It is the confrontation of opposites which is the very definition of development. It is not a straight-ahead, straight-line process; it is slow and tortuous, though in times of revolution, where the quantitative buildup has yielded to qualitative change there is a rush of *revolutionary* movement. "Evolution is what turns the cycle, revolution is what completes it!"

In Afro-American music, the rebellion and protest became an actual reaching back to go forward, a reassertion of the elemental and the essential. It was felt in all aspects as the R&B shook off its older Tin Pan Alleyisms in the burst of the shouters and the electricity and took it back to basic rhythm and blues. But out of this basic blues environment, which itself is constantly changing, the so-called jazz expression also takes its shape. This expression always begins by trying to utilize the fundamental Afro-American musical impulse, blues, and extend it, in all the ways it can: instrumentally (blues was basically a vocal music), technically and emotionally and philosophically. The harmonic, melodic and of course rhythmic innovations that jazz has made upon the blues impulse has produced some of the most exciting music of the twentieth century anywhere in the world. But this kind of Afro-American music utilizes a much broader musical palette with which to express itself than does blues. Jazz, so called, calls upon everything in the American experience it is aware of. It has borrowed more widely than blues (it is, in its best aspect, the blues doing the borrowing!). It has made use of and makes use of the music of the white national minority in the Black Belt homeland (called country and Western), "classical," semi-classical, quasi-classical, Latin, the American "popular" song—which it promptly transformed. Not to mention that it has continually gone back farther to where the blues came from to the shores of Africa, or when it wants to the Middle and Far East. It is intellectual and internationalist (but deeply emotional and with a national form), a working and oppressed, people's music; it has nevertheless affected every class in society!

Jazz is by its nature *ambitious.* It has succeeded in being the fullest expression of American life. At its most expressive it is exactly that, not just an expression of the Afro-American's life but with its borrowings and wanderings, its pretensions and strengths of character, it sums up the U.S. in a thousand ways. While blues is more specifically a *black music!*

John Coltrane returned to Philly from the still segregated Navy, as the whole of the U.S. armed forces in the Second World War were segregated! He had already been exposed to a certain extent to the heaviest expression of the music at that time, bebop. But not directly. People would say, "What made you *become* a bopper?" But the question does not understand that what was called bop had merely summed up musically where everything was at, including we ourselves. It was simply the most direct statement of our time, place and condition. If we were conscious, to the extent that we were, we would be boppers!

Trane came back playing in the clubs and cocktail lounges of Philly, mainly in the R&B groups which became the standard musical environment of Afro-American ghettoes. The blues sound of the day. He had started this work in the basic funky blues bands just before he went to the Navy. This was the easiest musical work to find, just as it is today in any black community, playing the blues in its contemporary forms. Trane played with dance bands, vocal groups, small blues combos, his entire early professional experience is with the rhythm and blues bands.

By the time the war was over the bop explosion was beginning to touch everywhere. Trane had resumed his studies with the Granoff Studios when he got back, but still clarinet and alto saw most of his attention, even though he did some studying of the larger tenor saxophone at the studios. What Bird and Diz Trane had heard on records had so impressed Trane that he set out to understand what they were doing theoretically, and at the same time this caused him to do even some deeper probing into music theory. The three fundamental struggles that push history forward are class struggle, the struggle for production and scientific experiment, though, as Mao Tse-tung has pointed out, among those three, while all are important, class struggle is key. Because finally it is class struggle that will transform the society politically.

The Afro-American people are, by the very nature of their lives in the U.S., an oppressed nationality, largely working-class, and they must wage a fierce class struggle to make any progress at all. This is not theoretical but a day-to-day fact of life. The struggle for production as well is a basic fact of the worker's life, which class constitutes the majority of the Afro-American nationality. And the innovators of the music, traditionally, have been, in the main, from the working class (though the roots of blues go back to a largely peasant people, and some contributions have been made by elements in the lower petty bourgeoisie).

In looking at the principal innovators of bop, for instance: Bird, from Kansas City (a key area in the thirties for the origin of the big blues bands and the shouters, it was where Charlie Parker first mastered his instrument with the Jay McShann band). Bird's father was a vaudevillian and Pullman car chef, his mother a domestic. Dizzy Gillespie, was born in Cheraw, South Carolina, the heart of the Black Belt, his father was a bricklayer who had musical instruments around because he led a band on the side. Dizzy's mother left Cheraw in 1935 and came to Philly, and as soon as Diz finished high school he came on up. Almost an identical tale to Trane's, just a decade before!

In Philly Trane lives and works as an Afro-American worker. He is in a factory job every day, as are his mother and cousin. He goes to music school in the evenings, and now he is beginning to work playing music an occasional weekend. This is a distinct change in many ways from the petty bourgeois life of High Point. Factory work is exacting in its discipline. The worker is there at a particular time each and every day, he does a certain work, goes through a specific routine, and this is repeated day in, day out. It is one of the reasons why the industrial proletariat is such a revolutionary class, specifically, its place in the production process of capitalism. It is the class that participates in the most advanced and modern aspect of social production. It is a class that is growing as modern large-scale industry further and further develops and forms the basis for modern life; all other classes are going out of existence as material conditions for their existence cease to exist. They are either driven into the proletariat with the degeneration of capitalism like the petty bourgeoisie, the small shopkeepers and professionals, the petty capitalists, and the small farmers, or destroyed by revolution like the bourgeoisie! It is not the meek who will inherit the earth, but the revolutionary proletariat! If the enraged worker but cease producing for capitalism, the entire society must come to a halt!

At the same time, however, Coltrane was moving more clearly toward the life of an artist; this was what his preparations were for. The money that did not go to sustain him went for his music studies. The factory work, living and playing among the Afro-American working class, provided strong ties with that culture and the depth of that expression, particularly musically. The very method by which Trane continued to make his living, even after leaving the factory, still connected him deeper to the Afro-American working class through the blues tradition, through the contemporary expression of it. But there was a duality in Trane too. He was the grandson of a petty-bourgeois nationalist preacher and son of a musical small-business man connected to black people inextricably by the experience of national oppression, yet with a class background that was not that of the Afro-American masses.

What made bop strong is that no matter its pretensions, it was hooked up solidly and directly to the Afro-American blues tradition, and therefore was largely based in the experience and struggle of the black sector of the working class—although there were some who took the surfaces of this new music and drug it off into other class expressions, and called it things like (some time later) "progressive jazz" and headed the music toward the expression of a younger petty bourgeoisie. (They cooled it and "classicized" it, so to speak.) But it is the connection to the experience of the black masses that gives Afro-American music its strength, and when it drifts from this it grows weak and expresses, finally, not the masses, but some other class.

THE REVOLUTIONARY TRADITION IN AFRO-AMERICAN LITERATURE

In speaking about the general ghettoized condition of Afro-American literature within the framework of the so-called American literature, Bruce Franklin, a professor at Newark Rutgers University, had this to say in the *Minnesota Review:* "If we wish to continue to use the term 'American literature,' we must either admit that we mean white American literature or construe it to include the literature of several peoples, including the Afro-American nation. The latter course leads to a fundamental redefinition of American literature, its history, and the criteria appropriate to each and every American literary work. For the viewpoint of oppressed people can then no longer be excluded from the criticism and teaching of American literature."

Franklin went on to say, "The most distinctive feature of United States history is Afro-American slavery and its consequences. This truth is at the heart of our political, economic and social experience as a nation-state. It is also at the heart of our *cultural* experience, and therefore the slave narrative, like Afro-American culture in general, is not peripheral but central to American culture."

These words are so important because Franklin sums up not only the fact that what is called American literature is basically the literature of certain white men; he also points out the importance to American culture and life itself of Afro-American life and culture. But if we look at the standard history of American literature, Franklin points to *The Literary History of the U.S.* by Spiller, Thorp, Johnson, Canby, Ludwig and Gibson, a college standard, revised in its fourth edition in 1974. We find in its 1555 pages of small print four black writers—Chesnutt, Dunbar, Hughes and Wright—and in the section of literature produced by the South during the Civil War, they devote three chapters, and discuss such literatury giants as Hugh Legare, William Wirt and George Fitzhugh, author of *Cannibals All, or Slaves Without Masters.* There is no mention of the slave narrative or slave poetry. There is no mention even of William Wells Brown, the nineteenth-century black novelist and playwright. They do not even mention Frederick Douglass!

So we must face the essential national chauvinism of what is taught as American literature. It should be obvious that it, like all other aspects of American life, represents the choice of a white elite, and what's more, even deemphasizes some aspects and confuses American literature, the white part of it, so that in many instances the anthologies and survey courses that we learn literature from are the choices of or have been influenced to a great extent by some of the most reactionary elements in this society. We have been raised up in literature too often on right-wing anthologies, and right-wing critics, pushing conservative and reactionary literature, playing down the progressive and revolutionary forces and excluding almost outright the oppressed nationalities and minorities and women.

It was the rebellions of the sixties, explosions in 110 U.S. cities, that created the few black studies and Afro-American studies departments that exist today. At the same time, these uprisings created the agonizingly small space that Afro-American literature takes up in the canon of academic and commercial written culture. A few authors got walk-on roles, to paraphrase Franklin again.

So first we must see the basic distortion that is given to all American literary history and to the official reflection of U.S. life and culture. This distortion occurs because the literary establishment and the academic establishment, far from being independent, represent in the main, the ideas and world view of the rulers of this country. These ideas, and the institutions from which they are mashed on us, constitute merely the superstructure of this society, a superstructure that reflects the economic foundations upon which they are built, the material base for U.S. life and culture, monopoly capitalism. So that in the main what is taught and pushed as great literature or great art, philosophy, &c, is mainly ideas and concepts that can help maintain the status quo, which includes not only the exploitation of the majority by a capitalist elite but also national oppression, racism, the oppression of women, and the extension of U.S. imperialism all over the world!

Afro-American literature as it has come into view fragmented by chauvinism and distorted by the same reactionary forces that have distorted American literature itself has indeed been laid out in the same confusing and oblique fashion. A method intended to hide more than it reveals, a method that wants to show that at best Afro-American literature is a mediocre and conservative reflection of the mediocre and conservative portrait that is given of all American literature.

In Afro-American literature, for instance, we have been taught that its beginnings rest with the writings of people like Phillis Wheatley and Jupiter Hammon. Ms. Wheatley, writing in the eighteenth century, is simply an imitation of Alexander Pope. First, it was against the law for black slaves to learn to read or write. So Ms. Wheatley's writings could only come under the "Gee whiz, it's alive" category of Dr. Frankenstein checking out his new monster! Also Wheatley's literature abounds with sentiments like " 'Twas mercy brought me from my pagan land," evincing gratitude at slavery—that the European slave trade had actually helped the Africans by exposing them to the great European culture. Which be the monster remarking how wise, how omniscient, be her creator!

Hammon is, if possible, even worse. In his stiff doggerel are such great ideas as Slavery was good for us Africans because it taught us humility, so when we get to heaven we'll know how to act around God. Pretty far out! (Both were privileged Northern house servants reflecting both their privilege and their removal and isolation from the masses of African/Afro-American slaves.)

But these two are pushed as Afro-American literature simply as a method of showing off trained whatnots demonstrating the glory of the trainer. But this is not the beginnings of Afro-American literature.

The black people of this country were brought here in slavery chains on the fast clipper ships of rising European capitalism. It is impossible to separate the rise of capitalism, the industrial revolution, the emergence of England and later America as world powers from the trade in Africans. And from the Africans' initial presence as commodities initiating world trade through the triangular trade route of slaves to the New World, cotton, rum, indigo, to England and manufactured goods to Africa for the African feudal ruling classes who had sold the other Africans into slavery, Black life has contributed to and animated the Anglo-American life and culture. But a formal artifacted presence (as art) cd be easily denied slaves. The African culture was banned by the slave masters as *subversive*. Christianity was used first as a measure of civilization (i.e., if you weren't a Christian you weren't civilized—the papal bull states it is cool to enslave non-Christians) but later it was used as a pacifier and bringer of social control (its present function). The development of a *specifically* Afro-American culture must wait for the emergence of the Afro-American people, the particular nationality composed of Africans reorganized by the fact and processes of slavery into an American people of African descent.

The most practical artifacts of that culture are the tools and environment of day-to-day living. In these practical pursuits are found the earliest Afro-American art—artifacted reflections of the life of that people. The music, because it is most abstract and could not therefore be so severely limited and checked by slave culture, must have been the earliest of the "nonpractical" arts to emerge, (tho a work song is to help one work!) the work song, chants, hollers, the spirituals, eventually the blues.

Afro-American literature rises as a reflection of the self-consciousness and self-expression of the Afro-American people, but to be an Afro-American literature, truly, it must reflect in the main the ideological and sociocultural portrait of that people! The Wheatleys & Hammons reflect the ideology of Charlie McCarthy in relationship to Edgar Bergen (is that before anybody's time?). The celebration of servitude is not the ideological reflection of the Afro-American masses, but of their tormentors.

In the slave narratives—the works of Frederick Douglass, Henry Bibb, Moses Roper, Linda Brent, W. Wells Brown, the Krafts, Henry "Box" Brown,

Solomon Nothrup, James Pennington and others—are found the beginnings of a genuine Afro-American literature—the stirring narratives of slave America, the exploits and heroism of resistance and escape, the ongoing struggle and determination of that people to be free. Beside this body of strong, dramatic, incisive, democratic literature, where is the literature of the slavemasters and -mistresses? Find it and compare it with the slave narratives and say which has a clearer, more honest and ultimately more artistically powerful perception of American Reality! (Yes, where are the William Gilmore Simmses, John Pendleton Kennedys, Augustus B. Longstreets and George Washington Harrises touted as the outstanding writers of the white slave South? Their literature is unreadable, even though overt racists like Allen Tate and the Southern Agrarians prated about it as a "gracious culture despite its defects," those defects consisting in the main of millions of black slaves, whose life expectancy by the beginning of the nineteenth century in the deep South, at maturity (18), was seven years). One of the main arguments for black slavery, Bruce Franklin points out in *The Victim as Criminal and Artist,* was that the blacks could do the manual labor "for which they were best suited," "leaving their owners free to create a fine, elegant and lasting culture" (p. 28). But check it out, at best such artistic efforts as represent this so-called lasting culture are embarrassing satires, the efforts of the Southern Agrarians to represent them as something else notwithstanding.

The slave narratives are portraits of a people in motion and they came into being created by the economic, social and political life of the U.S. The early part of the nineteenth century was marked by an intensification of slavery, the taking away of the limited civil rights of the free blacks as well. This was because slavery did not die out as was predicted towards the end of the eighteenth century. With the discovery of the cotton gin, to the feudalistic or patriarchal slavery imposed on blacks was now added capitalist exploitation. Karl Marx points out in *Capital* that once cotton became an international commodity, no longer used only in U.S. domestic markets, U.S. blacks were not only tied for life to domestic slavery but now had added to their inhuman burden the horrors of having to produce *surplus value* as a kind of slave and proletariat in combination. The seven-year life expectancy resulted "downriver" in the Black Belt cotton region because the slavemasters discovered that working slaves to death and then replacing them was more profitable than letting them live to grow old, less productive but still eating, wearing clothes and taking up space!

This period of intense repression is when Afro-American literature emerges. It is also the period when the resistance of the Afro-American people intensfies. It is now that Gabriel Prosser, Denmark Vesey, Nat Turner, lead their uprisings and rebellions and Harriet Tubman the Underground Railway.

At the approach of the Civil War, there is also another strong movement in

Afro-American literature, the pre-Civil War revolutionary black nationalists: David Walker, the activists—Henry Highland Garnett, Charles Lenox Redmond, C. L. Langston, as well as William Wells Brown, an escaped slave who became the first black playwright and novelist. It is a literature sparked by protest, an antislavery literature, a fighting oral literature that even when it was written was meant to be proclaimed from the lecterns and pulpits of the North and circulated secretly to inspire the black slaves in the South. These were black abolitionists, damning slavery in no uncertain terms, proclaiming death to slavery and calling for rebellion from the slaves. This was not the upperclass white abolitionists, morally outraged but politically liberal. These were black revolutionists, some, like Langston, even calling for black people to seize the land they toiled upon because it was only that land that provided a practical basis for the survival and development of the Afro-American people!

Usually in discussing Afro-American literature, the Wheatleys and Hammons are combined with perhaps Douglass and maybe Brown's *Clotel.* The other slave narratives and the pre-Civil War black revolutionary nationalists are largely ignored or their importance diminished. Charles Chesnutt, who lamented that "quality" black folks had to be lumped together with the ignorant black masses, is pushed as a kind of father of black literature. Next, Paul Laurence Dunbar and James Weldon Johnson are raised to the top rank, but an analysis of the content of these men's works is made vague or onesided, so that we are not aware perhaps that for all the positive elements of Dunbar's work, his use of dialect is positive insofar as it is the language of the black masses, but negative in the way that Dunbar frequently uses it in the context of parties, eating and other "coonery." Most of Dunbar's "serious" poetry is not in dialect.

Dunbar was deeply conservative and his short story "The Patience of Gideon" shows a young slave, Gideon, who is put in charge of the plantation as the massa goes off to fight the Civil War. Gideon stays despite the masses of slaves running away as soon as Massa leaves. Even Gideon's wife-to-be pleads with him to leave, but he will not: he has made a promise to Massa, and so even his woman leaves him alone with his promise to the slavemaster.

J. W. Johnson's quandary was how to create a "high art" out of Afro-American materials, not completely understanding that high art is by definition slavemaster, bourgeois' art, and that what was and is needed by all artists—or at least by those artists who intend for their works to serve the exploited and oppressed majority in this country—is that they be artistically powerful and politically revolutionary!

Johnson's *Autobiography of an Ex-Colored Man* tells of that quandary in social terms, with his protagonist existing in a never-never land between black and white and finally deciding because he is shamed and humiliated and horrified by the lynching of a black man that he cannot be a member of a race so disgraced. He disappears among the whites, forsaking art for commerce, pursuing the white lady of his heart!

The real giant of this period, the transitional figure, the connector between the nineteenth-century Reconstruction and the new literary giants of the twentieth century and the Harlem Renaissance, is W.E.B. Du Bois. His *Souls of Black Folks,* which issued the intellectual challenge to the capitulationist philosophy of Booker T. Washington, is the intellectual and spiritual forerunner of the writings of the Renaissance. Du Bois's *Black Reconstruction* remains the most important work on the Reconstruction period done by an American. He was a social scientist and historian, as well as a novelist, poet and political activist. He founded black theatrical troupes like Krigwa Players, organized international conferences of black activism as leader of the Pan-Africanist movement, led social movements in the U.S. like the Niagara Movement and NAACP, was a fighting literary editor, and his works of historical and sociological analysis are among the greatest written by an American. He studied and wrote about all aspects of black life and its connection with Africa and the slave trade. He was a socialist by 1910, and at the end of his life, inspired by and inspiring the African independence movements, residing in Nkrumah's Ghana, he became a communist. It is not possible to understand the history of ideas in the U.S. without reading Du Bois. Not to know his work is not to have a whole picture of Afro-American literature, sociology, history and struggle and to have a distorted view of American life in general.

Langston Hughes' manifesto *The Negro Artist and the Racial Mountain* is not possible without Du Bois and his total rejection of American racial paternalism and cultural aggression. The Harlem Renaissance is simply the flowering of a twentieth-century Afro-American intelligentsia which reflects the motion of black people in America. They reflect a peasant people in motion out of the South headed toward the urban north to serve as cheap labor for the developing U.S. imperialism cut off from its European immigrants by the coming of World War I. The Harlem Renaissance is a literature of the new city dwellers who have left their rural past. It is a literature of revolt, it is anti-imperialist and fights the cultural aggression that imperialism visits upon its colonial and nationally oppressed conquests—first by reflecting and proclaiming the beauty and strengths of the oppressed people themselves. By showing the lives of the people themselves in all its rawness, deprivation and ugliness. By showing them to themselves. It is a revolutionary nationalist literature at its strongest, especially the works of Claude McKay and Langston Hughes. It reflects the entrance into the twentieth century of Afro-American people and the U.S. in general. It is the sensibility of the Afro-American Nation that developed after the destruction of the Reconstruction governments and of the Reconstruction period, the most democratic period in U.S. life, the sensibility that survived the dark repression of the

1880s and 1890's, when the Northern industrial capitalists, no longer needing blacks to stabilize the South while the Wall Street conquerors stripped the Southern plantation aristocrats of economic and political independence, sold blacks back into near-slavery with the Hayes-Tilden Compromise of 1876, and crushed black political life with the Ku Klux Klan lynchings, the black codes, segregation and outright fascism!

The Harlem Renaissance influenced black culture worldwide, but it also reflected the fact that all over the world oppressed nations and colonial peoples were intensifying their struggle against imperialism. In Haiti, where the U.S. invaded in 1915, there was the *Indigisme* movement; in Puerto Rico it was called *Negrisismo;* in Paris, Senghor, Cesaire and Damas called it *Negritude,* and cited McKay and Hughes as their chief influences!

One aspect of the Harlem Renaissance in the "Roaring Twenties" as part of "the Jazz Age" was the stirring anti-imperialism, another part (showing how the bourgeoisie tries to transform everything to its own use) was the cult of exoticism which the commercializers and often pathological bourgeois "patrons" of the *New Negro* made of this cultural outpouring. This was the period, Hughes sd, when "the Negro was in vogue."

But by the beginning of the thirties, after the crash of 1929, and the Great Depression, which was only one of the many cyclical recessions, the bust part of the boom-bust cycle pointing toward the eventual destruction of capitalism, the exotic part of the Renaissance was over. The philanthropists turned to other pursuits, and just as in the factories where blacks are the last hired and the first fired, the literary flowering as manifested by U.S. publishers came to an end!

In the Depression thirties the revolutionary ideas of the Russian Bolsheviks, of Marx, Engels, Lenin and Stalin, had enormous influence on U.S. intellectuals. It was apparent that capitalism could not solve the problems of the exploited majority let alone black people, that the U.S. bourgeoisie was unfit to rule society. Black writers also show this influence, mostly as it was transmitted by the *then* revolutionary Communist Party U.S.A. The works of Hughes and McKay especially show this influence, and even though Hughes later copped out before the inquisitors of the HUAC, a collection of his thirties writings, *Good Morning Revolution,* is must reading to get at his really powerful works.

Richard Wright was one of the most publicized and skilled black writers of the thirties and forties. His early works, *Uncle Tom's Children, Native Son* and *Black Boy,* including the long suppressed section of this book called *American Hunger,* are among the most powerful works written by any American writer of the period. Wright was even more than Hughes influenced by Marxist-Leninist ideology, though Wright's individualism and idealism finally sabotaged him. He joined the CPUSA when he got to Chicago. (He came in from the John Reed Club, an anti-imperialist writers' organization. And if one believes *American Hunger,* the careerist aspect of this move vis-à-vis getting his early works published via the communists, &c is not insubstantial.) Wright had just come from Memphis and remained a member of the CPUSA until 1944. It was at this point, ironically, that the CP, burdened by opportunist reactionary leadership, sold out the black liberation movement by liquidating the correct revolutionary slogans LIBERATION FOR THE BLACK NATION! SELF-DETERMINATION FOR THE AFRO-AMERICAN NATION IN THE BLACK BELT SOUTH! The CP even liquidated itself, temporarily becoming the Communist Political Association, "a nonparty movement following the ideals of Washington, Jefferson, Lincoln and Tom Paine." But Wright's individualism and petty-bourgeois vacillation had begun to isolate him from the party years before, tho the errors and opportunism of CP leadership must be pointed out.

Many of the left, anti-imperialist, revolutionary, Marxist and even pro-Soviet ideas that grew to such prominence in the thirties were sustained into the forties because the U.S. by then had joined a united front with the U.S.S.R. against fascism. But by the fifties U.S. world dominance (which was enhanced by the fact of its emerging unscathed from World War II) dictated that it launch a cold war against the Soviet Union to try to dominate a world market. World War II allowed the insurgent colonial peoples to grow even stronger as the imperialists fought each other and in 1949 the Chinese Communists declared the People's Republic of China. This occasioned an attempted blockade and isolation of China as well by the U.S. and resulted in the Korean police action. This was accompanied by intense ideological repression inside the U.S.A. itself as McCarthyism emerged. The modern capitalist inquisition to purge all left and Marxist and anti-imperialist influences from U.S. intellectual life!

Hughes copped out before HUAC, sd he wdn't do it again and told James Eastland that all U.S. citizens had equality. A tragedy! Wright fled the U.S. to France and became an existentialist. Another event with tragic overtones. W.E.B. Du Bois was indicted as an agent of a foreign power! Paul Robeson was persecuted and eventually driven to his death as Jackie Robinson testified against him at HUAC. Powerful writers like Theodore Ward were covered with mountains of obscurity.

With the defection of the CPUSA to reformism, culminated by its 1957 pronouncement that it was now seeking socialism via the ballot in a "peaceful transition to socialism," that the road to socialism was integration not revolution, the late forties and the fifties were marked by the reevaluation of Wright's works. Both James Baldwin and Ralph Ellison condemned in spurious fashion "protest literature," and the general tone put out by well-published "spokespersons for black people" was that it was time to transcend the "limitations" of race, that Afro-American writing shd disappear into the mainstream like Lost Boundaries. Baldwin, of course, later refutes his own arguments by becoming a civil rights spokesman and activist, and by the sixties, with *Blues for Mr. Charlie,* he had even begun to question the non-violent, passive, pseudo-revolution put forward by the black bourgeoisie through its most articulate spokesman Dr. M. L. King.

Ralph Ellison's *Invisible Man* was the classic work of the fifties in restating & shifting the direction of Afro-American literature. The work puts down both nationalism and Marxism, and opts for *individualism.* This ideological content couched in the purrs of an obviously elegant technique was important to trying to steer Afro-American literature away from protest, away from the revolutionary concerns of the thirties and early forties, and this primarily is the reason this work and the author are so valued by the literary and academic establishments in this country. Both Ellison and Baldwin wrote essays dismissing or finding flaws in Wright's ultimate concern in his best work.

But the fifties civil rights movement was also superseded by the people's rapid intensification of the struggle in the sixties, and black literature like everything else was quick to show this. The emergence of Malcolm X to oppose the black bourgeois line of nonviolent passive resistance which duplicated the reformist anti-Marxists of the CPUSA in their "nonviolent transition to socialism." Where the black bourgeoisie had dominated the black liberation movement of the fifties with the aid of the CPUSA and the big capitalists themselves, in the sixties Malcolm X came forward articulating the political line of the black majority—Self-Determination, Self-Respect and Self-Defense—and struggled out in the open against the civil rights line of the black bourgeoisie,who could see black people beaten and spit on and bombed in churches and whose only retaliation wd be to kneel in the dust and pray.

Just as Malcolm's influence turned the entire civil rights movement around, from the student movement which was SNCC to the militance of Stokely Carmichael and Rap Brown, so the whole movement changed. Malcolm's line of self-defense was picked up in the South by people like Robert Williams in North Carolina, by Carmichael in Alabama with the *first* Black Panther Party, and by the young brothers and sisters in California who marched into the California legislature in 1967 to declare that black people had the right to armed self-defense . . . these were the Black Panthers led by Huey P. Newton and Bobby Seale. And by the end of the sixties even tho the bourgeoisie had assassinated Malcolm X, the movement had changed radically, the black bourgeoisie were no longer in control of the movement, and from civil rights we were talking next about self-defense and then after Rap Brown about rebellion itself.

All these moves were reflected by black literature, and they are fundamentally movements and thrusts by the people themselves, which the literature bears witness to and is a reflector of. The Black Arts Movement of the sixties basically wanted to reflect the rise of the militancy of the black masses as reflected by Malcolm X. Its political line at its most positive was that literature must be a weapon of revolutionary struggle, that it must serve the black revolution. And its writers, Askia Muhammad Toure, Larry Neal, Clarence Reed, Don Lee, Sonia Sanchez, Carolyn Rodgers, Welton Smith, Marvin X, &c its publications, its community black arts theaters, its manifestos and activism were meant as real manifestations of black culture/black art as weapon of liberation. On the negative side, the black arts movement without the guidance of a scientific revolutionary organization, a Marxist-Leninist communist party, was, like the BLM itself, left with spontaneity. It became embroiled in cultural nationalism, bourgeois nationalism, substituting the mistrust and hatred of white people for scientific analysis of the real enemies of black people, until by the middle seventies a dead end had been reached that could only be surmounted by a complete change of world view, ideology. It is my view that this is exactly what is going on today in many places in the country; that Afro-American literature is going thru the quantitative changes necessary to make its qualitative leap back into the revolutionary positivism of the thirties and the positive aspect of the black-arts sixties. For certainly the literature will always be a reflection of what the people themselves are, as well as a projection of what they struggle to become. The Afro-American nation and its people as an oppressed nationality spread out around the rest of the U.S. nation-state still face a revolutionary struggle. That nation is still oppressed by imperialism, and its liberation and self-determination can only be gained through revolution. The next wave of Afro-American literature, and of a genuine people's literature, will dramatically record this.

WHAT WAS THE RELATIONSHIP OF THE LONE RANGER TO THE MEANS OF PRODUCTION?

A Play in One Act
Characters

DONNA, worker in Colonel Motors

REG, worker in Colonel Motors

CLARK, worker in Colonel Motors

TUFFY, labor bureaucrat in union in Colonel Motors

MM, a person who is at first unknown

FELIPE, a worker in Colonel Motors

WORKERS in Colonel Motors

POLICE

REG. Hey, [*To his* CO-WORKERS] there's a man with a mask walking towards us!

CLARK. What the fuck is that ... is he, at? Maaaaan ... way out.

DONNA. Yow, it's the lone frigging ranger or who else that hip???

REG. Hip? maybee, you betta check him. Ras say they don't let yr ass in the country wit no mask.

DONNA. Naw, you probably be in there already ...
  [*All laugh. The* MASKED MAN *walks slowly directly towards them.* HE
  clean, with a blue pinstriped, chalk and red stripes, suit. A cigar, HE

smoke when he want to, a cane and homburg held in one hand. HE *is*
not *smiling. Remember. It is a grimace of the explorer walked here to
your house through miles of shit, and things* HE *killed. Bats, toads,
monkeys, shit* HE *ate to, like, survive. a grimace*]

MASKED MAN. [*Calling as* HE *walks*] Yoo! Yoo! Friends. Americans. Co Workers. Co Woikers. Co Blowed Minds.

CLARK. Co Stompers. Co Whompers. Co Parachuters. Naw. Co Beboppers!
Co Freakers! Co Hustlers. [*Does a step*]

MASKED MAN. Co Cos [*Laughs*] yeh, uh, yes, CoCos Co Co-Co's. I'm approaching in the new age. Post strike post strife, post worker post revolutionary post angry post nastyshit . . . I'm approaching [*A brief stop, turn, quickly
makes a humping prayer motion*] Thank you Marcuse, CPUSA, Jesse Jackson,
NAACP, all who urge righteous moderation!

REG. [*Assembly line begins whizzing by*] Hey the break's over, the line's
moving. I didn't hear no bell. Everybody else still out on break too!

CLARK. Wasn't no bell. These motherfuckers brains witherin up.

MASKED MAN. Don't fret. There wasn't any bell because we know you sense
when the line's moving. We've inter-rhythmed! We've cofucked, y'all! [*A
drawled implication*]

DONNA. What? [*Checking him*] Damn!

MASKED MAN. I said. We know the connection is complete. The final inter
bleeding interfeeling interknowing between us. [*Like dirty sex proposition*]
That we are one. Y'all and I or You all and us. [*Shows pictures of other
masked men*] These are my bros and sistoos. We together. [*Snaps fingers*]

DONNA. The shit you talk— Together.
REG. Well come on—together-ness—the line's moving.
        [WORKERS *at it*]

If you together, wherever your spot is, you betta start humpin sho nuff. This
line moving faster than before.

DONNA. They gonna work us to death now they fired that buncha people last
week.

CLARK. Times hard. You oughta be glad you got yr gig.

MASKED MAN. [*All the time line's moving* HE *posturing, like* HE *going to work, but* HE *actually turns it into a dance*] Ah, yes bright youth. Yout! [*Smiles*] You got it [*Whirls. Japanese accent*] iss true. All kinds cheap steel get in country. [*Changes*] Kraut cars, Japmobiles. Lucky, Lucky, Lucky!!! [*Bounces*] Lucky Lucky Lucky you are is to have has a job gig slave.

DONNA. What're you sposed to be Mr? I don't see Assbreath the super over here whining, so you must be part of the accepted ass environment.

REG. In a top hat and mask? The union send you?

CLARK. Advertising for the union picnic? Tryin to scare us into payin dues? Is that Bath Tub Tuffy the union rep in that get up? [*Checks*] Looks like it . . . uh not really.

REG. Mr. Tuffy—on the floor?

DONNA. Huh, Tuffy wdnt set foot near work of any kind. He claims it's unprincipled.

MASKED MAN. Just think about me as yr friend and guardian. As for Tuffy he is yr friend and guardian? That's two! I am yr friend and Guardian One. Capeesh?

DONNA. And a who are is am a you?

MASKED MAN. Public Relations!

CLARK. Public Relations?

DONNA. How's that?

MASKED MAN. Uh, better, Company-Employee relations.

REG. Why the get-up?

MASKED MAN. [*Grinning but slightly annoyed*] It's no get-up—uh, lads. It's my road uniform [*Dry laugh*] Ha Ha! At home I've a different set of threads. [*Blanches*] But wait—this is home, a part of it, the workshop. There used to be a time when there was more contrast between Home and away.

[WORKERS *busy on line*]

DONNA. Mad stuff! Hey man 're you for real? Company-Employee Relations?

MASKED MAN. Yes I'm here to help.

REG. The best way you could help wd be to get on this line.

DONNA. [*Looking at him closely*] A masked man? Where's Tonto?

MASKED MAN. [*Looking suddenly rather sheepish*] Ton-to? [*Looks off feigning sadness*] Yes, Tonto. Yes.

[WORKERS *looking at each other*]

CLARK. [*Aside*] What's with this dude.

MASKED MAN. I can explain about Tonto. You see hostile Indians killed him. You know the kind ... Geronimo, Crazy Horse and that Bunch. I had a deep love for Tonto .. he was my main negotiator ... and friend. He helped me cool out more bad scenes ... really. [HE *looks like* HE *could cry if* HE *knew how*]

REG. You mean Tonto is dead?

MASKED MAN. [*Head hung sad-like*] Yes ... Tonto was a very advanced Indian you know. He could explain about the reservations so thoroughly. We've got a few boys now who can run it about the African problem. Various up and coming chiefs. The blacks have a few trouble makers too ya know.

DONNA. Who are you, mister?

MASKED MAN. You can call me MM.

REG. MM ... what's that stand for?

MASKED MAN. It could be Masked Man ...

CLARK. This guy talks wacky.... [*Looking around*] Why don't Tuffy show.

DONNA. The guy is from management, in that get-up. He's an owner. MM stands for masked man, alright.

MASKED MAN. It could, but my friends call me mmmmm, for sweet.

REG. Who are you, mister, you must be with management otherwise they'd toss you out. No visitors or strangers on the plant floor.

MASKED MAN. My real name is Money's Master.

/   255

DONNA. Of course, and Masked Man too, and mmmm because we in the united snakes and bourgeois ideology dressed up sweetlike.

MASKED MAN. [*At mention of bourgeois,* MASKED MAN *turns suddenly*] Bourgeois? What? How dare you? Do you know who I am?

CLARK: Tell us ... I don't understand why the foreman or union rep don't come over here and look you up and down.

REG. He wd be management straight out just come from a late/early banquet except for the mask ...

DONNA. He's trying to tell us something ...

CLARK. Like what?

DONNA. That we can see their real Face and not be put off by illusions [*To* MASKED MAN] Money's Master. An owner. Not a slave.

MASKED MAN. An owner ... [*Puffing slightly over the "bourgeois"*] ... yes even bourgeois ... young lady I don't mind the name, I know the game, whatever you call me it's still the same ... MM is me. I.

REG. This a publicity stunt?

MASKED MAN. No, the young lady's right ... I'm an owner, *the* owner, I'm a collective spirit.

DONNA. Collective ... ? A class spirit. This is *your* factory?

MASKED MAN. Of course, but forgive me, you wanted to know about the mask.

DONNA. I got it figured. You're trying to tell us something. Robbers wear masks, the inquisition, the klan ...

MASKED MAN. Also superheroes, my good woman. [*To the* GROUP] By the way, don't slow down, I'm here to relax you, to give you something ... gifts, tokens, badges of honor, gold booty for you ... [*Loud*] You're American workers! American Workers. [*Draws it out*] And I am your leader, your guide, your spiritual father. I wear the mask for the same reason Batman, Robin, Captain America, Spider Man and so many other superheroes wear the mask, to hide my identity from evil doers.

REG. Hey what's with this dude?

CLARK. Sound like he got a warped gourd. Head screwed on backwards, like in the Omen.

MASKED MAN. You liked the Omen?

CLARK. It was alright.

DONNA. [*Holding her nose*] Metaphysical claptrap. Bloody religious spook story. Economic crisis in the U.S. now the rulers want to send us off into thinking about monsters and goblins. Sex, police, money, metaphysics and nostalgia. Anything but how to change things.

MASKED MAN. A great flick. Did you like Jaws 1 and 2, Omen 2, all Clint Eastwood films, Deathwish ... great films. I helped make those great pictures. If you look carefully in almost all scenes my initials are spelled out in the speeches, on the furniture, slobber coming out of the dead people's mouth. M-M.

REG. What is this an in-plant gig to get our minds off our wage demands. Where's the whiskey, and dope?

MASKED MAN. [*Oblivious to them*] You see, Tonto left me ... but I cd replace him easy ... but he was bright ... He cd have been the first colored UN ambassador from this country ... before Amos' walking buddy in there now.

DONNA. Oh, man ...

CLARK. The dude looks crazy ... He says he owns this factory ... and he walking around like a circus reject, crazy as a bedbug.

DONNA. Bedbugs suck blood.

CLARK. Can't no crazy people run no big factories like this.

REG. Man, look around you, that's exactly who's running it, this death hole. No safety, speedups all the time, layoffs.

DONNA. Yeh, but don't go for the crazy bit ... crazy in the sense that what they're doing is gonna fail ... exploiting all these people ...

MASKED MAN. [*Wheels around*] Ex-ploiting ... now wait just a minute ... [*Remembers his goodwill mission*] ahh ... ahhh now, yes, just a minute ... you see you misunderstand us Money Masters. You have a job because of us, MM and his class mates. It is the MM's of the world—and there's not a hell of a lot of us . . . who create the jobs for people like you. [*Brightens*] But we love it . . . love to do it . . . love to help you.

REG. Well then help us, we've laughed a bunch now help us. First thing I want, first help I want's a raise? Can you deal with it?

MASKED MAN. I thought you'd never ask . . . that's what I'm about . . that's exactly why I'm here, to give you, you all, a much needed raise!

CLARK. So we don't have to strike huh?

MASKED MAN. Strike? That doesn't solve anything.

REG. Talk on the raise mister . . . what're yall talking about?

DONNA. Raise? I gotta hear this.

MASKED MAN. And well you should, I have come to show you how to be raised, to give you a raise in spirit.

REG. What?

DONNA. [*Laughing*] Yeh . . .

CLARK. Man, what the fuck, scuse the expression, you talking about. A raise in spirit. Whatta you Rev. Ike or somebody like that?

DONNA. Must be . . . a raise in spirit . . . huh.

MASKED MAN. Wait, before you grow cynical . . . hear me out.

DONNA. Hey man, my spirit can only get as raised as my material conditions. Right now my spirit is urban innercity ghetto stretched out, huh, my spirit's in hock, and the part of it that's not is tied to this damned machine. Are you some kind of clown, labor psychologists tell you to walk around the plant depressing the workers . . . cause you damn sure can't cheer none up with the bullshit you belching.

CLARK. Oh you sposed to cheer us up, make us laugh . . . well you was funny except that last shit drug the hell outta me for one.

MASKED MAN. Money is not everything.

DONNA. Well give yours to us then!

MASKED MAN. If you understand how important the work is yr doing, then you'll be filled up with that pride of accomplishment.

DONNA. Why? We don't even own these machines. We don't own nothing but bills. Mister why are you here talking shit, it's bad enough we got to work, but we do not want to listen to and be distracted by no unfunny non-clown clowns.

REG. Ditto.

MASKED MAN. You have a stake in this system.

REG. What system?

MASKED MAN. The free enterprise system! You're free. You can do anything, go anywhere, because you live in a free society . . . you can't have this much freedom in a totalitarian country like—

DONNA. Crown Heights, South Bronx, Newark, Lower East Side, for instance.

MASKED MAN. Ahh that's just cynicism . . . you need really to have yr spirits raised Miss. We can't have that cynicism running loose in here. You make ten dollars an hour, a fantastic salary, same as the men.

DONNA. Yeh, but in the same hour I help make you five hundred thousand dollars. Plus got to give you the ten back the minute I get outta here.

REG. Groceries, rent, auto payments, clothes . . . all to the money masters huh?

DONNA. Ten dollars an hour . . . his boy the philanderer Henry Ford II makes only two dollars an hour . . . but two dollars an hour clear profit on each worker he owns. Two hundred thousand workers, that's four hundred thousand an hour clear profit.

CLARK. Philanderer?

REG. Womanizer.

DONNA. Male Chauvinist is more like it . . . and that bastard never done any real work in his life. Got people going down in the coal mines, tophatted white shirt wearing dudes snatching the wealth from the people who spend half their lives under the ground digging coal. Then while we working winter summer, six days a week, ten hrs a day, Dudes like our man here layin up in Bermuda, or Cannes or somewhere slick . . . rollin in dough that we made for them.

REG. Truc—but what is the gimmick with this dude tippin around in here?

MASKED MAN. Young lady, you're hardly being fair. You don't know anything about me.

DONNA. You said you own this factory . . . if that's true I know your class . . .

MASKED MAN. My class?? Now come on, you know in America there is no class system. Here we're all equal.

REG. Well how come you not working then . . . humpin at this machine?

MASKED MAN. I'm doing my job now, raising yr spirits—it's also sometimes called character guidance.

CLARK. So no raise just some more bullshittin. What kinda car you drive mister MM?

MASKED MAN. I don't drive, personally, my driver drives a modest Bentley to spread me around the place.

CLARK. I gotta chevy, to spread me around this factory and back home. Gotta have it too, public transportation closes down after you go back and forth to work. Excuse me, let me see your hands Mister.

MASKED MAN. You going to tell my fortune?

CLARK. Damn, smooth as a baby's behind . . . whatever work you doin mister its pretty slick.

MASKED MAN. The USA is still growing—expanding—The American Century goes on [*Snide aside*] contrary to the newspaper sensationalism of the mercantile interests. You all . . . all even the lowliest . . . the blackest the reddest the yellowest the brownest . . . all even we the whitest . . . all have a place in it.

DONNA. Korea, Vietnam, Cambodia, Guinea Bissau, Mozambique.

[MASKED MAN *shrinks like* HE *is being whipped*]

MASKED MAN. Cruel sensationalism. [*Leaping in the air*] We are still rrrricher than anybody!

> [TUFFY *the union rep appears,* HE *is dressed like a "poor"* MASKED MAN, *cheaper versions of everything* MASKED MAN *has on*]

MASKED MAN. Ahh, here's my man, yr leader, stalwart Tuffy. He'll have some further clarifying word. What's the word, friend Tuff?

TUFFY. [*Like Ojays*] Money-Money-Moneeeeeee. [HE *is pushing wheelbarrow with a dead person in it under a tarp. As* HE *speaks* HE *unceremoniously dumps the body next to the machines*] Don't fuck with God! Niggers spicks greasers slanteyes broads all eat shit. You play you pay. America the beautiful, vote fusion and for god sakes no strike.

> [WORKERS *look at the body, and at* TUFFY *and* MASKED MAN]

REG. Hey, a body what the hell's going on.

TUFFY. Instruction day friend woiker. (Hear my working class accent???) I'm your leader.

DONNA. You don't even want us to strike, misleader sounds more real . . . now killer out front . . . what's wrong with this dude you dropping on the floor . . . this is a crazy ass place alright . . .

CLARK. A dead man on the plant floor? What the hell is going on?

MASKED MAN. [*Laughs and snaps fingers*] Life has its lessons, and if you learn them you prosper, if you don't, still on the floor, or booted out the door?

DONNA. Or become a bureaucrat whore.

> [*The* WORKERS *move to look at the dead body*]

REG. What's going on madass Tuffy now? What're you all crazy?

MASKED MAN. It's coming it's coming, be patient.

DONNA. What's coming . . . you murdering workers out in the open now??

TUFFY. We want to explain the game full up. We want you to know what side your bread is buttered on, or what side your butter is breaded on.

MASKED MAN. And so today we will reveal the totality of our establishment. Its grime and its rime. Its beauty and its booty.

TUFFY. This is undoubtedly the best system in the world.

DONNA. Capitalism and Racism you mean, women's oppression . . .

TUFFY. Whatever you call it . . . the rule of the cool is more like it. [*Aside to* MASKED MAN] IIcy, chicfic, this broad sounds like a lefty . . . [*Sd in a dopey singsong*]

MASKED MAN. Don't call me Chiefie . . . Go on with yr demo Tuffy, I do the the-inkking around here.

TUFFY. No offense intended Chief . . . but watch it . . .

MASKED MAN. Go on!

DONNA. What kind of foolishness you guys running, you're even interrupting production, and I know you don't want to do that.

MASKED MAN. No, no, no we're not doing that. [*Like Bert Lahr*] We're not lady . . . we're raising yr, giving you, the spiritual food.

TUFFY. Yeh, [*Giggles*] yer gettin yer raise . . . for days . . .

CLARK. Whatta we crazy or you crazy . . . I never seen nothing like this during work hours, somea those union meetings come on nearabout like it tho, come to think about it . . .

DONNA. I'm interested in why you got this dead man in here.

TUFFY. To tell you the truth ahh troot . . . times is getting harder . . . very hard out there now . . . very hard. Jobs hard to come by.

MASKED MAN. MMMMMMMMMM [*Smiling*] indeed, indeed.

REG. Indeed? What's going on?

TUFFY. [*Pacing, mock serious*] Jobs, jobs, jobs, it's what our world lives by alright. And there's few of 'em, alright. Few of em . . .

MASKED MAN. MMMMMMMM [*Smiling as before*] indeed, indeed . . .

REG. What's with this indeed? I knew I shdn't have gone for this overtime. Factory get a little deserted all kinds of ghosts and monsters come out.

DONNA. Yeh . . . whatta you dudes want . . . and why's this man dead?

TUFFY. You see there's no more jobs anywhere . . . [*Sudden frenzy*] None! none! [*To* DONNA] And don't let these commie bastids bullshit ya there's no jobs nowhere no more. Not in russia china or greasball coon fantasies of everybody bein equal bullshit.

REG. Tuffy you gonna get yr ass broke off and set afire you keep up with the nasty language, you hear?

DONNA. Russia is not a socialist country if that's why you mentioned it. It's the same shit going on there as here. Ghouls own the tools. And the people got nothin but a hard way to go.

MASKED MAN. Tuffy, Tuffy, will you go ahead with the presentation? I shd've done it myself . . .

TUFFY. [*Aside*] Yrself?? But chief you know I got to give the presentation because I'm a, scuse the expression, woiker like them dem. Right?

MASKED MAN. [*Looks drugged*] It sounds scientific . . . and don't think it's a rip off [*At audience*] it works too. And when you give the presentation tuf-guy think of the great ones of yr ilk, the great bribereenies of the past & present— and you can take yr place in the future . . . MEANY [*Looks ecstatic*] WOODCOCK,

TUFFY. MILLER, [*Does pirouette, spin*] REUTHER, [*Louder, more animated*] JOHN L. LEWIS,

MASKED MAN. [*An ecstatic peak*] SAMUEL H. GOMPERS!!!

TUFFY. [*Sweating and moved*] Yeh, Yeh, Yeh, Yeh, Yeh, I can do it Chief I can. Check me out right now.
        [*Whirls . . .* WORKERS standing staring with mixture of unbelief and
        cynicism]
You woikers, Listen. Listen, I've got the word. I'm gonna raise yr spirits and tell you the troot, at the same time. Call me Archie Bunker if it makes you feel better.

MASKED MAN. Nice, nice . . . [*Beaming, cupping his hand around his mouth*]

TUFFY. You all, and all of us here, together . . . get that . . . together, we're really lucky as hell lucky as blazes lucky as the dickens well we're very very lucky to be amuricans . . . lucky as shit lucky as pizza pie eatin lucky luciano lucky lucky lucky, to be amuricans. [*Hands up like tricky dick*] I hope you understand, I hope that's perfectly clear how fuckin lucky we are. Get it?? Get it?

DONNA. No [*Joined by* OTHERS] Nooo, you're drunk probably you acting crazier than usual.

REG. You always go out like this on the overtime shift? You won't catch me on this number again if I can help it.

CLARK. Yeh, but you can't help it, they want our ass for overtime we in overtime.

TUFFY. Right.

MASKED MAN. Well said my backward friend. Go on Tuffy.

TUFFY. Luck-keeee, that's the name of our game. Lucky to be in this great country. Lucky to be allowed in here some of us . . . my people were lowly potato pickin irish immigrants and look at me, baby look at me, now. Me and the Kennedys and John Wayne really made it big. Yeh. All courtesy of MM and his class mates.
    [MM *bows modestly*]
And you greasers . . . [*A beer can flies past his head*] Excuse me, I didn't mean that, you PRs and Mexs you guys know you wdna hada chance to get through the gates, poor starving bastids, you wdna hadda chance except MM here, and kind word on yr behalf from yrs truly! We have to drag tons of grease-balls back across the rio grande tryin to sneak in here and take all the jobs every day.

DONNA. Sneak in where . . . California, Arizona, New Mexico, Texas is Chicano land.

TUFFY. [*In dopey singsong aside to* MM] A lef-ty, I'm tellin you boss! But listen to reason mates. You woogies . . .

REGGIE. [*Goes in his pocket and comes out with a blade which* HE *flicks open behind his back*] I told you . . .

TUFFY. I didn't mean it . . . you cullid guys you cullid people MM brought you from where? [*Shrinks up in gesture of extreme disgust*] Africa! Geez, think of it, the freakin dark continent, savages and shit.

REG. [*Moves forward*] God dam it.

TUFFY. Wait wait.

MASKED MAN. Please my good man don't get upset, Tuffy tends to be overly dramatic.

DONNA. Tuffy tends to be a racist, he always going around spreading those kind of bourgeois lies among us . . . that's part of his goddam job.

REG. Yeh, well he gon lose parta his goddamn ass about it.

MASKED MAN. Wait, wait. [*Perturbed*] Tuffy come here, let me speak to you.

TUFFY. Yeh boss.

MASKED MAN. Look, you've got to be more subtle with your characterizations [*Whispers*] true tho they may be—discretion is the soul of valor.

TUFFY. Friends I'm sorry I've offended some of youse [*Looks over his shoulder for* MM's *approval*] check the language boss?? I'm sorry if I've offended some of you or somea youse—insert correct answer where indicated—But all I was tryin to say in my crude but innocent (wow!) fashion is that we've got to love MM. We've got to love MM.
> [MM *does sex dance*]
We've got to love MM.

MASKED MAN. MMMMMMMMMMMMM love me, love me, love me . . .

TUFFY. We've got to love MM because because because MM LOVES US yes. That's it now all repeat after me.

> [*Only* CLARK *begins and then is stopped by* DONNA's *look. But* TUF *and* MM *shout as loud as* THEY *can*]

TUFFY AND MASKED MAN. WE'VE GOT TO LOVE MM BECAUSE MM LOVES US! WE'VE GOT TO LOVE MM BECAUSE MM LOVES US! WE'VE GOT TO LOVE MM BECAUSE MM LOVES US!

TUFFY. [THEY *are sweating and puffing*] You see how easy it is? All of us have got to develop a deep love for MM . . . because MM loves us and does so much for us. He brought us all here from backward places because he wanted us to make progress. He wanted to teach us to read and write. He wanted to give us culture and religion. He wanted to teach us to speak proper.

[MM *meanwhile is going through Sex dance and alternating like highly moral xtian preacher figure*]

DONNA. If MM loves us so much why does he wear a mask?

MASKED MAN. What? What is she saying?

TUFFY. Mask? What Mask. MM don't wear no mask, you must be kidding. That's just a shadow from his hat.

DONNA. What? Where am I the crazy house? Is this really Colonel Motors or did I get a contact high when I took my kid to school this morning and walked through those halls?

TUFFY. MM does not wear a mask!

REG. What're you wastin our time with this bullshit now for Tuffy? The guy told us he wears a mask because he was like Superman and Spiderman a superhero. And first of all we see the fuckin mask so what's the bullshit?

MASKED MAN. I do not wear a mask I was humoring you with intellectual stimulation. I was reciting a highart poem. No wonder you don't understand it. I'll refrain in the future.

CLARK [*Frowning*] Mask?

DONNA. Clark will you please stop fooling around.
      [CLARK *screws up face*]

REG. Brother you got trouble seeing or you looking for some stale crumbs in your 8 year old sears roebuck refrigerator?

CLARK. I see it, for a second it didn't look like he had one on, really. It just looked like a shadow, really.

DONNA. I don't care about this dumb shit you all talking, you come in here with a body and then start rantin and ravin about how lucky we are. Who is that dead dude and why's he here?

MASKED MAN. Tuffy!

TUFFY. He's dead because he cdn't get a job so he killed hisself. Shot hisself in the personnel office. No jobs anywhere, nowhere in the world. So he's suffering, cdn't take it, so he killed hisself. Never seen nuthin like it before. He stood up and strangled himself to death.

266   /

REG. Strangled himself? What?

DONNA. I don't wanna hear that. Hey you all we need to get to the bottom of this. We need to get some more workers over here and find out just what's happening.

TUFFY. No, no, you have to hear the special presentation all by yrselves.

MASKED MAN. It's best you hear the presentation together alone together and alone. Everything always sounds better in isolation, remember that. Other people just confuse the issues.

TUFFY. Right Chief. And besides all those others who stayed out on break have been sent home.

REG. Sent home.

TUFFY. Yeh, yeh, let's say it's a temporary layoff. No more strikes. No more bullshit, no more nothin, but good clean honest work. Work work work overtime over over time and over over over time. That's our goal more work, we gotta stay ahead of the commies, the krauts, the japs, the frogs, all of em, we gotta stay ahead and it means work. Woik for the american way. You remember when we added that to the Jack Armstrong promos, "he fights for truth justice and the american way"?

DONNA. Make sense Tuf. We're the only ones here?

MASKED MAN. MMMMMMMMMM Quaint isn't it. A new, so to speak, order ... speak on it Tuffy lad.

TUFFY. Yeh, we taking some time, because there's no more jobs and we gotta get more work. We takin some time for a special character guidance. A special orientating session with THE NEW AGREES.

REG. Agrees?

TUFFY. Yeh, we givin out new agrees. New point of unity, a whole new contract for labor and management.

MASKED MAN. A whole new—uhh relationship!

DONNA. What? Make sense.

TUFFY. This is sense ... We've selected you all to lead the way, because from now on [*An eruption of menace in his voice*] absolutely no work without a pledge to uphold the new agrees!

DONNA. What?

TUFFY. And so now, all over the industry we have management-labor leader teams getting smart cookies like yrselves to sign the agrees, make the first move to insure the new harmony between labor and management.

MASKED MAN. You see for too long there's been strife between us, but ultimately we have the same interests [*Tearfully*] to make this country a great place in which to live.

TUFFY. Right?

CLARK. Is that right, we have the same interests?

TUFFY. Right!

DONNA. Wrong.

TUFFY. This is the new détente!

MASKED MAN. [*Dancing*] Buy it buy it buy it! It's real! Peace in our time!

TUFFY. The New Agrees!
       (REGGIE *begins laughing, almost doubling over*]

DONNA. Reg, it's not funny . . . as sick and silly as this shit seems, it's real.
       [*A* POLICEMAN *is wandering slowly on the set from one side*]

TUFFY. Point one—MM is always right!

DONNA. Far Right!

TUFFY. And what he and his class mates do is done for the good of all of us!
[*To* WORKERS] Cheer!

DONNA. Bullshit!

TUFFY. Point two. Tuffy and his Bribereenoes are the true servants of MM & company, and as such are the true leaders and benevolent hard-working brothers of workers everywhere. Cheer!

REG. Doublebullshit!

TUFFY. Point three. Working for MM is great and under no circumstances will we jeopardize this by complaining, bitching, or striking. Anyone urging these madnesses will be pointed out by all of us, isolated and fired for the *common good!*

DONNA. Yr crazy!

CLARK. Is this shit for real? They mean this?

DONNA. Yeh they mean it. It seem crazy? It is crazy. This whole thing, the whole society don't have to be this way. These money freaks run everything, got the world sick and crazy like this, like those weird pictures in the museums with 3 eyes and twisted up heads ... that's them—that dead spooky music you hear in there is running through their brains. Dracula runs this country and that's Frankenstein bullshitting us right now.

TUFFY. That broad has got to shut up boss. She was a bad choice. Not that I'm against women. But ... fucking bitches all they got is big mouths and complaints. We shdnta hired her in the first place. A cunt's place is on her back in the sack with a hard joint jammed up in her.

DONNA. Go to hell!

TUFFY. Point four. Woman's place is in the sack on her back with an erect penis inserted where appropriate. Post this, her place is in the crib minding the issue of such union. Hooray for the ERA!

DONNA. Go to hell. I don't have to stay around for such bullshit!

MASKED MAN. No, you don't ... right you are ... you have some rights ... [*Laughs nasty.*]

> [DONNA *thinks again about it. Another* COP *drifts slowly on scene, stands in background trying to be unobtrusive*]

TUFFY. Point five. Colored, Mex's, PR's, Slants, Blanket Heads, All must make slightly less than the chump change paid to white workers.

REG. Fuck you.

MASKED MAN. Shut up and listen, it's for your own good!

DONNA. Bullshit!

TUFFY. Point six. Bourgeois Democracy has not worked well enough!

CLARK AND DONNA. What?

TUFFY. And so we must *retreat* for a short period . . . to a sterner form, a more gutsy style of government. Do-What-We-Say-Ism or as it is sometimes called Straight-Out-Ism where no one has to worry about choices—there is only one choice, ours.

DONNA. It's always been like that.

TUFFY. Oh no . . .

MASKED MAN. [*Miffed*] Fucking-a-tweety it has . . . But now it's straight out!!! We won't have this . . . this truculence. What we do we do for *your* benefit.

TUFFY. For our benefit!

CLARK. Our benefit?

REG. Clark will you wise up and stop takin this dope??

MASKED MAN. MMMMMMMMMMM [*Mock smile*] for your benefit!

TUFFY. Point seven. Commies are poison and there is no such thing as socialism. Anyone talking that shit, thinking that shit, looking like talking like or smelling like a commie must be isolated and liquidated for the common good.

DONNA. You got the camps open yet Mr. Masked Man. Looks like you finally taking off your mask.

MASKED MAN. I told you I didn't have on a mask. Now you're beginning to understand.

DONNA. Like I said Dracula and the 30 vampires, you all run it all.

MASKED MAN. You don't understand . . .

DONNA. Whatta you holding us in here hostages while you got the rest of the workers locked out? Is that what's really happening?

TUFFY. Hostage??

MASKED MAN. Too dramatic my dear. Much too dramatic.

TUFFY. We know you all are a cross section of all the guys and dolls in this joint.

DONNA. Not really.

MASKED MAN. Really ... the really backward are already with us ... or the really advanced, however you choose to look at it ... you see we present both sides.

TUFFY. We are making peace and prosperity for everyone, and we want you to join in the leadership ...

DONNA. Have you finished with the agrees. Can we go?

TUFFY. Go? You haven't finished yr shift. You haven't said either what you think of the agrees.

REG. You haven't heard all the constructive criticism we been giving you guys. Like bullshit and go to hell. Fuck you was in it too I believe.

MASKED MAN. [*Hissing*] She told you one thing right, this is no laughing matter. There are no more jobs, either sign up with us or go starve.

[TUF *laughs almost uncontrollably*]

CLARK. If we sign those agrees what do we get?

TUFFY. You get to work ... you get a steady slave my friend, a guaranteed income. Dignity. Prosperity for you and your families. All the things you need and rightfully demand. Those are the agrees. And I've got the contracts where you can sign on the dotted line.

MASKED MAN. Our little cross section.

DONNA. And the dead worker there. Shot, strangled ... murdered by you.

MASKED MAN. Died of a broken heart, because he wasn't intelligent enough to sign the agrees. That hurt him so badly. Something burst within his head.

DONNA. [*Begins to move toward the body*] Who is this ...

MASKED MAN. Yes, go ahead look ...

DONNA. Aggghh. [*In horror*] It's Felipe . . .

REG. Felipe . . . goddamn, what bullshit you all talking here, Felipe didn't die of no goddam broken heart . . .

DONNA. A bullet in the center of his head.

MASKED MAN. Really? MMMMMM things are getting serious . . .

TUFFY. We know you and this guy Felipe are around in this plant to upset things to organize the sweet workers against their own interests.

MASKED MAN. There were 3 of you in this section of the shop right . . . One we know is the woman. I'd make a guess and say the other is you sir. [*Pointing at* REGGIE]

REG. Whatta you talking about? You killed Felipe motherfucker you deserve to die. [HE *leaps at* TUFFY]

TUFFY. Hey Hey.

[*The* POLICEMEN *now run forward with guns drawn*]

DONNA. Reggie, cool it, this is just provocation . . . You bastids wanna accuse us of anything just do it. But dragging dead bodies around and the rest of the mad shit going on you can can all that. We ain't going for it. Let us out of here. It's after hours.

TUFFY. And the agrees?

REG. Fuck you and Fuck MM and Fuck the agrees, sabe??

MASKED MAN. Yes Kemosabe. I sabe. [*Looks off*] It all reminds me of how the last battle with my old companion went down . . . we were surrounded, backed up to the edge of Mass Line Canyon. Bullets whizzing around us, and flame tipped arrows. We battled down to our last ammunition, and suddenly Tonto was gone. [HE *is crouching as if firing . . . we hear war cries whoops and hollers now rising*] Tonto, I sd, Tonto, we're surrounded . . . but help is on the way . . . help is on the way good friend . . . and then he reminded me that I was the *Lone* Ranger, that there was no help, that I was a lonely superpower whose destiny was . . . was [*As if* HE *cannot bear to remember*]

[*Suddenly rising off the floor, in the midst of the fantasy with the lights dimming just slightly to give off the effect of being slightly removed from reality,* FELIPE *becomes* TONTO]

FELIPE (TONTO). . . . a lonely superpower who's destiny is doom, doom.

MASKED MAN (NOW THE LONE RANGER). But you're with me . . . I can't be lonely and I won't be doomed alone . . . you're with me . . .

FELIPE (TONTO). Me, a scared house servant about to skip out the backdoor yr honor? I won't be with you. I ain't even with myself.

MASKED MAN (THE LONE RANGER). Don't talk like that . . . we're a team . . . we work together to keep the range free for democracy.

FELIPE (TONTO). Do you know Indian history, kemo sabe. All this was ours, the Indians' . . . and you bathed us in our own blood to get it . . . Your Manifest Destiny! Even Walt Whitman went for it. And if I ain't a house servant then I'm something better, a field hand, a worker, an oppressed nationality, spawn of an oppressed nation. And if I am not a house servant, if I am not a comprador or a traitor, then I am one of the millions who right now ride out there threatening you, whose arrows and bullets whiz ever closer to your frightened ass! And then even if I am in your field or factory I plot against you, I form nuclei of scientific revolutionaries to plan your downfall, your death or imprisonment, the destruction of yr system.

MASKED MAN (THE LONE RANGER). Tonto! Tontoooo! Don't make me kill you!

FELIPE (TONTO). Adios motherfucker.

[*A shot as the lights go down*]

MASKED MAN. You see he made me kill him . . . he made me . . . I thought he was my friend, my companion . . . I wd have let him fuck my sister any time . . . or me for that matter. He cd've lived in a nice neighborhood with hip stores and a mall, street musicians and foreign films. He gave it all up.

[*Lights back up* . . . FELIPE/ TONTO *is back on the floor*]

CLARK. Whew . . . some strange shit alright . . .

DONNA. And now what, you bringing on fascism cause yr shit is exposed and all the Indians, black red people, white red people, brown red people, yellow red people, red red people, they all read your shit and hate it.

TUFFY. Shutup Willya. Ya'll get a fat lip.

REG. Fuck you Bureaucrat . . . you're the real tonto, the new tonto, a bribed goddam worker living off the extra blood Dracula can drip your way . . . a white chauvinist, a male chauvinist, a goddam dull ass assistant ghoul tied up to some dying shit.

TUFFY. Sign the agrees or be with your dead friend.

CLARK. You serious? You'll kill us?

MASKED MAN. Yr friend here is very slow.

DONNA. They will.

CLARK. But why me. I go along with all this shit. I put up with all of it . . . all I want's a raise, that's all. The other bullshit, all that talk about oppression capitalism and the like I don't know from nothing. I just need more money . . . to live . . . and for my family. That's all I want mister MM that's all.

MASKED MAN. But we have no more money for you . . . in fact we're raising yr spirits so we can lower your material . . . paycuts all around is the order of the day.

CLARK. Whatta you mean paycut . . . Hey paycut? You kidding can't get no paycut mister . . . don't have nuthin now. Can't make it on no paycut.

TUFFY. He told you Clark, MM told you, there's no money for you . . . you've got to take a cut, you'll learn to love it just like you learned to love everything else we've done to you.

CLARK. Yeh, yeh, but mister, I need more money. I don't want to make trouble really. I really do not want to make no trouble. I go home I just want to throw my feet up and watch the ballgame, but paycut I can't go for that. I ain't no trouble maker, you know that . . . Tuffy'll tell you that . . . but I can't live with this money you givin me and I just can't make no cut . . . that's the truth.

TUFFY. The agrees. Bullshittin times over.

MASKED MAN. Yes, the agrees . . . Sign, or disappear, join yr friend old Tonto.

REG. The shit has gone that far, Straight-Out-Ism pure and simple huh? You need to grow a halfa mustache Tuffy and pull yr bangs down over one eye. You'll look great with a goosestep.

MASKED MAN. How crude. We are much more modern . . .

DONNA. Whatever you are, however you package it, you'll get yr ass kicked again and again, no matter how many times you make trouble, you'll get yr ass kicked another time for the asking, and finally one day your ass will get kicked for once and for all, and you and your class mates mister MM and you Tuffy and yr bribereenoes, will be under *our* gun.

TUFFY. More lefty bullshit . . .hahahahaha.

MASKED MAN. Rave on, Lady Macbeth, but remember your time is running out . . . sign or lay on the floor with Tonto . . . Sign the agrees!

TUFFY. The agrees . . . Sign.

> [*Now we hear the same war cries and whoops as during the* TONTO *segment. They are at first like the Indians attacking but later they begin to change. Another* COP *runs in the plant*]

COP. Boss Boss, the workers are back. The streets are packed with em. They got signs.

MASKED MAN. What? Tuffy . . .

TUFFY. What're you talking about . . . There were supposed to be cops guarding the workers' neighborhoods so they cdn't leave. Cops and troops. They promised us.

DONNA. Time's running out for who?

> [*The* WORKERS *chant "Strike, Strike, Strike, Strike . . . Free Donna, Free Reggie, Free Clark—Free the Colonel Motors Three! Avenge the Death of Felipe! Free the Colonel Motors Three. Strike Strike Strike Strike Strike"*]

DONNA. We're walking outta here you two, call off your goons.

REG. Yeh get outta our way . . . you coming Clark??

CLARK. You goddam right. Whatta you mean am I coming? What I look like to you a goddam fool?

REG. No brother . . . not that . . .

TUFFY. Boss you want to kill them . . .

[MASKED MAN *turns to look at the window from which the chants are coming*]

DONNA. It won't do you no good, bloodsucker, to kill us ... they'll always be more ... you'll have to kill all the workers all the oppressed nationalities to get rid of the likes of us ... and you can't do that.

REG. Before it's over they'll kill *you.*

DONNA. Let us out of here, we'll come back. But when we do, it'll be to run this place for ourselves.

MASKED MAN. And so why let you go, so you'll help lead this mess ... oh no ... you'll ...

[*At this point the door bursts open and* WORKERS *surge into the factory chanting "Free Donna! Free Reggie! Free Clark! Avenge the Murder of Felipe!" The* WORKERS *come in, some with clubs, and sticks, some with pistols and rifles. They stand menacing* MM, TUF *and* CO.]

DONNA. See you later MM and Tuffy ... we'll see you real soon ... we'll be back right after we finish our party ...

REG. Yeh, we gotta party to go to ... party of a new type ...

DONNA. And then we'll be back ...

[*The* WORKERS *rush to greet them, the cry goes back up "Strike"* ... *the* POLICE, MM *and* TUFFY *line up on one side* ... *the* WORKERS, DONNA, REG *and* CLARK *on the other. Some* WORKERS *rush over to* TONTO's *body* ...]

WORKERS. Strike! Strike! Strike! Strike!

BLACKOUT